# ANATOMY, PHYSIOLOGY AND PATHOLOGY

## for Complementary Therapists

### Level 2 and 3

Francesca Gould

Nelson Thornes

Published in 2012 by:
Nelson Thornes Ltd
Delta Place
27 Bath Road
CHELTENHAM
GL53 7TH
United Kingdom

13 14 15 / 10 9 8 7 6 5 4 3 2

A catalogue record for this book is available from the British Library

ISBN 978 1 4085 1569 3

Cover photograph by Shutterstock/VladGavriloff
Illustrations by Beehive Illustration
Page make-up by Hart McLeod Ltd, Cambridge
Printed in China by 1010 Printing International Ltd

## Acknowledgements

The author and the publisher would also like to thank the following for permission to reproduce material:

Fig 2.6 iStockphoto/Beboy_ltd; Fig 2.7 iStockphoto/Jacob_Wackerhausen; Fig 2.9 Science Photo Library/JOTI; Fig 2.10a&b Science Photo Library/ Kate Jacobs, Science Photo Library/Ian Hooton (3), Science Photo Library/ Lea Paterson, Science Photo Library; Fig 2.11 Science Photo Library/ISM; Fig 2.12 Science Photo Library/Western Ophthalmic Hospital; Fig 2.13 Science Photo Library/Dr. P. Marazzi; Fig 2.14 Science Photo Library; Fig 2.15 Science Photo Library/Dr. Chris Hale; Fig 2.16 Science Photo Library; Fig 2.17 Science Photo Library/Dr. P. Marazzi; Fig 2.18 Science Photo Library/Dr. P. Marazzi; Fig 2.19 Science Photo Library/David Parker; Fig 2.20 Science Photo Library; Fig 2.21 Science Photo Library/ Dr. P Marazzi; Fig 2.22 Science Photo Library/Dr. H.C. Robinson; Fig 2.23 Alamy/Stefan Sollfors; Fig 2.24 Science Photo Library/Dr. P. Marazzi; Fig 2.25 Science Photo Library/Custom Medical Stock Photo; Fig 2.26 Getty/Paul Burns; Fig 2.27 iStockphoto/fanelie rosier; Fig 2.28 Science Photo Library/JOTI; Fig 2.29 Alamy/Medical-on-Line; Fig 2.30 Science Photo Library; Fig 2.31 Alamy/Medical-on-Line; Fig 2.32 Science Photo Library/Dr. Harout Tanielian; Fig 2.33 Science Photo Library/Dr. P. Marazzi; Fig 2.34 Science Photo Library; Fig 2.35 Science Photo Library/CNRI; Fig 2.36 Science Photo Library/Dr. H.C. Robinson; Fig 2.37 Science Photo Library/St Bartholomew's Hospital; Fig 2.38 Science Photo Library/ Dr. Harout Tanielian; Fig 2.39 Science Photo Library/Dr. P. Marazzi; Fig 2.40 Science Photo Library/Dr. P. Marazzi; Fig 2.41 Science Photo Library/ Dr. P. Marazzi; Fig 2.42 Science Photo Library/Jane Shemilt; Fig 2.43 Science Photo Library; Fig 2.44 Science Photo Library/James Stevenson; Fig 2.47 Alamy/Medical-on-Line; Fig 2.48 Science Photo Library/John Radcliffe Hospital; Fig 2.50 iStockphoto/Osuleo; Fig 2.52 Science Photo Library/Dr. P. Marazzi; Fig 2.53 Science Photo Library/John Radcliffe Hospital; Fig 2.54 Science Photo Library/ Dr. P. Marazzi; Fig 2.55 Science Photo Library/Pascal Goetgheluck; Fig 2.56 Science Photo Library/ Dr. Harout Tanielian; Fig 2.57 iStockphoto/Clayton Cole; Fig 2.58 Science Photo Library/ Dr. P. Marazzi; Fig 2.59 Science Photo Library/ Dr. P. Marazzi; Fig 2.60 Science Photo Library/Mike Devlin; Fig 2.61 Science Photo Library/ Dr. P. Marazzi; Fig 2.62 © Mediscan; Fig 2.63 Science Photo Library; Fig 2.64 © Mediscan; Fig 2.65 © Wikimedia; Fig 2.66 Science Photo Library/Dr. P. Marazzi; Fig 2.67 Science Photo Library/ Dr. P. Marazzi; Fig 2.68 Science Photo Library/Dr. Harout Tanielian; Fig 2.69 Science Photo Library/Dr. Jeremy Burgess; Fig 3.23 Science Photo Library/Alex Bartel; Fig 7.2 Fotolia/Memi; Fig 8.1 iStockphoto/Baris Simsek; Fig 8.2 iStockphoto/Henrik Jonsson; Fig 8.3 Fotolia/popyconcept; Fig 8.17 iStockphoto/Diamond Images; Fig 9.9 Science Photo Library/ Dr. P. Marazzi; Fig 12.1 iStockphoto/Christian Jasiuk

Fig 1.8 adapted from diagram of 'Facilitated Diffusion' Copyright © The McGraw-Hill Companies Inc; Fig 1.20 adapted from Great Ways to Learn Anatomy & Physiology by Charmaine McKissock published by Palgrave Macmillan (2009). Reproduced with the permission of Palgrave Macmillan; Fig 12.3 adapted from DuoFertility.com © 2007-2012 Cambridge Temperature Concepts Ltd.

Every effort has been made to trace the copyright holders but if any have been inadvertently overlooked the publisher will be pleased to make the necessary arrangements at the first opportunity.

# Contents

FREE answers and crosswords are available
on our Planet Vocational website
www.planetvocational.co.uk

Planet
Vocational

# Introduction

Welcome to the third edition of *Anatomy, Physiology and Pathology for Complementary Therapists.*

This book contains twelve chapters, which each relate to a body system. It is written primarily for those undertaking an anatomy and physiology course, and those who are considering gaining professional qualifications in complementary, beauty or sports therapy.

The requirements for both VTCT and ITEC anatomy and physiology qualifications have been studied to ensure the book contains all that you need to pass these courses. Being both VTCT and ITEC qualified, and having taught VTCT and ITEC complementary and beauty courses myself, means that the book contains relevant and important information to help you succeed and pass your exams.

The book has been reviewed by lecturers experienced in teaching VTCT and ITEC qualifications to ensure it is fully up to date with the requirements of these awarding bodies.

I have tried to explain complex information as simply as possible. Anatomy and physiology isn't an easy subject to understand, there are many Latin and Greek names to learn, and understanding the way our incredible bodies work requires a lot of commitment and hard work.

Included at the end of most chapters is a section on pathology. You would never be expected to diagnose a disease or disorder, but it is important to have an understanding of these conditions, as it is likely that during your career you will come across people that may either suffer with a specific illness or have previously suffered with one.

I hope you enjoy reading this book as much as I enjoyed writing it. A lot of effort has been put into ensuring this book is user friendly and easy to understand, and it assumes no previous knowledge of anatomy and physiology.

Whichever career path you decide to take, I wish you luck. With hard work and perseverance you will do well in both your exams and career.

Francesca Gould

# How to use this book

This book is set out to help ensure maximum learning and the activities will help to assess your knowledge. Many of the activities are fun tasks and involve colouring in or completing puzzles such as crosswords, so make sure you have some colouring pencils to hand!

## Level 3 content
Level 3 content has been flagged throughout the book and is colour coded on a purple background.
If you are studying at Level 2 you don't have to worry about learning this information!

## Key words
During your course you will come across new words and terms that you may not have heard before. These key words and their definitions can be found in the glossary at the back of the book.

**ASK FRAN...**

This feature consists of commonly asked questions relating to anatomy and physiology. The answers I have given are explained clearly.

**FAST FACT**

Fast Fact provides you with a variety of interesting snippets of information relating to anatomy and physiology.

*don't forget*

The 'don't forget' feature provides you with useful reminders that will be invaluable to your learning and will enhance your knowledge.

**MEMORY JOGGER**

This feature will help you to remember important information so that you can recall it in an exam situation. These types of mnemonics (memory aids) have proven to be effective – and have been invaluable in helping me to pass my exams.

**What you should know**

At the end of each chapter you will find a checklist to mark off what you have learned so far, in order to check your progress. Level 3 knowledge is underlined in purple.

# 1 Cells and tissues

Anatomy and physiology is the study of the body and how it works. Anatomy refers to the study of the body's structures, for example the heart, and physiology relates to the functions of the body parts, for example how the heart beats.

Every structure in the human body is made up of specific types of cells. Like the bricks of a house, cells are the building blocks of the body. The body is made up of over 100 000 billion cells. Although minute, cells are organised and complex structures. Different cells have certain functions, such as muscle, blood and fat cells, and can vary in size and shape. A single cell is ineffective, but if grouped together with similar cells it can form tissues. Two or more tissue types make up an organ, such as the skin, eye and heart. A **system** is made up of various organs, an example is the cardiovascular system. Systems make up an **organism**, such as a human being.

**Figure 1.1** A heart muscle cell

**FAST FACT**

The body is made up of over 100 000 billion cells.

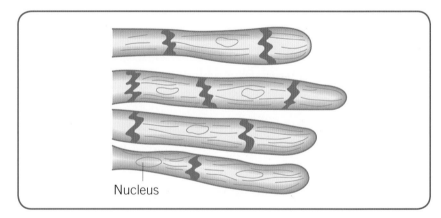

Nucleus

**Figure 1.2** Heart muscle tissue

✻ **Cell**, for example a heart muscle cell (Figure 1.1)

✻ **Tissue**, for example heart muscle tissue (Figure 1.2)

* **Organ**, for example the heart (Figure 1.3)

* **System**, for example the circulatory system (Figure 1.4)

* **Organism**, for example a human being

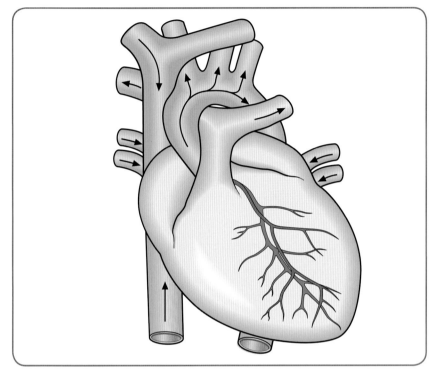

**Figure 1.3** The heart

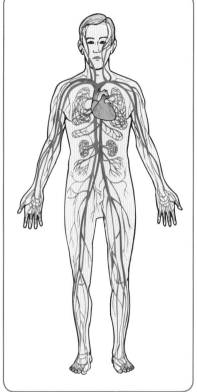

**Figure 1.4** The circulatory system

# Structure of cells

Nearly all cells have the same basic structure. They are surrounded by a ⓵ **membrane**, which encloses the contents of the cell. Cells contain organelles (small organs), which are responsible for the functioning of a cell.

⓶ **Cytoplasm** is a jelly-like liquid consisting mostly of water, but it also contains nutrients required by the cell for growth, reproduction and repair. The cytoplasm contains many organelles.

The ⓷ **nucleus** is the largest organelle and is surrounded by the nuclear membrane. The function of the nucleus is to control the cell's activities, such as movement and reproduction, and is often described as the 'brain' of the cell.

*don't forget*

Many structures in the body are made from protein, for example keratin, which is found in hair and nails. The cell membrane is also partly made of protein.

Almost all cells have a nucleus, which contains **chromosomes**. Chromosomes are strings of DNA (deoxyribonucleic acid) and carry all the information needed to make an entire human being. Within the nucleus will be the ④ **nucleolus**. It is a dense area of almost pure DNA.

**don't forget**

DNA inside the nucleus is the genetic material of the cell and controls the cell's activities.

**Phagocytosis (Fay-go-sy-toe-sis)** is the process used by certain cells (**phagocytes**) to engulf and ingest (take in) particles such as nutrients, and is also an important part of the immune system as these cells can destroy bacteria or other foreign bodies. **Pinocytosis (Pin-no-sy-toe-sis)** is the process by which certain cells can ingest liquid into a cell. The liquid is carried in vesicles.

**Vesicles** are bubble-like structures that store and transport products made by the cell. **Lysosomes** are vesicles and are the cell's waste disposal units. They are little sacs that release substances called **enzymes** to destroy bacteria, worn out parts of the cell and other unwanted substances. Enzymes are made from protein and are substances that increase the rate of chemical reactions without being used up.

There are two types of **endoplasmic reticulum** (ER): smooth and rough.

⑤ **Smooth ER** (SER) produces and transports fats, known as steroids and lipids. The **hormones oestrogen** and **testosterone** are produced by the smooth ER.

⑥ **Rough ER** (RER) is covered with tiny granules called **ribosomes**. The function of ribosomes is to make protein. The rough ER transports these proteins through the cytoplasm to the ⑦ **Golgi body**, also known as Golgi apparatus. The Golgi body sorts and packages the proteins. Some proteins will be used inside the cell and other proteins, such as hormones and enzymes, will be transported out of the cell. Many structures in the body are made from protein, such as **keratin**, which is found in hair and nails.

**don't forget**

Cells that require little energy to carry out their functions, for example fat cells, have few mitochondria. The cells that use a lot of energy, for example muscle and liver cells, have many mitochondria.

Sausage-shaped organelles called ⑧ **mitochondria** (singular: mitochondrion) are the powerhouses and help to produce energy for the cell. Cells that require little energy to carry out their functions, for example fat cells, have few mitochondria. The cells that use a lot of energy, for example muscle and liver cells, have many mitochondria.

⑨ **Vacuoles** are empty spaces that store and transport substances such as waste products and water.

A ⑩ **centriole** is a barrel-shaped structure that is made up of microtubules, and plays a role in cell division. A pair of centrioles can be found inside a structure called a centrosome (see cell division on page 12).

## ACTIVITY 1.1

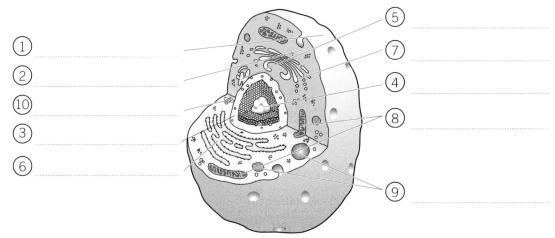

① ........................
② ........................
⑩ ........................
③ ........................
⑥ ........................

⑤ ........................
⑦ ........................
④ ........................
⑧ ........................
⑨ ........................

**Figure 1.5** Structure of a cell

Label the diagram in Figure 1.5 matching the numbers to the numbered terms in the text above. Use the key below to colour the diagram.

Blue – cell membrane
Yellow – cytoplasm
Red – nucleus
Green – Golgi body

Orange – mitochondria
Brown – SER
Pink – RER
Purple – centriole

## Cellular respiration

For the cells to produce energy to carry out their work they require fuel. The food we eat provides the fuel. It is absorbed from the intestines into the bloodstream. Tiny food molecules, for example glucose, eventually pass into the tissue fluid – this is fluid that surrounds and nourishes the cells. The process whereby fuel molecules are broken down and energy is released is known as **cellular respiration**. A tiny molecule called ATP (**adenosine triphosphate**) contains a small amount of energy. The cell can use ATP to help it carry out tasks, such as taking in food molecules or getting rid of unwanted substances from the cell. ATP is also needed for body activities, such as muscle contraction and the passing of nerve messages. Mitochondria are the major sites of ATP production.

## Glucose

Glucose is a type of sugar that is produced when the body breaks down carbohydrates from foods such as potatoes and bread (see Chapter 10 for more details).

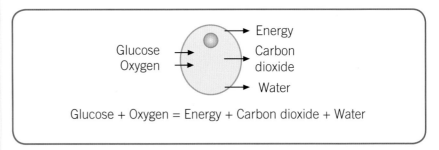

Glucose + Oxygen = Energy + Carbon dioxide + Water

**Figure 1.6** Simplified equation of cellular respiration

Glucose is a fuel that is often used by the cell for cellular respiration. However, other food groups, such as fat, carbohydrates and protein, can also be used as fuel.

Oxygen is also vital for cells to burn up the glucose. Oxygen enters the body through the lungs and passes into the bloodstream. The oxygen passes into the tissue fluid that surrounds the cells. Cells use the glucose and oxygen to make energy for the cell's activities.

When cells respire they form the by-products carbon dioxide and water. Carbon dioxide is a gas that is toxic to the body, so it is removed by the blood and taken to the lungs to be breathed out. The water is utilised by the body.

## Basal metabolic rate

Energy is required for activities of the body, such as breathing, digestion, heartbeat and the functioning of the brain. The **basal metabolic rate (BMR)** is the minimum energy needed to keep the body alive. BMR varies from person to person and will rise when an individual carries out exercise. Food and drink provide the energy in the form of calories.

## Metabolism

The body gets the energy it needs from food through metabolism, which converts the fuel from food into energy. Every living cell has a metabolism that involves the intake of food and the disposal of waste products. **Anabolism** and **catabolism** are chemical processes that are together known as metabolism. Anabolism is when the body uses food to build or repair cells; catabolism is when the body uses food for energy. Without glucose and oxygen the cells would die, as the many chemical reactions constantly taking place inside the cell would stop happening. These chemical reactions are important for maintaining life. **Cell metabolism** is the sum total of all these chemical reactions. It is the production of energy in the cell that is essential for cell respiration, growth and division.

## Transportation of molecules across cell membranes

Substances, such as glucose and water molecules, pass into cells by various methods.

### Cell membrane

The **cell membrane** consists of mainly lipids (fat) and some protein. It is partially permeable, that is, it will only allow certain substances to pass through it. The membrane controls and regulates what gets into and out of the cell.

*don't forget*

Molecules are made up of atoms joined together. For example, $CO_2$ (carbon dioxide) has one carbon atom (C) and two oxygen atoms ($O_2$). The joining of the carbon atom and the oxygen atoms makes one molecule.

FAST FACT

Generally, the heavier the body, the higher the basal metabolic rate as more energy will be needed to maintain it and move it about.

FAST FACT

The daily intake of energy should equal the energy needs of metabolism; otherwise a person will gain or lose weight.

## Diffusion

**Diffusion** is the process by which small molecules, such as oxygen and carbon dioxide, pass through the cell membrane. Diffusion is the movement of molecules from an area of high concentration (where there are lots of them) to an area of low concentration (where there are less). An example of diffusion in the body is the exchange of oxygen and carbon dioxide molecules in the lungs.

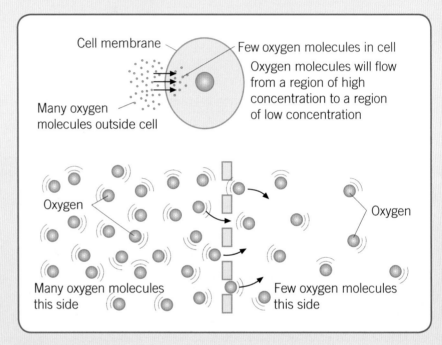

**Figure 1.7** Diffusion

## Facilitated diffusion

Facilitated diffusion involves special carrier proteins, which are embedded in the cell membrane and allow substances to pass across it into the cell. Molecules, such as glucose (sugar), sodium ions (salt) and chloride ions, are unable to pass directly through the membrane so carrier proteins transport them into the cell. They do this by binding to a molecule, such as a glucose molecule, and then changing shape to allow it to enter the cell.

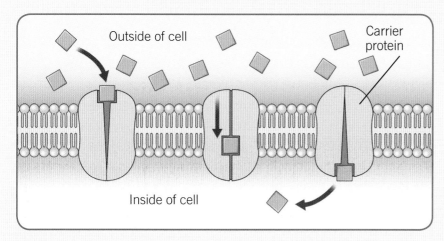

**Figure 1.8** Facilitated diffusion

## Osmosis

**Osmosis** involves the movement of water molecules from a region of higher concentration of water to a region of lower concentration of water through a partially permeable membrane, such as the cell membrane.

If the cell contains little water compared to the surrounding tissue fluid, it will draw water into the cell from the tissue fluid by osmosis. If the cell contains too much water compared to the tissue fluid, then the excess will pass into the tissue fluid.

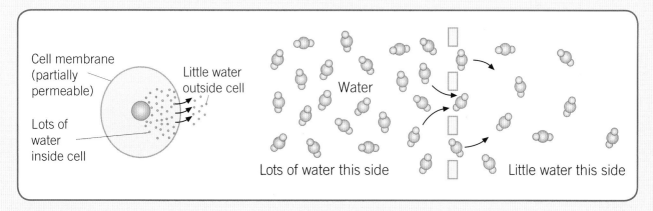

**Figure 1.9** Osmosis

## Active transport

This process involves the movement of molecules across a cell membrane from a region of lower concentration into a region of higher concentration. A carrier protein is required to transport the molecules. As the molecules are being moved the opposite way to which everything else is moving, energy is required in the form of **ATP**. ATP stores the energy required to carry out active transport. Active transport takes place during the **digestion** of food, such as glucose, in the **small intestine**.

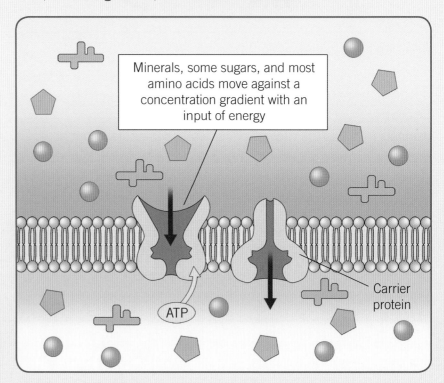

Minerals, some sugars, and most amino acids move against a concentration gradient with an input of energy

ATP

Carrier protein

**Figure 1.10** Active transport

## Filtration

**Filtration** is the movement of water and solute molecules (dissolved substances) across the cell membrane owing to hydrostatic pressure (pressure of fluid) from the cardiovascular system. This pressure of fluid against the cell membrane forces substances into the cell. An example of where filtration takes place is the kidneys, which filter the blood. Blood pressure (the pumping action of the heart provides this pressure) forces water and small molecules (known as filtrate) out of the blood into a **nephron** of the kidney (see Chapter 11).

Dissolution

**Dissolution** involves one substance (solute) dissolving into another (solvent).

## Homeostasis

For each cell to survive and carry out its functions, the body must maintain a constant internal environment, known as **homeostasis**. The body systems work together to help maintain this inside the body. The main organs concerned with homeostasis are the lungs, skin, liver and kidneys. There are different bodily activities that need to be controlled, which include the sugar levels, water levels, oxygen levels, salt levels and body temperature. These are all important to the body and need to be at just the right levels, not too high or low, to ensure survival of the cells.

Oxygen, carbon dioxide and food particles need to be transported into and out of cells. This is carried out by processes such as diffusion and osmosis. These methods of transport across a cell membrane depend on the body's water and salt balance, which are maintained by homeostasis.

The **hypothalamus**, in the brain, is about the size of a pearl and is one of the main regulators of homeostasis. It produces hormones that control body temperature, hunger, thirst, sleep and emotional behaviour, such as rage, pleasure, fear and sexual behaviour.

## Cell division (mitosis)

A cell does not keep on growing in size but divides into two daughter cells. The cells further multiply by splitting in half again and again. The cells continue to divide until the billions of cells needed to make up the body are produced. This process of cell division is called **mitosis**. Mitosis of cells is also needed for growth and the replacement of dead cells.

FAST FACT

No red blood cells are filtered into the kidney as they remain within the blood vessels. Therefore, no blood should appear in the urine. If there is blood within the urine, it may be a sign of kidney problems.

*don't forget*

**The body needs to maintain a constant stable internal environment to ensure health. This is known as homeostasis.**

The growth and division of a cell consists of five phases (the letters refer to Figure 1.11):

**A** The cell spends most of its life in **interphase**. During this phase the cell actively grows.

**B** **Prophase** is the first phase of mitosis. The **chromatin** (strands of genetic material) coil tightly to form dark X-shaped structures, known as **chromosomes**. They are arranged in pairs, called **chromatids**, and are attached to a part of the chromosome called the **centromere**. During prophase, the nucleus becomes smaller and disappears. Two pairs of organelles, called centrioles, go towards each end of the cell and form cell fibres, also known as spindles.

**C** During **metaphase**, chromosomes line up in the middle of the cell.

**D** During **anaphase**, the chromatids separate and become individual chromosomes, rather than a pair. One set of chromosomes moves to one end of the cell and the other set moves to the opposite end. So, there are 46 chromosomes on each side.

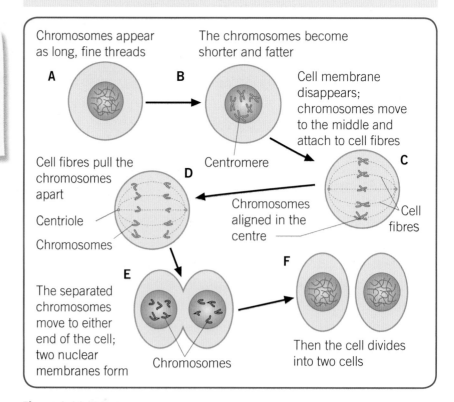

**Figure 1.11** Mitosis

**E, F Telophase** now begins. A nuclear membrane starts to form around each set of chromosomes. The cell will begin to constrict around its middle and then divide to form two cells. The division of cytoplasm of a cell following the division of the nucleus is known as **cytokinesis.**

## Meiosis

To make a human being, 46 chromosomes are needed. There are only 23 chromosomes in an egg and 23 chromosomes in a sperm. As these sex cells undergo a special process called meiosis, their number of chromosomes is halved compared to cells undergoing mitosis. When fertilisation takes place, the egg and sperm join together (so result in 46 chromosomes) and form a **zygote**. The zygote is able to reproduce by cell division (mitosis).

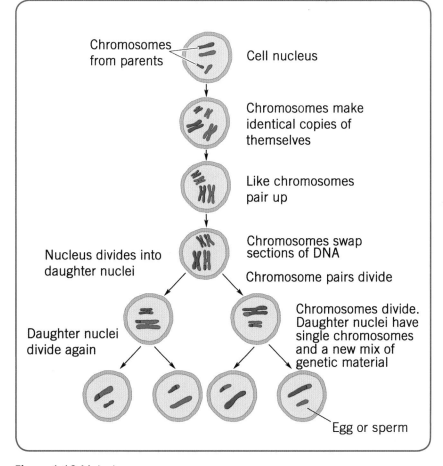

**Figure 1.12** Meiosis

The division of cells leads to a big group of cells being formed, which is known as tissue. Different types of tissue have specific functions in the body.

# Tissues

## Epithelial tissue

This kind of tissue provides protective covering for surfaces inside and outside the body. Certain cells within this tissue can make and release (secrete) substances, such as mucus. The tissue also has to allow material, such as oxygen, carbon dioxide, nutrients and hormones, to pass through it. There are two types of epithelial tissue: simple and compound.

## Simple epithelial tissue

This type of tissue consists of a single layer of cells and includes the following.

- ✖ **Pavement** or **squamous epithelial cells** are flat, thin cells placed edge to edge, like the slabs of a pavement. Their thinness allows for rapid movement of substances through them. These cells are found in the alveoli (air sacs) of the lungs, in the lining of the heart and in blood and lymph vessels.

- ✖ **Columnar cells** are tall, column-shaped cells. They line the ducts of most glands, the **gall bladder** and nearly the whole of the digestive tract.

- ✖ **Cuboidal cells** consist of cube-shaped cells and can be found covering the **ovaries**, in the kidneys and within the eye. They are involved in absorbing and releasing substances.

- ✖ **Ciliated cells** are columnar in shape but have the addition of fine, hair-like structures, called **cilia**, attached at the head. These cells line the respiratory passages and also the **Fallopian tubes**. In the respiratory tract, the constant movement of the cilia help to prevent dust and bacteria from entering the lungs. In the Fallopian tubes, cilia help move the ovum (egg) along the tube.

# Compound epithelial tissue

This type of tissue consists of two or more layers. There are two types of compound tissue.

**Stratified epithelium** (stratified means in layers) consists of two or more layers of cells. It is more durable and can protect underlying tissues from the external environment and from wear and tear. It forms the top five layers of the skin, known as the epidermal layers. It lines the mouth, throat (pharynx), food pipe (**oesophagus**), the anal canal and the vagina. It also covers the surface of the eye.

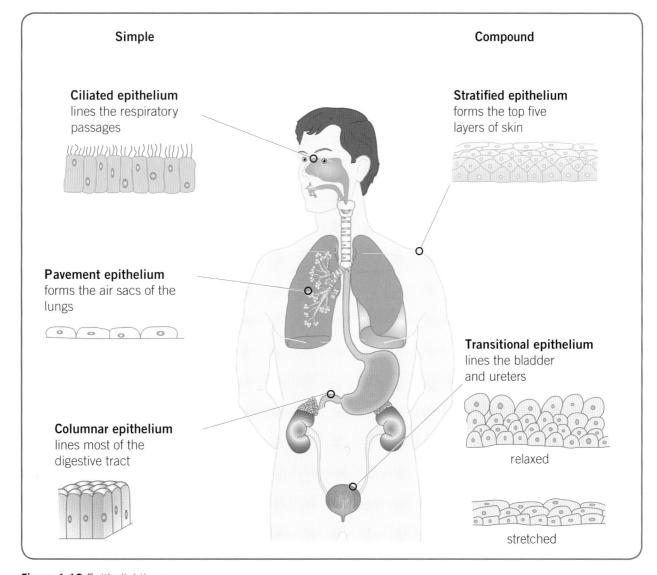

**Figure 1.13** Epithelial tissue

Stratified epithelial tissue can be classified as **keratinised** and non-keratinised. Keratinised surfaces are protected by keratin, a tough, insoluble protein, which prevents the deeper layers from drying out and include skin, hair and nails. Non-keratinised surfaces must be kept moist by the body to prevent them drying out, and include the mouth, oesophagus and the surface of the eyes. The oesophagus contains many tiny glands that make mucus, which helps to keep the surface moist and aids the passage of food.

**Transitional epithelium** is variable in appearance, depending on whether it is relaxed or stretched, and consists of several layers of cells. It lines the bladder and **ureters** (tubes entering the bladder from the kidneys). Its function is to help prevent the rupture of organs.

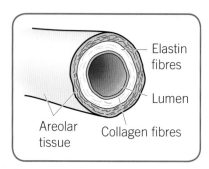

**Figure 1.14** Areolar tissue

## Connective tissue

Functions of connective tissue are to protect, bind and support. There are several types.

**Areolar tissue** is widely distributed throughout the body. It consists of a network of fine, white fibres that are found inside a watery gel. These fibres are made of collagen, which gives the tissue strength. It forms a thin, transparent tissue surrounding vessels (such as a **blood vessel**), **nerves** and muscle fibres in muscle. It also has the function of connecting skin to tissues and muscles. Areolar tissue contains stretchy fibres of **elastin**, which is made from protein.

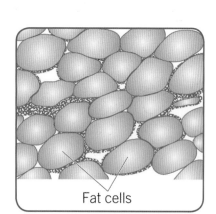

**Figure 1.15** Adipose tissue

**Adipose tissue** consists of fat cells. This fatty tissue is found in most parts of the body. It helps to support and protect organs, such as the kidneys. It forms a protective covering for the whole body to help protect against injury, and provides insulation and a store of energy if the body requires it.

**don't forget**

Histology – study of the microscopic structure of tissues.

**Fibrous tissue** is found in muscles, bones, **tendons** (which join muscle to bone) and **ligaments** (which join bone to bone). Fibrous tissue is made of collagen fibres; collagen is a type of protein that helps to give strength to the tissues.

**Elastic tissue** contains elastic-type fibres. It is found in the walls of the arteries (thick blood vessels) and in the air tubes of the respiratory tract in the chest, where elasticity is needed to allow stretching of various organs.

Muscular tissue includes skeletal, smooth and cardiac muscle (see Chapter 4).

**Bone tissue** consists of fibrous material, which gives the bone its strength. The addition of salts, such as calcium phosphate, gives the bone its rigidity (see Chapter 3).

**Lymphoid tissue** is found in lymph nodes (lymph nodes help with the body's defence system and inflame when infected). It is also found in the spleen, **tonsils** and **appendix** (See Chapter 9).

Blood is also a type of connective tissue and is made up of red blood cells, white blood cells, platelets and plasma (see Chapter 8).

Nerve tissue consists of **neurones** and neuroglial cells (see Chapter 5).

## Types of cartilage

**Cartilage** is a type of connective tissue and there are three types found in the body: hyaline cartilage, elastic cartilage and fibrocartilage (see Table 1.1).

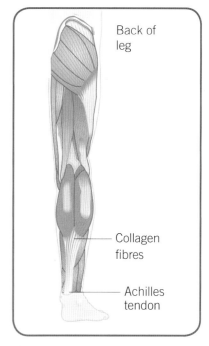

**Figure 1.16** Fibrous tissue

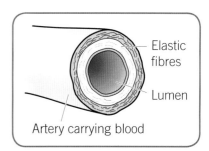

**Figure 1.17** Elastic tissue

**Table 1.1** Types of cartilage

| Cartilage | Description | Where found in body |
|---|---|---|
| Hyaline cartilage | Most common type of cartilage found in body. It is firm, elastic and reduces friction and absorbs shock at joints. | At joints. The C-shaped rings that keep the windpipe open. |
| Elastic cartilage | Also called yellow elastic cartilage as it contains yellow elastic fibres. It is flexible and readily springs back into shape. | At the tip of the nose and the upper part of the ear (the earlobe is made of adipose and fibrous tissue). |
| Fibrocartilage | Also known as white fibrocartilage and is made up of bundles of fibres with cartilage cells in between. | Where great strength is required, such as in the discs between the bones that form the spine. |

## Membranes

There are three types of membrane in the body: mucous, synovial and serous (see Table 1.2).

**Table 1.2** Types of membrane

| Membrane | Description | Where found in body |
|----------|-------------|---------------------|
| Mucous membrane | Produces a slimy, sticky fluid called mucus, which lubricates the surfaces and prevents them from drying out. | Lines the surfaces in the body that open to the outside, such as the digestive tract, air passages, urinary tract and reproductive tract. |
| Synovial membrane | Produces a thick fluid, rather like egg white, called synovial fluid. The fluid cushions and lubricates the ends of the bones. | Lines the spaces around certain joints, such as the knee joint. |
| Serous membrane | Produces a watery fluid called serous fluid, which enables organs to slide freely against each other to prevent friction. | Surrounds the lungs, the heart and the organs in the abdomen. |

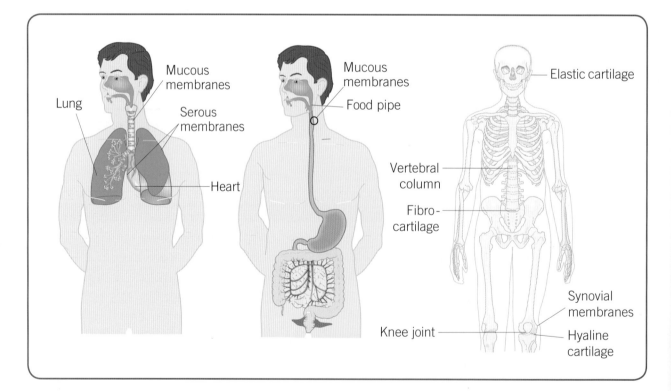

**Figure 1.18** Types of cartilage and membrane

## ACTIVITY 1.2

Match the terms in the bubbles with the correct description in the list.

- Produces fluid to enable organs to slide freely over each other ...........
- Produces mucus, which prevents surfaces from drying out ...........
- Helps to absorb shock at joints ...........
- Produces a thick fluid and is found at joints ...........
- Found where great strength is needed, such as between the discs in the backbone ...........
- Flexible and springy and found in the upper part of the ear ...........

1. Synovial fluid

2. Fibrocartilage

3. Serous membrane

4. Mucous membrane

5. Hyaline cartilage

6. Elastic cartilage

## ACTIVITY 1.3

**Brainstorming ideas**

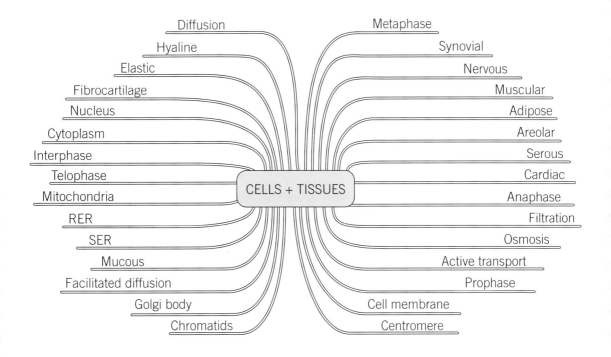

**Figure 1.19** Mind map for cells and tissues

## MEMORY JOGGER

Brainstorming ideas is helpful for revision and can be used for all body systems.
First, write your subject matter, in this case it's 'Cells and tissues', in the middle of a blank page. Now think of key terms relating to cells and tissues and list the terms as shown in Figure 1.19.

## ACTIVITY 1.3 (cont.)

Use coloured pencils to shade terms (found in Figure 1.19) that relate to each of the following headings.

Cell mitosis – use a blue colour

Cell structures – use a green colour

Transport methods across the cell membrane – use a red colour

Connective tissues – use a brown colour

Types of membrane – use an orange colour

Types of cartilage – use a yellow colour

## ACTIVITY 1.4

Copy out the table below. Look at the terms in Figure 1.19 and decide which should be inserted under each heading.

| Cell mitosis | Cell structures | Transport methods across the cell membrane | Connective tissues | Types of membrane | Types of cartilage |
|---|---|---|---|---|---|
|  |  |  |  |  |  |

## Anatomical directional terms

To understand these directional terms, the body has to be viewed in the correct anatomical position. The body stands erect with arms by the side and palms facing forwards. There is an imaginary vertical line that runs through the middle of the body and is known as the **midline**.

**Medial** – nearer to the midline of the body. The ulna is medial to the radius. The inside of the leg and foot is the medial side.

**Lateral** – towards the outer side, or further away from the midline of the body. The humerus is lateral to the clavicle. The outside of the leg and foot is the lateral side.

**Anterior or ventral** – nearer to, or at the front of, the body. The sternum is anterior to the heart.

**Posterior or dorsal** – nearer to, or at the back of, the body. The heart is posterior to the sternum. The top of the foot is the dorsal surface.

**Plantar** – on, or towards, the sole of the foot.

**Proximal** – closer to the midline. In the limbs, it is the part nearer to the trunk. The humerus is proximal to the radius.

**Distal** – further away from the midline. In the limbs, it is the part that is further away from the trunk. The phalanges are distal to the carpals.

**Superficial** – towards the surface of the body. The skin is superficial to the heart.

**Deep** – away from the surface of the body. The heart is deep to the skin.

**Superior** – located above or towards the upper part. The heart is superior to the liver.

**Inferior** – located below or towards the lower part. The stomach is inferior to the lungs.

**Parietal** (pa–rye-et-al) – relating to, or forming, the wall of a body part, organ or cavity. For example, the parietal pericardium of the heart is the outermost layer.

**Visceral** (vis-ser-rall) – refers to the internal organs of the body, specifically those of the chest or abdomen.

**Ipsilateral** – located, or affecting, the same side of the body.

**Contralateral** – affecting the other, opposite, side of the body.

## ACTIVITY 1.5

True or false?

Put a circle around the correct answer.

The lungs are superior to the kidneys.
– True or False

Plantar relates to the top of the foot.
– True or False

The lungs are anterior to the heart.
– True or False

The stomach is deep to the skin.
– True or False

Joints allow several different types of movement to be made. There are some basic terms used to describe these movements.

## ACTIVITY 1.6

Use Figure 1.20 to make up a poster showing all the movements. Ensure you practise each movement while repeating its name. This will help you to remember them.

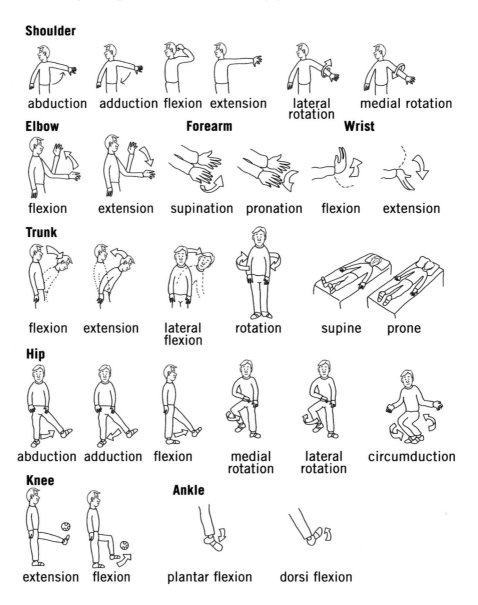

**Figure 1.20** Directional terms

**Table 1.3** Anatomical planes

| Plane | Divisions |
|---|---|
| Sagittal (an example of a longitudinal plane) | Divides the body into left and right parts. |
| Frontal (also an example of a longitudinal plane) | Divides the body into anterior and posterior (front and back) parts. |
| Transverse | Divides the body horizontally at any point. |
| Oblique | Refers to a diagonal or slanted direction, which passes from one side of the body, or body part, to the other side. |

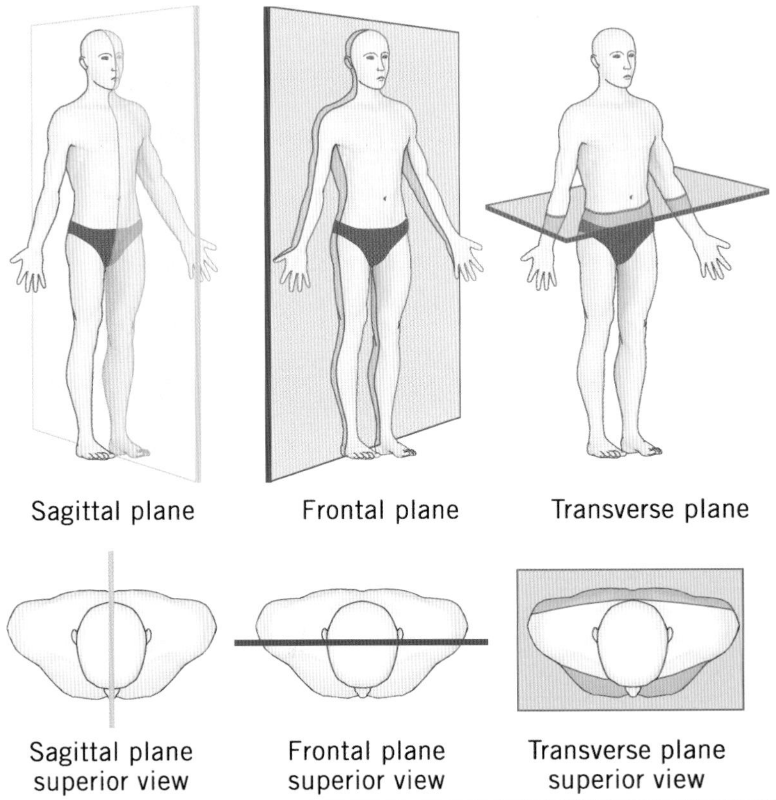

Figure 1.21 Anatomical planes

Sagittal plane     Frontal plane     Transverse plane

Sagittal plane superior view     Frontal plane superior view     Transverse plane superior view

**Figure 1.21** Anatomical planes

## ACTIVITY 1.7

Use books and the internet to research the following directional terms.

- Protraction
- Retraction
- Depression
- Elevation

## MEMORY JOGGER

To help you remember 'sagittal', consider that *sagitta* means arrow (think of Sagittarius, the Archer).
Imagine shooting an arrow at an object and seeing it strike the front and pass through to the back, so the object splits into two halves. This marks out the sagittal plane.

# Anatomical regions of the body

Understanding anatomical regions allows you to be specific when talking about certain areas of the body. Figure 1.22 shows the anatomical regions of the body. Learning the names of these regions will help you learn the names of many structures in the body, such as bones, muscles and lymph nodes.

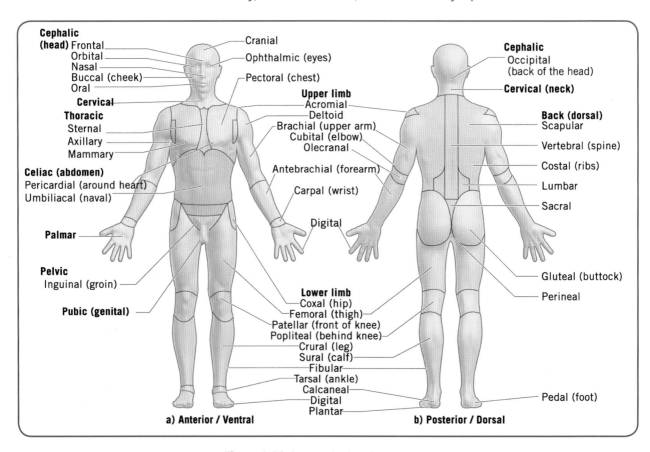

**Figure 1.22** Anatomical regions

## ACTIVITY 1.8

Where would you find the following anatomical regions?

- Cubital .................................................
- Cervical .................................................
- Patellar .................................................
- Gluteal .................................................

- Brachial .................................................
- Crural .................................................
- Costal .................................................

# What you should know

## Organisation of the body

- [ ] Simple chemicals – oxygen, carbon dioxide
- [ ] Nutrient chemicals (see Chapter 10) – carbohydrates, lipids (fats), proteins, vitamins, minerals, fibre, water
- [ ] Complex chemicals – ATP (see Chapter 4), DNA
- [ ] Cells, tissues, organs, systems, organisms (such as a human body)

## Structure and function of cells

- [ ] Components of cells – cell membrane, nucleus, nucleolus, cytoplasm, vacuoles, vesicles, centrioles, centrosome, organelles, Golgi, lysosomes, ribosomes, mitochondria, endoplasmic reticulum
- [ ] Process of transport across cell membrane – diffusion, osmosis, facilitated diffusion, active transport, dissolution, filtration, phagocytosis, pinocytosis

## Cell growth and repair

- [ ] Process of mitosis – interphase, prophase, metaphase, anaphase, telophase
- [ ] Growth and repair – cells, tissues, bone formation (see Chapter 3)
- [ ] Homeostasis (see Chapter 6), influencing factors, hormones (see Chapter 6), nutrition, environmental, pathologies

## Major tissues types and locations

- [ ] Epithelial tissue – protective and secretory
- [ ] Simple epithelial tissue – squamous, cuboidal, columnar, ciliated
- [ ] Stratified epithelial tissue – keratinised, non-keratinised, transitional
- [ ] Connective tissue – fibrous, areolar, adipose, lymphoid, cartilage, bone
- [ ] Blood – red blood cells, white blood cells, platelets, plasma (see Chapter 8)
- [ ] Muscular tissue – skeletal, smooth, cardiac (see Chapter 4)
- [ ] Nervous tissue – neurones, neuroglial cells (see Chapter 5)
- [ ] Membranes – serous, mucous, synovial

## Anatomical regions of the body

- [ ] Definitions and locations – abdominal, axillary, brachial, buccal, calcaneal, carpal, celiac, cephalic, cervical, costal, cranial, crural, cubital, cutaneous, femoral, forearm, frontal, gluteal, groin, inguinal, lumbar, mammary, leg, ophthalmic, orbital, palmar, patellar, pectoral, pedal, pelvic, perineal, pericardial, plantar, popliteal, sacral, tarsal, thoracic, umbilical

## Directional terms

- [ ] Definitions and examples – superior, inferior, medial, lateral, superficial, deep, anterior, posterior, proximal, distal, parietal, visceral, contralateral, ipsilateral
- [ ] Planes – Frontal, sagittal, transverse, longitudinal, oblique
- [ ] Pathologies – viral, bacterial, fungal, congenital, heredity, hormonal, allergic (see Chapter 2), hormonal (see Chapter 6).

# 2 Skin, hair, nails and common pathologies

The skin is a large organ and forms a protective, waterproof covering over the entire surface of the body. It is thinnest on the eyelids and thickest on the soles of the feet. The skin is continually shedding and renewing itself. It is made up of layers called the **epidermis**, **dermis** and **subcutaneous layer**.

## Epidermis

The upper portion of the skin is called the epidermis. It mainly consists of four layers. However, five layers are found in regions such as the palms of the hands and soles of the feet. The layers include the horny layer, clear layer, granular layer, prickle cell layer and basal layer.

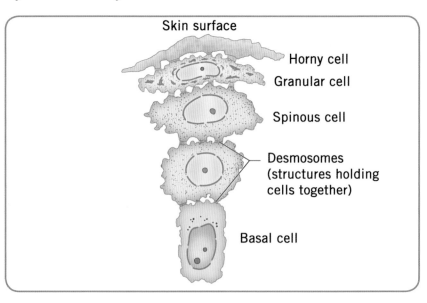

**Figure 2.1** A cell from each layer of the epidermis

26

# ① Horny layer (stratum corneum)

The top layer of the epidermis is called the horny layer and consists of flat, overlapping, keratinised cells. Keratin is a protein responsible for the hardening process (keratinisation) that cells undergo when they change from living cells with a nucleus to dead cells without a nucleus. Cells that have undergone keratinisation are therefore dead.

The keratinised cells help to prevent bacteria entering through the skin and protect the body from minor injury. Cells of the horny layer are continually being rubbed off the body by friction and are replaced by cells from the layers beneath. The shedding of dead skin cells is known as **desquamation**.

**don't forget**

Around 95% of cells within the epidermis are keratinocytes, which are responsible for producing keratin.

# ② Clear layer (stratum lucidum)

The clear layer is found below the horny layer and consists of dead, keratinised cells without a nucleus. The cells are transparent and the layer is thin. This layer is mainly found on the fingertips, the palms of the hands and the soles of the feet, and provides cushioning and protection.

**don't forget**

The top two layers – the horny and clear layers – are made up of dead cells that constantly shed from the skin. The granular layer also contains some dead skin cells.

# ③ Granular layer (stratum granulosum)

The granular layer contains cells that have a granular appearance. As the cells die, they fill with tiny granules called **keratohyalin** granules and so keratinisation (hardening of cells) begins to take place. This layer consists of living and dead cells. The keratin in this layer helps to prevent water loss from the skin.

# ④ Prickle cell layer (stratum spinosum)

In the prickle cell layer, the cells are living. The cells interlock by arm-like fine threads, which give the cells a prickly appearance. Pigment granules called **melanin** may be found here.

## ⑤ Basal layer (stratum germinativum)

The basal layer is the deepest layer in the epidermis and is in contact with the dermis directly beneath it. It consists mainly of a single row of tall, narrow basal cells. These cells are living, contain a nucleus and divide (mitosis) to make new skin cells. As new cells are produced, they push older cells above them towards the surface of the skin, until they finally reach the horny layer. It takes three to six weeks for the skin cells to be pushed up from the basal layer to the horny layer.

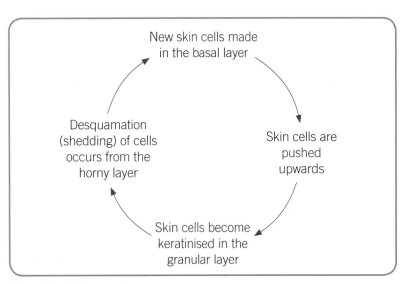

New skin cells made in the basal layer

Skin cells are pushed upwards

Skin cells become keratinised in the granular layer

Desquamation (shedding) of cells occurs from the horny layer

**Figure 2.2** Skin growth cycle

### ACTIVITY 2.1

Label the diagram in Figure 2.3, matching the numbers to the numbered terms in the text that describes the epidermal layers. Use this key to colour the diagram.

Yellow – layers 1 and 2
Red and yellow (that is, some cells red, some yellow) – layer 3
Red – layers 4 and 5

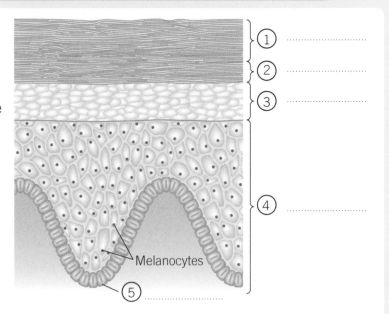

Melanocytes

**Figure 2.3** Epidermis

## Skin pigmentation

Melanin is the natural pigment responsible for the colour of skin, hair and eyes. Cells called **melanocytes** are found within the basal layer and produce granules of melanin. Melanin is stimulated by ultraviolet rays from the sun. This is why the skin develops a tan after sunbathing. Its function is to protect the deeper layers of the skin from damage. Approximately one in every ten basal cells is a melanocyte. Everyone has the same amount of melanocytes but produces varying quantities of melanin. This will determine the depth of skin colour. More melanin is produced in black skins than white skins, and this extra protection can help black skins to age more slowly than white skins.

### ACTIVITY 2.2

Mark the following statements true or false.

1. The basal layer contains dead cells. True/False

2. Keratinisation is the hardening process of cells, which occurs when they change from living to dead cells. True/False

3. Melanocytes are found in the horny layer of the epidermis. True/False

4. Melanin is the natural pigment responsible for the colour of skin and hair. True/False

### don't forget

Around 95% of cells within epidermis are keratinocyles, which are responsible for producing keratin.

### MEMORY JOGGER

To help you remember the layers of the epidermis, and depending on which names you need to learn, think of:
**Happy** – horny
**Clever** – clear
**Girls** – granular
**Pat** – prickle cell
**Back** – basal
or
**Corny** – stratum **corne**um
**Lucy's** – stratum **luci**dum
**Granny** – stratum **gran**ulosum
**Spins** – stratum **spin**osum
**Germs** – stratum **germi**nativum.

# Dermis

Below the epidermis lies the dermis, which connects with the basal layer and helps to protect, support and nourish the skin. It consists of two layers.

1. The upper section is called the **papillary layer** and contains small tubes called **capillaries**, which carry blood and lymph. There are also nerve endings. This layer provides nutrients for the living layers of the epidermis.

2.  The **reticular layer** is thicker and contains many thick **collagen** fibres, and also **elastin** fibres, which float in a gel-like substance. Collagen and elastin fibres are proteins made by cells called **fibroblasts**. Collagen fibres help to give the dermis resistance to strain and also give the skin strength. Elastin, a similar protein, gives the skin its elasticity and helps to keep it flexible. Wavy bands of tough collagen fibres restrict the extent to which the skin can be stretched, and elastin fibres return the skin back to shape after it has been stretched.

The dermis also contains nerves, hair follicles, sebaceous glands, sweat glands and arrector pili muscles; these are known as **appendages**.

## MEMORY JOGGER

Collagen will firmness bring, elastin will ensure a spring!

## ACTIVITY 2.3

Label the diagram in Figure 2.4, matching the numbers to the numbered terms in the text describing skin structures. Use this key to colour the diagram.

Pink – arrector pili muscle and the muscle below the subcutaneous layer
Blue – sweat gland and sensory nerve ending
Yellow – adipose tissue and sebaceous gland
Red – blood vessels
Brown – lymph vessels

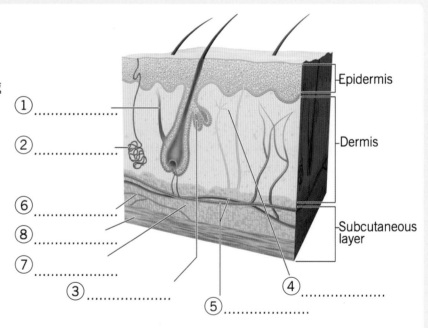

Figure 2.4 The skin and its structures

① **Arrector pili** muscles are small muscles attached to the hair **follicles** (the pits into which hairs sit). When we are cold, the contraction of these muscles causes the hairs to stand on end. This results in the appearance of goose bumps. Air is trapped between the skin and hair and is warmed by body heat. This can help to keep the body warm.

## Sweat glands

There are two types of sweat gland in the body.

② **Eccrine glands** excrete sweat and are found all over the body. The sweat duct opens directly onto the surface of the skin through an opening called a **pore**. Sweat is a mixture of water, salt and toxins. Black skins contain larger and more numerous sweat glands than white skins.

**Apocrine glands** are found in the armpits, around the nipples and in the groin area. They secrete (produce and release) a milky substance. These glands are larger than eccrine glands and are attached to the hair follicle. Apocrine glands are controlled by hormones, becoming active at puberty. Body odour is caused by the breaking down of the apocrine sweat by bacteria.

③ **Sebaceous glands** are small, sac-like structures that produce a substance called **sebum**. Sebum is a fatty substance that protects the skin from losing moisture. These glands are found all over the body, but are more numerous on the scalp and areas of the face, such as the nose, forehead and chin. Hormones control the activity of these glands and, as we get older, the secretion of sebum decreases, causing the skin to become drier. Sebum and sweat mix together on the skin to form an **acid mantle**. The acid mantle maintains the pH (acid/alkaline level) of the skin at 5.5–5.6; this helps to protect the skin from harmful bacteria. Some soaps affect the acid mantle and cause irritation and drying of the skin.

### FAST FACT ▶

The apocrine sweat contains substances called pheromones; the smell is thought to play a part in sexual attraction between individuals and the recognition of mothers by their babies.

### MEMORY JOGGER

To help you remember the position of the sweat glands think of **E** (eccrine glands) for **e**verywhere and **A** (apocrine glands) for **a**rmpits.

### FAST FACT ▶

The skin releases toxins through sweat; therefore, the skin helps to detoxify the body.

### FAST FACT ▶

Sebum is a Latin word meaning fat. The body uses fat to make sebum.

### *don't forget*

**Apocrine glands are also found on the feet.**

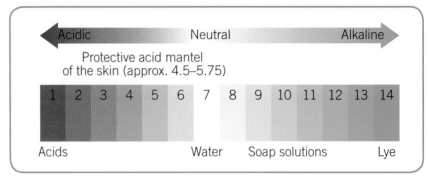

**Figure 2.5** pH scale and pH level of the skin

(4) **Sensory nerve endings** are found all over the body but are particularly numerous on the fingertips and lips. These nerves will make us aware of feelings of pain, touch, heat and cold by sending messages through sensory nerves to the brain.

Messages are sent from the brain through **motor nerves**. Motor nerves stimulate the sweat glands, arrector pili muscles and sebaceous glands to carry out their functions.

Blood within the (5) **blood vessels**, which form a **capillary network** (see the cardiovascular system in Chapter 8), provides the skin with essential oxygen and nutrients. The living cells of the skin produce waste products, such as carbon dioxide and other **metabolic waste**. These waste products pass from the cells and enter into the bloodstream to be taken away and removed by the body.

(6) **Lymph capillaries** carry a liquid substance called lymph (see the lymphatic system in Chapter 9). Like blood, lymph circulates throughout the body in tube-like structures.

## Subcutaneous layer

The subcutaneous layer is situated below the dermis. It consists of (7) **adipose tissue** (fat) and areolar tissue. The adipose tissue helps to protect the body against injury and acts as an insulating layer against heat loss, helping to keep the body warm. The areolar tissue contains elastic fibres, making this layer elastic and flexible. (8) **Muscle** is situated below the subcutaneous layer and is attached to bone.

## ASK FRAN...

**Q.** What causes the skin's inflammatory response during an allergic reaction?
**A.** You may have experienced an allergic reaction after applying make-up or using a certain cosmetic. During an allergic reaction, a chemical called **histamine** is produced by mast cells and is released in the skin. Histamine causes the blood vessels to dilate (widen) and become more permeable (leaky), so that fluid seeps out into the skin. This leads to inflammation, reddening and irritation of the skin. Extra blood is brought to the skin to help repair the tissues. Despite being the cause of unpleasant symptoms, the main function of histamine is to protect the body against invaders such as bacteria and viruses.

## ACTIVITY 2.4

Match up the bubbles with the correct definition in the list.

- Process of keratinisation takes place here ...........
- Dead cells of this layer are rubbed off by friction ...........
- Contracts, causing hair to stand on end ...........
- Layer found on palms of hands and soles of feet ...........
- Send messages informing the brain about the sensations of pain, heat and cold ...........
- Deepest layer in epidermis and in contact with the dermis ...........
- Found all over the body and excrete sweat ...........
- Stimulate sweat glands and sebaceous glands to carry out their functions ...........
- Release a moisturising substance called sebum ...........
- Living cell with a prickly appearance ...........
- Release milky substance and found in armpits and groin area ...........
- Bring supplies of oxygen and nutrients vital to skin ...........

1. Motor nerves

2. Prickle cell

3. Eccrine glands

4. Sensory nerve endings

5. Clear layer

6. Basal layer

7. Blood vessels

8. Sebaceous glands

9. Granular layer

10. Arrector pili

11. Apocrine glands

12. Horny layer

# Functions of the skin

## Sensation

The skin contains sensory nerve endings that send messages to the brain. These nerves respond to touch, pressure, pain, cold and heat, and allow us to recognise objects from their feel and shape.

**FAST FACT**

Metabolic waste results after oxygen and nutrients have been used by cells, and include carbon dioxide, water and sodium chloride.

ASK FRAN...

**Q.** Can massage help to break down fat?

**A.** If only it were that simple! The only way to break down body fat to lose weight is by adopting a healthy diet and to do regular exercise. However, massage treatment is beneficial in a number of ways.

- It can help support exercise and weight loss by warming up muscles in preparation for activity.
- It can reduce soreness and stiffness in muscles.
- It increases flexibility.
- It reduces the risk of injury.
- It increases the metabolic rate.
- It aids the digestive function.
- It helps to motivate an individual by increasing feelings of well-being.

## Heat regulation

It is important for the body to have a constant internal temperature of around 37 degrees Celsius (°C). The skin helps to maintain this temperature by:

1. **Vasoconstriction**. This occurs when the body becomes cold. The blood vessels constrict (become narrower) reducing the flow of blood through the capillaries. Heat lost from the surface of the skin is therefore reduced, so helps the body to stay warm.
2. **Vasodilation**. This occurs when the body becomes too hot. The capillaries expand and, becoming wider, so the blood flow increases. This allows heat to be lost from the body by radiation. The loss of heat from the body will help to cool it down.
3. **Goose bumps**. Contraction of the arrector pili muscle, when the body is cold, causes the hairs to stand on end, keeping a layer of warm air close to the body. This was probably of more use to our ancestors, who were generally hairier.
4. **Shivering**. Shivering, when cold, helps to warm the body, as the contraction of the muscles produces heat within the body.
5. **Sweating**. In hot conditions the rate of sweat production increases. The eccrine glands excrete sweat on to the skin surface and heat is lost as the water evaporates from the skin.

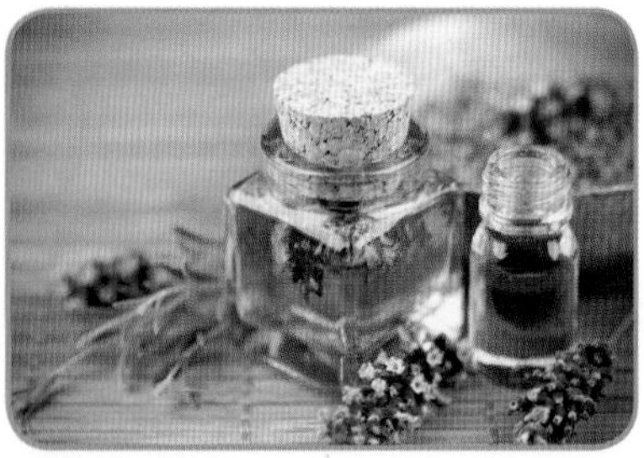

**Figure 2.6** Essential oils can be absorbed by the skin

## Absorption

The skin is largely waterproof and absorbs very little, although certain substances are able to pass through the basal layer. Essential oils can pass through the hair follicles and into the bloodstream. Certain medications, such as hormone replacement therapy (HRT), can be given through patches placed on the skin. Ultraviolet (UV) rays from the sun are also able to penetrate through the basal layer.

## Protection

The skin protects the body by keeping harmful bacteria out and by providing a covering for all the organs inside. It also protects underlying structures from the harmful effects of UV light by forming **melanin**. The other functions of the skin also help to protect the body.

## Excretion

Eccrine glands excrete sweat on to the skin's surface. Sweat consists of 99.4% water, 0.4% toxins and 0.2% salts.

## Secretion

Sebum is a fatty substance secreted from the sebaceous glands on to the skin's surface. It keeps the skin flexible, helps to waterproof it, and also reduces the loss of moisture from the skin, helping to ensure it doesn't become dry.

## Vitamin D

Vitamin D is often known as the sunshine vitamin. It is produced in the body when the UV rays from the sun penetrate through the skin's layers and activate a chemical found in the skin, turning it into vitamin D3. This vitamin is carried to the liver and then the kidneys to be transformed into active vitamin D (calcitriol). Then it is released into the blood circulation and taken to various organs. Vitamin D is stored in the liver and is essential for healthy bones.

---

**MEMORY JOGGER**

A good way of remembering the functions of the skin is the mnemonic SHAPES VitD.
S – sensation
H – heat regulation
A – absorption
P – protection
E – excretion
S – secretion
VitD – vitamin D formation.

**FAST FACT**

A deficiency of vitamin D can cause rickets in children, a condition in which the bones are malformed. In adults, it can cause osteomalacia, which features bones that are soft and weak and easily break.

**don't forget**

Vitamin D helps bones to grow strong and is made by the body when exposed to the sun!

## ACTIVITY 2.5

Fill in the gaps in the following text.

- ........................................ nerve endings respond to touch, pressure and pain. They send the information to the brain.

- It is important for the body temperature to remain at around ........................................ .

- To reduce heat loss from the skin, the blood vessels ........................................ . This is known as ........................................ .

- When the body becomes too hot, the capillaries dilate so heat can be lost. This is known as ........................................ .

- Goose bumps are caused by the contraction of the ........................................ ........................................ muscles.

- Shivering helps to ........................................ the body because of the contraction of the muscles.

- Sweating helps to ........................................ the body as heat is lost when the sweat evaporates.

- The skin can absorb certain substances, including ........................................ and ........................................ .

- Sweat consists of water, ........................................ and ........................................ .

- A fatty substance called ........................................ is secreted on to the skin's surface.

- Vitamin ........................................ production is stimulated by the penetration of UV rays through the skin.

**Figure 2.7** Massage can be beneficial to the skin

# Skin ageing

Some ageing of the skin occurs naturally over time, but premature ageing can occur because of various factors, including a person's genetic make-up, environmental factors (perhaps working outside in all weathers), inadequate diet, smoking or ill health.

The skin is at its best from birth to the early 20s as there is good collagen production and the elastin has a lot of 'spring', allowing the skin to easily snap back into place if it is stretched. However, in adolescence, hormonal factors can lead to an overproduction of sebum, resulting in spots and acne.

In the late 20s and 30s, fine lines appear on the skin's surface, especially around the eyes, where the skin is thinner. Collagen production slows and the elastin has less spring.

From age 40, hormone activity in the body slows down, so the sebaceous glands produce less sebum and the skin becomes increasingly dry. Lines and wrinkles appear on the surface. Wrinkling is caused by changes in the collagen and elastin fibres of the connective tissue in the dermis. The collagen fibres in the dermis begin to decrease in number, stiffen and break apart. The elastin fibres lose some of their elasticity and break down, so that when the skin is stretched it does not immediately snap back into place. Constant facial expressions cause wrinkles, such as crow's feet, to be found at the sides of the eyes.

From the late 50s, darkened, flat spots called lentigines (**liver spots**) may appear because of an increase in the size of some melanocytes. Liver spots are commonly brown in colour and are seen on sun-exposed areas of the skin, such as around the temple areas of the face and on the backs of the hands.

The blood flow to the skin is reduced and the rate of mitosis (cell division) in the basal layer slows down. The horny layer is therefore thinner, making the skin more fragile. Broken capillaries appear on the face, especially on the cheeks and nose.

The sweat glands are less active and the sebaceous glands decrease in size, which leads to dry and cracked skin. The skin of older people heals poorly and becomes more susceptible to infection. Loss of underlying fat leads to hollowed cheeks and eye sockets.

Skin cells are continually dying and being replaced by new cells in a process known as cell renewal or cell turnover. The appearance of the skin is influenced by the rate at which cell turnover occurs. At a young age, skin cells turn over about every

## ASK FRAN...

**Q.** What are the effects of massage on the skin?
**A.** Massage is beneficial to the skin in a number of ways.

- The circulation is improved and so fresh blood brings nutrients to the sebaceous glands; therefore, sebum production is increased. Sebum helps to make the skin soft and supple.
- The sweat glands become more active and so more sweat is excreted. Toxins, such as urea and other waste products, are eliminated from the body in this way.
- Massage also causes the top layer of dead skin cells to be shed (desquamation), which improves the condition of the skin, giving it a healthy glow.
- The sensory nerve endings can either be soothed or stimulated, depending on the massage movements used.
- When massage and essential oils are used together, the skin's health and appearance can be greatly improved.

## FAST FACT

In people who are regularly exposed to UV light or who smoke, the loss of elasticity of the skin is greatly accelerated (speeded up).

### ASK FRAN...

**Q.** How does botox treatment work?

**A.** Botox treatment involves injecting a protein, derived from botulism toxin, underneath the skin to paralyse facial muscles, which helps to minimise frown lines, forehead lines and crow's feet. Botox works by blocking signals (known as neurotransmitters) that pass messages from nerves to the muscles. Normally, passing of these massages results in contraction of the muscles and, therefore, wrinkling of the skin. Blockage of the signals causes relaxation of the muscle, therefore wrinkled areas appear smoothed out. When the neurotransmitter production returns to normal, usually within three to six months, the muscle receives the signal to contract once again, which leads to skin wrinkling. Botox treatment is also used to treat migraine headaches and excessive underarm sweating.

30 days. As we get older, the cells divide more slowly. At 80 years old, cell turnover takes twice as long as when a person was 30. This causes the top of layer of skin to become thinner and more fragile, and the complexion becomes dull because the dead skin cells at the top of the skin slough off more slowly.

### ACTIVITY 2.6

List five changes that take place in the skin as it ages.

1. ........................................................................................

2. ........................................................................................

3. ........................................................................................

4. ........................................................................................

5. ........................................................................................

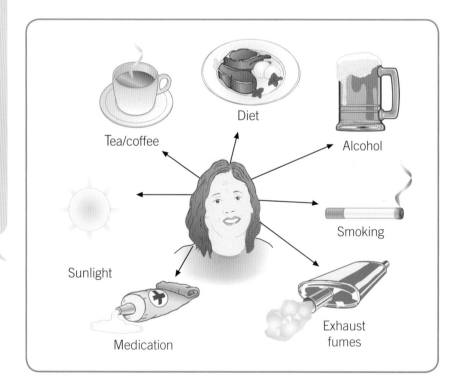

**Figure 2.8** Factors affecting the skin

Various factors can affect the condition of the skin and include those listed below.

## Diet/Nutrition

The best nutritional recommendation to ensure healthy skin is to eat a well-balanced diet. The Western diet generally contains the essential vitamins and minerals required for a healthy skin. These include vitamins A, C and E.

Vitamin A helps to control the rate of keratinisation in the skin, so deficiency of this vitamin can result in dry skin. Good sources include vegetables, eggs, butter and cheese.

Vitamin C is required by the body to produce collagen, which makes up a large part of the skin, and deficiency of this vitamin can lead to dermatitis. A lack of vitamin C may cause blood capillaries to become weakened and so lead to bruising. Good sources of vitamin C include fruit and vegetables.

Vitamin E helps to keep the skin hydrated, reduce inflammation and aids healing. Vitamin E is found in most foods, but good sources include vegetable oils, eggs and meat.

## Alcohol

Alcohol is not harmful to the skin in moderation, but large amounts dilate the blood vessels and, over time, may weaken the capillary walls. This can lead to broken capillaries and redness, which can often be seen on the face.

Alcohol also dehydrates the skin, by drawing water from the tissues, and robs the body of vitamins B and C, which are required for a healthy skin.

## Caffeine

Caffeine is found in tea, coffee, chocolate and some fizzy soft drinks. Drinking moderate amounts will cause no harm, but excessive amounts can interfere with the absorption of vitamins and minerals, which can result in an unhealthy and dry skin.

**FAST FACT**

Vitamins A, C and E are all antioxidants, which help to prevent premature ageing of the skin.

**don't forget**

An antioxidant is a substance that helps to fight free radicals. Free radicals are molecules that damage the cells, such as skin cells.

## Sunlight/UV

Of all the factors that cause premature ageing, exposure of the skin to sunlight is the most important. UV radiation from the sun penetrates the dermis of the skin and causes damage. With repeated exposure to the sun, the skin loses the ability to repair itself. This is often termed photoageing, and is, without doubt, the leading cause of skin ageing. It causes dehydration, breaks down collagen and interferes with the making of new collagen. It also attacks the elastin in the skin, which then loses its strength and elasticity, resulting in severe wrinkling and sagging.

**Figure 2.9** Wrinkling of the skin can be caused by several factors

## Smoking

Smoking interferes with cell respiration and slows down the blood circulation as nicotine is a vasoconstrictor (it causes the blood vessels to become smaller). This makes it harder for nutrients to reach the skin cells and for waste products to be eliminated. Cigarette smoking also releases a chemical that destroys vitamin C. This interferes with the production of collagen and so contributes to premature ageing.

In addition, continual puckering of the lips while smoking can result in wrinkles forming around the mouth. People who have smoked for a long time will generally look older than non-smokers of the same age.

## Medical conditions and medication

Some medical conditions can affect the skin. For example, an underactive thyroid can cause dry and pale skin, and an overactive thyroid can cause oily skin, blemishes and, possibly, acne. Thyroid problems can also lead to flushing and increased redness of the skin, and can cause the skin to thicken.

Medications, such as antidepressants, antihistamines and antibiotics, can also affect the skin.

Antidepressants and antihistamines can cause skin dryness.

Antibiotics can cause temporary drying of the skin, although it will improve after the course of drugs has finished. Antibiotics can also make the skin more photosensitive (sensitive to sunlight), so it is more likely to burn. Some antibiotics can cause hives and flushing of the skin.

Beta blockers are used to treat heart problems, high blood pressure, anxiety and migraine. In some people, they may cause the skin to become dry or lead to the development of hives. Also, the skin may bruise more easily or develop purplish marks.

Steroids are used to treat inflammatory conditions, such as arthritis, asthma and some skin conditions. Taken by mouth they can lead to skin dehydration, fluid retention or swelling of the tissues.

Hydrocortisone creams are a type of steroid that are applied externally and are used to treat skin conditions such as psoriasis and dermatitis. These creams should only be used for short periods of time and in small quantities, otherwise thinning of the skin may occur. However, this does depend on the type of hydrocortisone cream used.

## Environment/climate

The moisture content of the epidermis can be affected by factors such as central heating, which creates a dry environment. This causes moisture to be lost from the epidermis and can lead to dehydration.

When a person moves between a cold and a warm environment, their capillaries contract (become narrower) and dilate (become wider) to adapt to the change in temperature. If someone does this frequently, for instance if they work outdoors, over time the capillary walls may become weak, leading to permanently broken capillaries. These are also known as dilated capillaries or thread veins and are commonly seen on the cheeks and nose. Excessive alcohol consumption, hereditary factors, vigorous scrubbing to the face, excessive sun exposure and certain skin conditions can all result in broken capillaries.

Air pollution from industry, car fumes, for example, harms the skin and causes dehydration. It can also lead to dirt building up on the skin, resulting in blocked pores.

## Stress

People suffering with stress are more likely to neglect their skin, which can result in it looking unhealthy. Stress can have a harmful effect on the skin, and conditions that are particularly sensitive to it include acne, eczema, psoriasis, hives and cold sores. Chronic stress can also lead to premature ageing of the skin. Tense facial muscles may cause lines and wrinkles to form, and may also restrict oxygen and nutrients to the skin. Stress may lead to excessive alcohol intake and rapid weight loss or gain, resulting in changes to the skin, such as dehydration and sagging.

## ACTIVITY 2.7

Fill in the gaps in the following text.

- Vitamin ............................... is required by the body to produce collagen.

- Excessive alcohol intake can lead to weakening of the ............................... walls.

- UV rays cause ............................... of the skin and also damage the structure of the ............................... and ............................... fibres.

- Smoking causes a chemical to be released that destroys vitamin ............................... .

- Long-term smokers are more prone to ............................... ageing than non-smokers.

- Long-term use of certain hydrocortisone creams may cause ............................... of the skin.

- While using antibiotics the skin can become ............................... and ............................... .

- Central heating and air pollution can lead to the skin becoming ............................... .

- If the skin alternates between cold and warm environments, damage to the capillaries may result, which leads to permanently broken ............................... .

# Skin types

Skin types vary from person to person and can be described as being normal/young/balanced, dry, oily, combination, sensitive, dehydrated or mature. Essential oils can be chosen to suit each individual skin type.

## Normal/Young/Balanced

This skin type will look healthy, clear and fresh. It is often seen in children, as external factors and ageing have not yet affected the condition of the skin, although the increased activity of hormones at puberty may cause the skin to become greasy. A normal skin type will look neither oily nor dry and will have a fine, even texture. The pores are small and the skin's elasticity is good, so it feels soft and firm to the touch. It is usually free of spots and blemishes.

## Dry

This skin type may look thin and fine, and broken capillaries can often be seen around the cheek and nose areas. The skin will feel and look dry because little sebum is being produced and it is also lacking in moisture (water). This skin type will often tighten after washing, and will not generally contain comedones (blackheads) or visible open pores. This skin type is prone to premature wrinkling, especially around the eyes, mouth and neck.

## Oily

This skin type will look shiny, dull and slightly yellowish (sallow) in colour because of the excess sebum production. Oily skin is coarse, thick and will feel greasy. Enlarged pores can be seen; these are due to the excess production and build-up of sebum. Open pores can let in bacteria, which cause spots and infections. Blocked pores often lead to comedones. Oily skin tends to age more slowly as the sebum absorbs some of the UV rays of the sun and so can protect against its damaging effects. The sebum also helps to keep the skin moisturised and prevents drying.

**Figure 2.10a** Various skin types

**Figure 2.10b** Various skin types

## Combination

Most clients will have a combination skin type. With this skin type there will be areas of dry, normal and oily skin. Usually the forehead, nose and chin are oily (this is known as the T-zone). The areas around the eyes and cheeks are usually dry and may be sensitive.

## Sensitive

This skin type is often dry, transparent and reddens easily when touched. Broken capillaries may be present, especially on the cheeks, which gives the face a red colour. Hereditary factors may be a cause of sensitive skin. Certain substances may easily irritate a sensitive skin, so care should be taken when choosing products for this skin type. If a white skin is sensitive to a product it will show as a reddened area; on black skin it will show up as a darkened area.

## Dehydrated

This skin type lacks moisture (water) and so is dry. The causes include too much sun, illness, medication, dieting and working in a dry environment with low humidity (little water in the air), such as an air-conditioned office. Sebum helps to prevent evaporation of water from the skin, so when insufficient sebum is produced, moisture is lost from the skin. The skin feels and looks dry and tight. There may be flaking and fine lines present on the skin. Broken capillaries are also common with this skin type.

## Mature

This skin type is dry, as the sebaceous and sweat glands become less active as we age. The skin may be thin and wrinkles will be present. There are usually broken capillaries, often around the nose and cheek areas. The bone structure can become more prominent as the adipose (fat) and supportive tissue become thinner. Muscle tone is often poor, so the contours of the face become slack. Owing to the poor blood circulation, waste products are removed less quickly, so the skin may become puffy and pale in colour. Dark patches, known as liver spots, may also appear on the face and hands. The cause of this skin type is ageing and altered hormone activity.

## ACTIVITY 2.8

Write the characteristics of each skin type into the table below.

| Skin type | Brief description |
| --- | --- |
| Normal/young/ balanced | |
| Dry | |
| Oily | |
| Combination | |
| Sensitive | |
| Dehydrated | |
| Mature | |

*don't forget*

A <u>congenital condition</u> is a disease that is present from birth.

# Skin diseases and disorders

**FAST FACT**

An acute disease is one that generally begins rapidly but lasts for a short period of time. A chronic disease starts more slowly but lasts for a longer period of time and is often persistent.

There are several classifications for skin diseases and disorders, including bacterial infections, viral infections, fungal infections, infestations, allergies and non-infectious conditions. Some infections, such as ringworm and athlete's foot, can be caught by direct contact with an infected person. Infections can also be caught by indirect contact with contaminated items, such as towels, coins, door handles and crockery, which can store germs such as bacteria.

## Bacterial infections

**Bacteria** are tiny, single-celled organisms and can multiply very quickly. They are capable of breeding (increasing in numbers) outside the body, so can be caught easily by direct contact or by touching a contaminated article. Regular hand-washing and ensuring items in your environment are clean will help to keep bacteria levels to a minimum.

There are two types of bacteria: **pathogenic** (harmful) and **non-pathogenic** (harmless). Infections occur when harmful bacteria enter the skin through broken skin or through hair follicles. The most common are listed below.

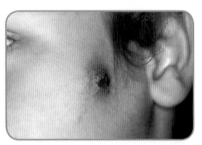

**Figure 2.11** Boil

### Boils

A boil is an infection of the hair follicle with staph bacteria, which usually enter through a cut, scratch or other break in the skin. It begins as a tender, red lump and develops into a painful **pustule** containing pus. It extends deep into the skin, and grows larger and more painful until it ruptures. Once a head is formed the pus is discharged, leaving a space, and so scarring of the skin often remains after the boil has healed.

Poor general health and inadequate diet are factors increasing the chances of developing a boil. Sufferers are treated with antibiotics. Boils are infectious so the area affected should be avoided during complementary therapy treatment. **Carbuncles** are a group of boils involving several hair follicles.

**Figure 2.12** Stye

A stye is a small boil on the edge of the eyelid and is caused by an infection of the follicle of an eyelash. The area becomes inflamed and swollen, and there may be pus present. Styes are infectious and are mostly caused by bacteria entering the skin, so it is important that the eyelid area is kept clean to prevent them occurring. A doctor may prescribe antibiotics if the infection spreads.

## Conjunctivitis

This is inflammation of the conjunctiva, the membrane covering the eye. The inner eyelid and eyeball appear red and sore. It is caused by a bacterial infection following irritation to the eye, such as grit or dust entering the eye, and is further aggravated by rubbing. Pus is often present and may ooze from the area. Conjunctivitis is infectious, and cross-infection can occur through using contaminated towels or tissues.

**Figure 2.13** Conjunctivitis

## Impetigo

This infection begins when bacteria invade a cut, cold sore or other broken skin. It can be seen as sores and weeping blisters that form golden/yellow-coloured crusts. The area around the crusts is inflamed and red. Impetigo is highly infectious and spreads quickly on the surface of the skin. Usually the outbreaks are among children. If this condition is suspected, the sufferer must be referred to a doctor and treated with antibiotic creams.

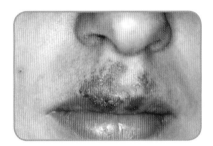

**Figure 2.14** Impetigo

## Folliculitis

Folliculitis can be caused by a bacterial or fungal infection of the hair follicles and sebaceous glands. It may develop because of friction from shaving, excessive perspiration or tight clothing. It can also be a side effect of certain medicines, such as steroids. Symptoms include skin inflammation, itching, red swellings

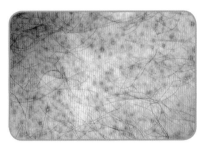

**Figure 2.15** Folliculitis

## ACTIVITY 2.9

Fill in the table below.

| Disorder | Brief description | Is it infectious? |
|---|---|---|
| Boil | | |
| Carbuncle | | |
| Conjunctivitis | | |
| Impetigo | | |
| Folliculitis | | |

(**papules**) and pus-filled swellings (pustules). The area should be avoided during complementary therapy treatment. More severe cases of folliculitis may require antibiotics or antifungal medications to help control the problem.

## Viral infections

Although very small, **viruses** are responsible for a great deal of human disease. They are protein-coated particles. Cells in the body are taken over by invading viruses and so break down. Viruses need living cells in which to live and multiply – they cannot live outside their host (the body). Many viruses take up residence along nerve pathways, which accounts for the pain associated with viral infections, such as shingles. They can be transmitted by direct and indirect contact.

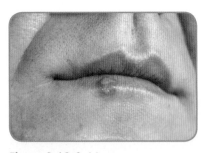

**Figure 2.16** Cold sore

### Cold sore

Cold sores are a common skin infection caused by the **herpes simplex** virus. It is usually passed on in early childhood, probably as a result of being kissed by someone with a cold sore. The virus passes through the skin, travels up a nerve and lies dormant at a nerve junction. When the virus is stimulated, it travels back down the nerve and forms a cold sore. It begins as an area of erythema (redness) on the skin, which blisters and forms a crust, usually around the mouth. Cold sores often appear after a period of stress. They can also be triggered by exposure to bright sunlight, menstruation or can accompany colds and flu. Cold sores are highly infectious so the area must be avoided during complementary therapy treatment.

### Shingles (herpes zoster)

Shingles is an infection caused by the Varicella zoster virus, which also causes chickenpox. It is an infection of the nerves supplying certain areas of the skin and is more common in middle-aged and older people, and in people with a poor immune system. It appears as areas of redness and inflammation on the skin and there is itching too. Blisters (sacs of fluid) develop along nerve pathways, and there may be fever and lethargy. It can be painful and persist for many months.

After suffering with chickenpox, the virus remains in the body at the nerve roots. However, if it becomes active again it can cause shingles. Most people will only get shingles once. You may catch chickenpox from someone with shingles, if you have not had chickenpox before, but you cannot get shingles from someone who has shingles. The virus is passed on by direct contact with the blisters. No massage treatment should be given over the affected area.

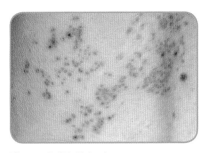

**Figure 2.17** Shingles

## Warts

Common warts are firm, raised, pink or skin-coloured lumps with a bumpy surface that may look like a cauliflower. They may be alone or in groups on the hands, elbows or knees, and will generally disappear on their own within two to three years. Warts are caused by infection with the human papillomavirus (HPV), which can take anything from one month to two years after contact to cause a wart to form. They often invade warm, moist places, like small cuts or scratches on the fingers, hands and feet.

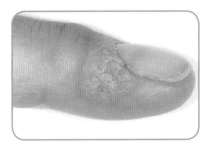

**Figure 2.18** Warts

## Verrucas (or verrucae)

Verrucas appear on the soles of the feet and grow inwards. They appear as flat, thickened skin and have a rough surface. Small black spots may be present; these are actually small blood vessels caused by tiny blood clots getting trapped within blood capillaries. They can be painful and make standing or walking uncomfortable.

The virus responsible for warts and verrucas is spread by direct contact with an infected person, or by touching surfaces or items, such as towels, which are carrying the virus. It may also be picked up in places such as swimming pool floors and changing rooms, which have been in contact with a person who has warts.

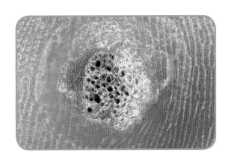

**Figure 2.19** Verruca

*don't forget*

Warts and verrucas are infectious and so should not be touched.

## ACTIVITY 2.10

Fill in the table below.

| Disorder | Brief description | Is it infectious? |
| --- | --- | --- |
| Cold sore | | |
| Shingles | | |
| Wart | | |
| Verruca | | |

## Fungal infections

Disease-causing (pathogenic) fungi produce infectious conditions. Microscopic fungi spores reproduce by the process of cell division (cells multiply to make new cells). Fungi need other cells to survive and often affect dead tissue, such as hair and nails.

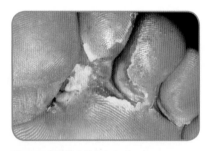

**Figure 2.20** Athlete's foot

### Athlete's foot (tinea pedis)

This common infection is caused by a type of fungus (tiny microscopic organisms that include yeasts and moulds). The fungi like warm, moist environments. They feed on keratin – a protein found in hair, nails and skin. Many people have fungi present on their skin but are unaffected by them. Breaks in the skin allow the fungus to enter and may cause athlete's foot, which mostly affects the area between the toes and on the sole of the foot. The skin becomes cracked and itchy with flaking pieces of dead, white skin, which may give off an unpleasant smell. The skin may also be swollen and blisters may form. It is more common in men and teenagers and, as the name suggests, it is more common in people who play a lot of sport.

A fungal infection is commonly spread in places such as communal showers and changing rooms. It can be spread through direct contact with the infection and by skin particles left on towels, shoes, floors of shower cubicles and around swimming pools, and in changing rooms.

Athlete's foot is infectious so the affected area should be avoided during treatment. The client should be encouraged to keep the feet cool, dry and clean. Antifungal powders can be used to treat the condition.

### Ringworm (tinea corporis)

Ringworm is a fungal infection, not caused by a worm, and can be caught through touching animals, skin-to-skin contact with an infected person, and contact with infected objects. It affects the horny layer of the skin and shows itself as itchy, red, scaly, circular patches that spread outwards. The centre of the patch heals, forming a ring shape. It usually appears on the trunk of the body, the limbs and the face. Ringworm is highly infectious so the area must be avoided during massage treatment and the client should be referred to their GP.

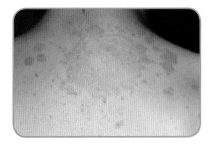

**Figure 2.21** Ringworm

## ACTIVITY 2.11

Fill in the table below.

| Disorder | Brief description | Is it infectious? |
|---|---|---|
| Athlete's foot | | |
| Ringworm | | |

## Infestations

There are various types of parasitic infestations that cause disorders of the human skin.

### Scabies

The eight-legged scabies mite burrows into, and lays its eggs, in the horny layer of the skin. It can affect most areas of the body, although it is commonly found in the webs between the fingers and in the crease of the elbow. There is a four- to six-week incubation period before the outbreak and the new mites work

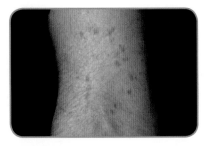

**Figure 2.22** Scabies

their way to the surface of the skin and spread to other areas. The female mite leaves a trail of eggs and excrement in the skin, which appear as wavy greyish lines. The condition is very itchy and highly infectious; it can be spread quickly through physical contact in a family, school or nursing home. No massage treatment should be given and the client should consult their doctor. Scabies is easily treated with medications that, when applied to the skin, kill the mites that cause scabies.

**Figure 2.23** Head lice

### FAST FACT ▶

Head lice cannot jump or fly; they are spread by head-to-head contact or via contaminated objects, such as a hairbrush or towel.

### Head lice (pediculosis capitis)

Head lice are a very common problem, especially among school-aged children owing to close head contact. They are tiny insects that live in hair, preferably clean hair, and feed on the blood from the scalp. The female lays 4–10 eggs each day and attaches them to hair close to the scalp. This condition is itchy, so infection can occur through scratching. Specialist shampoos are available and the whole family should be treated. No complementary therapy treatment should be given as the condition is highly infectious.

### Pubic lice (pediculosis pubis)

Pubic lice are tiny insects that are found in pubic hair, and are also known as crabs as they resemble sea crabs. They are commonly caught through having sex with an infected partner. Pubic lice feed on blood, and their bites may cause severe itching. The infection can be readily treated by the use of special lotions and creams that kill the parasites and their eggs.

## ACTIVITY 2.12

Fill in the table below.

| Disorder | Brief description | Is it infectious? |
|---|---|---|
| Scabies | | |
| Head lice | | |
| Pubic lice | | |

# Pigmentation disorders and factors affecting the colour of skin

### Chloasma (melasma)

This condition shows itself as patches of increased pigmentation on areas of the skin, often the face, and is the result of an increase in the level of melanin and melanocytes. The condition can be caused by sunburn, pregnancy or the contraceptive pill. Chloasma is not infectious so massage treatment can be carried out.

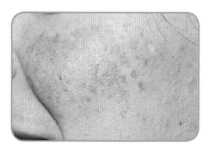

**Figure 2.24** Chloasma

### Vitiligo (leucoderma)

This condition shows itself as a complete loss of colour in areas of the skin, causing white patches to appear. The affected areas have either lost their pigment (melanin) or were never pigmented. The lightened patches of skin are very sensitive to sunlight and burn easily. The cause of vitiligo is unknown. This condition is not infectious so complementary treatment can be carried out.

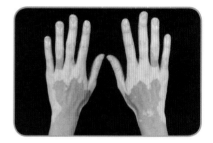

**Figure 2.25** Vitiligo

### Albinism

In this condition, the skin and hair are abnormally white and the irises of the eyes are pink, as there is little or no production of the pigment melanin. Most people with albinism are sensitive to sun exposure and are at increased risk of developing skin cancer. It is a hereditary disorder and a result of faulty genes. Albinism is not infectious so complementary therapy treatment can be given.

**Figure 2.26** Albinism

**FAST FACT**

Melanin is involved in the development of optic nerves (nerves in the eyes). Therefore, people with albinism have problems with the development and function of the eyes, and so experience vision impairment.

### Freckles (ephelides)

Freckles show themselves as small, pigmented areas of skin. The UV rays from sunlight stimulate the production of melanin and therefore either darken freckles or create new ones. Freckles are not infectious so can be worked over during complementary therapy treatment.

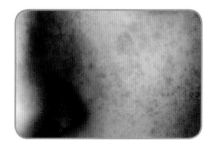

**Figure 2.27** Freckles

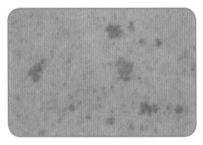

**Figure 2.28** Lentigines

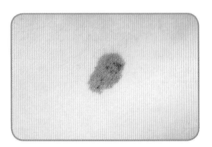

**Figure 2.29** Naevus

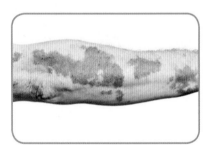

**Figure 2.30** Port wine stain

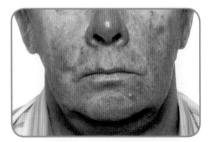

**Figure 2.31** Erythema (a person blushing)

## Lentigines (len-tij-gin-knees) (liver spots)

Lentigines (singular: lentigo) are also known as **liver spots** or **age spots**. Although larger than freckles, they are also pigmented areas of skin, but lentigines do not darken when exposed to UV rays. They are usually brown in colour and oval-shaped, and are commonly seen on the face and hands. Liver spots are mainly caused by years of exposure to UV light from the sun. They are not infectious so can be worked over during complementary therapy treatment.

## Naevus (knee-vus) (birthmark)

A naevus (plural: naevi) is a birthmark; however, there are many different types. They can be found anywhere on the body and vary in size. Naevi are not infectious so complementary therapy treatment can be carried out over the affected area.

## Port wine stain (nevus flammeus)

A port wine stain is a birthmark that consists of a large area of dilated capillaries, causing a reddish colour. It looks like maroon-coloured wine was spilled or splashed on to the skin, and most port wine stains occur on the face, neck, scalp, arms or legs. They are caused by insufficient supply of nerve fibres to an area of skin. Small blood vessels keep expanding, as they are not controlled by nerves, and allow a greater amount of blood to flow into the blood vessels. Blood is constantly supplied to that area of the skin and causes a red stain to develop. Laser therapy is commonly used to treat them and will make them much less noticeable. They are not infectious so can be worked over during complementary therapy treatment.

## Erythema

There are different types of erythema; however, it generally refers to redness of the skin. It occurs when blood capillaries expand (dilate) to allow a greater amount of blood to reach the skin. It can be the result of many factors, including injury, allergy or an infection, but it can also be caused by massage and skin blushing.

## ACTIVITY 2.13

Fill in the table below.

| Disorder | Brief description | Is it infectious? |
|---|---|---|
| Chloasma | | |
| Vitiligo | | |
| Albinism | | |
| Freckles | | |
| Lentigines | | |
| Naevus | | |
| Port wine stain | | |
| Erythema | | |

## Skin allergies

### Allergies

An allergy, such as hay fever, is an abnormal response by the body's immune system to a usually harmless substance (**allergen**). Allergens include pollen, house dust mites and food. Some people's skin can react to ordinary substances, such as cosmetics or plants, which are normally harmless to most people. This results in irritation to the skin, causing some of its cells to release histamine. Histamine is released by mast cells in the skin and causes it to become warm, red and swollen. Antihistamines can be used to help control the symptoms caused by the release of histamine. They work by blocking the effect of histamine.

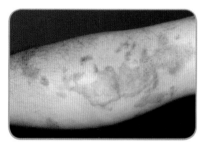

**Figure 2.32** Allergic reaction to skin

It is advisable to give an allergy test to someone with sensitive skin; there may be a reaction to the essential oils or carrier oils. You should also ensure that the client is not allergic to wheat or nuts if you intend to use wheatgerm or carrier oils extracted from nuts. An irritated skin caused by an allergy is not infectious, but it is advisable not to carry out complementary therapy treatment over the affected area.

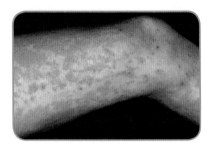

**Figure 2.33** Urticaria

## Urticaria (ur-tee-care-ree-er)

Urticaria is an allergic skin condition often called **nettle rash** or **hives**. The rash may appear anywhere on the face or body and is accompanied by itching. There are numerous causes of urticaria; it can occur as an allergic response to substances such as certain foods and drugs. It can also be caused by heat, cold, sunlight, scabies, insect bites and contact with plants. This condition is not infectious, but it is advisable not to work over the affected area during complementary therapy treatment.

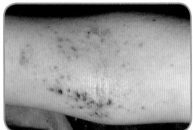
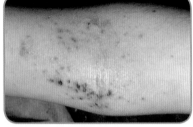

**Figure 2.34** Eczema

## Eczema

Eczema is the name for a group of skin conditions that cause skin inflammation and feature itchy, dry, scaly red patches. Small blisters may form and burst, causing the skin to weep. Hereditary factors or external irritants, such as detergents, cosmetics and soaps, can cause eczema. Internal irritants, such as dairy products, can also be a trigger. This condition is not infectious, although it is advisable to avoid working over the affected areas during complementary therapy treatment, especially if there is weeping or bleeding.

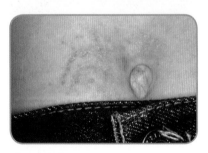

**Figure 2.35** Dermatitis

## Dermatitis

Contact dermatitis is a form of eczema and there are two types.

**Allergic contact dermatitis** is caused by a substance (allergen) that stimulates an immune response in the skin. The first time this happens, the body becomes 'sensitised' to the allergen. However, the following time it comes into contact with it, the body 'remembers' the previous encounter and so a skin reaction will occur. Common allergens that cause allergic contact dermatitis include hair dye, textiles, glue and plants. Certain metals, such as nickel, found in watch straps, earrings and bra hooks, can irritate the skin and lead to dermatitis in sensitive people.

**Irritant contact dermatitis** is caused by a substance (irritant) that damages the skin and causes a burning and stinging sensation.

Common irritants are detergents, soaps and chemicals found in perfumes, cosmetics and toiletries. These irritants can produce allergic reactions that can lead to this type of dermatitis.

Symptoms of both types of dermatitis include erythema, dryness, itching and flaking of the skin and, in severe cases, blisters can develop. Although the condition is not infectious, it is advisable not to work over the affected area until it has cleared up.

**FAST FACT**

An abrasion is a minor injury that only affects the surface of the skin.

## ACTIVITY 2.14

Fill in the table below.

| Disorder | Brief description | Is it infectious? |
|---|---|---|
| Allergies | | |
| Urticaria | | |
| Eczema | | |
| Dermatitis | | |

## Sebaceous gland disorders

### Milia

If skin keratinises over the hair follicle it causes sebum, dead skin and other substances to accumulate and become trapped in the follicle. It is the keratinised skin cells that cause the hard lump. A milium (plural: milia) can be seen as a small white spot, so is often termed a **whitehead**, and may accompany dry skin. Milia usually occur on the cheekbones, eyelids and sometimes the forehead. Beauty therapists are often trained in the removal of milia. This condition is not infectious.

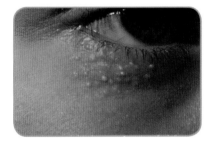

**Figure 2.36** Milia

### Comedones

Comedones (singular: comedo), also known as **blackheads**, occur when sebum and dead skin cells become trapped in a hair follicle. This may happen if the sebaceous glands produce too much sebum. Keratinised skin cells mix with the sebum and form a

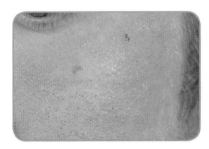

**Figure 2.37** Comedomes

plug. The head of the comedo becomes black in colour because it combines with the oxygen in the air (oxidises). Comedones generally occur on oily skin types and are not infectious. Complementary therapy treatment can be carried out over them.

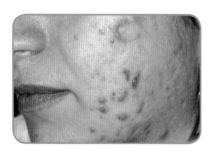

**Figure 2.38** Acne vulgaris

### Acne vulgaris

Acne is a common skin condition and usually affects teenagers. It is caused by an overproduction of sebum, usually because of stimulation of the sebaceous glands by hormones called testosterone and **progesterone**. During adolescence the levels of these sex hormones rise. The pores become clogged as the sebum, along with dead skin cells, becomes trapped in the openings of the sebaceous glands and, if the pores become infected, red and swollen spots will appear. Comedones (blackheads) also form and, if they become infected, the typical red and swollen spots appear. The spots are mainly found on the face, neck and back.

Acne often runs in families and may be triggered by hormonal changes, medications (such as steroids, oestrogen and testosterone), oily cosmetics and hair products, Acne is not infectious, but the skin must be handled with care.

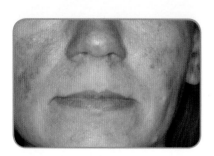

**Figure 2.39** Rosacea

**don't forget**

Papules are also known as pimples, and are inflamed, raised, irritated spots. Pustules are spots that contain pus.

### Rosacea (roe-zay-sha)

This condition is often referred to as **acne rosacea**. It mainly affects people over the age of 30 and is more common in women than men. Rosacea affects the nose, cheeks and forehead, giving a flushed, reddened appearance. The blood vessels, which are dilated in these areas, produce a butterfly shape. Pus-filled spots may appear and the affected area may also become lumpy, because of swollen sebaceous glands. The exact cause of rosacea is unknown, but triggers include exposure to sunlight, stress, alcohol, eating spicy or hot food, and cold weather. Fortunately, most cases of rosacea can be effectively treated with medication. It is not an infectious condition but care needs to be taken when massaging over the affected areas. It is wise to avoid the area if the client has a severe case of rosacea.

## ACTIVITY 2.15

Fill in the table below.

| Disorder | Brief description | Is it infectious? |
|---|---|---|
| Milia | | |
| Comedones | | |
| Acne vulgaris | | |
| Acne rosacea | | |

# Skin disorders involving abnormal growth

### Psoriasis

Psoriasis is a common skin condition that involves skin cells reproducing too quickly in certain areas of the skin. This results in thickened patches of skin, which are red, dry and covered in whitish scales. They may also be itchy and painful. Psoriasis may be mild and only affect the elbows and knees, or it may cover the whole body, including the scalp. The cause is unknown although the condition can be hereditary, and stress and an unhealthy lifestyle can also be factors. There are many treatments for psoriasis, such as UV therapy and cortisone creams, but there is no cure. Psoriasis is not infectious so complementary therapy treatment can be given providing there is no bleeding or weeping and that the client will not feel any discomfort.

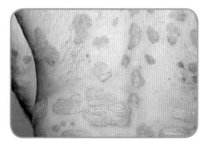

**Figure 2.40** Psoriasis

### Skin tags

Skin tags can affect most parts of the body, often the neck, and are soft lumps that are attached to the skin by a stalk. They are made of loose fibrous tissue, which protrudes out from the skin, and are mainly brown in colour. They are harmless and are not infectious. Removal of skin tags can be carried out by a doctor or certain beauty clinics. It is advisable to work gently over skin tags as it may be uncomfortable for the client.

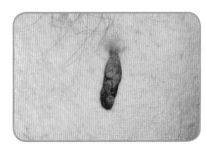

**Figure 2.41** Skin tags

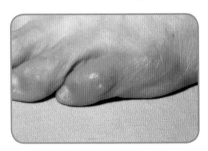

**Figure 2.42** Corns

**don't forget**

Basal cell carcinoma begins in the basal cells.

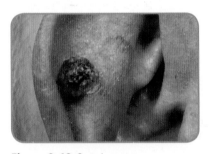

**Figure 2.43** Carcinomas

**don't forget**

A melanoma can affect anyone so we should all be vigilant. The danger signs to look out for are:
- any new moles that appear
- a mole that gets bigger
- a mole that bleeds, itches or ulcerates
- a mole that gets darker or lighter in colour.

## Corns

Corns are areas of thick, hard and dry skin that build up in order to protect parts of the feet from friction or pressure. Hard corns are pea-sized and have a hard centre that can press into the skin causing pain and swelling; they commonly form over bony areas such as the little toe. Soft corns are whitish and feel rubbery; they often occur between the toes where the skin is kept moist. They may be painful and can become infected by bacteria or fungi. They are usually caused by badly fitting shoes. If a corn is infected or painful do not treat the affected area.

## Skin cancer

There are three main types of skin cancer, named according to the types of skin cell from which they develop.

### Basal cell carcinoma

Basal cell carcinomas account for most cases of all skin cancers. They are usually found on areas of the body that are often exposed to the sun, such as the face, neck, arms and hands. This type of skin cancer may begin as a small lump that increases in size, and may have shiny-looking edges. The middle of it may be sunken and sometimes develops into an ulcer or a crusty patch. They are usually painless but may be itchy. They are mostly diagnosed in middle-aged or older people, and it is rare for a basal cell skin cancer to spread to another area of the body. They are not infectious but should be avoided during complementary therapy treatment as they may cause discomfort to the sufferer if touched, and can easily bleed.

### Squamous cell carcinoma

This type of cancer is less common than basal cell skin cancer, but it is also found on areas of the body that are commonly exposed to the sun. It begins in keratinocytes and as it develops may become a crusty, scaly ulcer or be bumpy and hard. It may develop in scars, areas of skin that have been previously sunburned, and ulcerated skin. This cancer can spread, commonly to the deeper layers of the skin, but sometimes to lymph nodes and other organs close by, which may cause secondary cancers.

### Melanoma

A melanoma, also called malignant melanoma, is a skin growth caused by overactivity of the melanocytes, usually the result of excessive exposure to the sun. Melanocyte overactivity may be benign, as in a mole, or malignant, as in a malignant melanoma. Although rare and not infectious, malignant melanomas are extremely dangerous as the cancer can spread to other organs in the body. They can occur anywhere on the body, but often at the site of a mole. The first sign of a melanoma may be the development of a new mole or a change in the appearance of an existing mole. They are usually irregular in outline, patchy in colour, itchy or sore and may bleed. They spread very quickly and need prompt medical attention.

**don't forget**

A mole is a pigmented area of the skin and is also known as a <u>papilloma</u>.

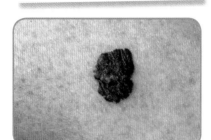

**Figure 2.44** Melanoma

**FAST FACT**

The main cause of melanoma is thought to be overexposure to the sun. Overuse of sunbeds may increase the risk of developing melanoma.

## ACTIVITY 2.16

Fill in the table below.

| Disorder | Brief description | Is it infectious? |
|---|---|---|
| Psoriasis | | |
| Skin tag | | |
| Corn | | |
| Basal cell carcinoma | | |
| Squamous cell carcinoma | | |
| Melanoma | | |

## Other skin diseases, disorders and conditions

Here are some brief descriptions of other skin conditions including their causes and whether they are infectious. Use the internet to find images of these conditions.

### Dermatosis papulosa nigra

These are small black or dark brown papules on the face and neck. It is common in black skin types. The cause is unknown although it can be hereditary. It is not infectious.

### Blisters

When the outer layer of skin is damaged a blister may develop. It is filled with a clear fluid that helps to protect the area from further damage. Blisters are not infectious.

### Cyst

This is a sac of air, liquid or semi-solid substance that can form in body tissue. It is not infectious. There are various causes, which include infection and hereditary factors.

### Candidiasis

This is a yeast infection (a type of fungus), which results when there is an overgrowth of yeast on the skin. It causes a rash, which may be sore and itchy. Antifungal powders and creams are commonly used to treat it.

### Keloid scars

This is abnormal healing of the skin resulting in the formation of lumpy scar tissue. It is more common in dark-skinned people, especially black skin types. It is not infectious.

### Striae (stretch marks)

These are areas of skin that show (often whitish) bands, lines or stripes. They may be caused by rapid weight loss or weight gain. Stretch marks may develop following pregnancy and can be caused by medical conditions, such as **diabetes**, and certain medications. They are not infectious.

### Xanthomas

These are slightly raised bumps under the skin that are yellow in colour. They are fatty deposits and may be a sign that fat levels in the blood are too high. The cause is unknown and they are not infectious.

### Chillblains

These are painful itchy areas on the skin that can vary in colour from blue to red. They may be caused by poor blood circulation, which is worsened by cold and damp conditions. They are not infectious.

# Hair

Most of the body is covered by hairs, with the exception of the palms of the hands and the soles of the feet. Hairs mainly consist of the protein keratin and grow out from **follicles**. Follicles are deep pits that extend into the dermis. Hairs help to keep the body warm and are also a form of protection. The eyelashes prevent substances from entering the eyes, and the hairs that line the nose and ears help to trap dust and bacteria.

The ① **bulb** is found at the base of the hair and has an upper and lower part. The ② **matrix** is the lower part of the bulb and this is where cell division takes place to create the hair. When cells reach the upper part of the bulb they quickly fill with keratin and die.

Melanin can be found in the upper part of the bulb and will determine the colour of hair. The hair bulb surrounds the ③ **dermal papilla**, an area containing many blood vessels, which provides the necessary nutrients needed for hair growth.

*don't forget*

The functions of hair include heat regulation and protection.

**FAST FACT ›**

Hereditary factors, in other words, patterns that run in families, will determine the specific hair growth characteristics of a person.

**FAST FACT ›**

Hormones are responsible for stimulating the growth of the hairs so will determine the quantity, thickness and distribution of hair on the body.

## ACTIVITY 2.17

Label the diagram in Figure 2.46, matching the numbers to the numbered terms in the text. Use this key to colour the diagram.

Blue – cortex (avoid the bulb area)
Red – dermal papilla
Yellow – bulb
Green – inner root sheath
Orange – outer root sheath

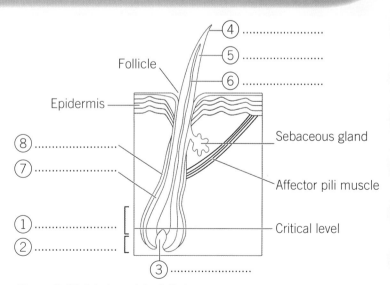

Follicle

Epidermis

④ .....................
⑤ .....................
⑥ .....................

⑧ .....................
⑦ .....................

① .....................
② .....................

③ .....................

Sebaceous gland

Affector pili muscle

Critical level

**Figure 2.45** A hair and its follicle

The hair is made up of three layers.

1. The ④ **cuticle** is the outer part of the hair and consists of a single layer of scale-like cells. These cells overlap rather like tiles on a roof. No pigment is contained within this layer.

2. The ⑤ **cortex** lies inside the cuticle and forms the bulk of the hair. It contains melanin, which determines the colour of the hair. The cortex helps to give strength to the hair.

3. The ⑥ **medulla** is the inner part of the hair and is not always present. Air spaces in the medulla determine the colour tone and sheen of the hair because of the reflection of light.

The ⑦ **inner root sheath** can be found between the outer root sheath and the hair shaft. It is made up of three layers: cuticle, Huxley's layer, and Henle's layer. The cuticle of the inner root sheath consists of cells that interlock with the cuticle scales of hair and helps to keep the hair in place. Huxley's layer is in the middle and is the thickest of the three layers. Henle's layer is found on the outside and lies next to the outer root sheath.

The ⑧ **outer root sheath** surrounds the inner root sheath and is continuous with the basal layer of the epidermis. It contains hair germs cells, which make new hairs. The new hair cells are produced at the base of the follicle by mitosis (cell division).

The vitreous membrane (also called basal lamina) separates the outer root sheath and the connective tissue.

## Types of hair growth

There are different types of hair growth.

1. **Lanugo hair** is the hair found on the foetus and is usually shed by about the eighth month of pregnancy.

2. **Vellus hair** is soft and downy and is found all over the body except on the palms of the hands and soles of the feet.

3. **Terminal hair** is longer, coarser and the follicles are deeper than vellus hair. These hairs can be found on the head, eyebrows and eyelashes, under the arms and in the pubic region.

**FAST FACT** ❯

When a hair is removed from the body it may have a white substance surrounding the bottom of it; this is the inner root sheath.

**don't forget**

The inner root sheath only grows as far as the sebaceous gland and is not part of the epidermis.

**don't forget**

Connective tissue connects, supports or surrounds other tissues and organs. Examples include bone, blood and adipose (fat) tissues.

# The hair growth cycle

The hair grows in stages known as **anagen**, **catagen** and **telogen**. All hairs will be at different stages of growth at any one time.

1.  The **anagen** stage is the active growing stage. It lasts from a few weeks up to several years and accounts for 85 per cent of hairs at any one time. The hair bulb surrounds the nutrient-giving dermal papilla and a hair begins to grow from the matrix in the bulb. The anagen stage ends when the hair begins to separate from the dermal papilla and so no longer receives nutrients.

2.  **Catagen** is the transitional stage and lasts for about two weeks. Only 1 per cent of hairs will be at this stage. The hair is now fully grown and cell division has stopped. The hair has separated from the papilla and the follicle begins to shrink.

3.  **Telogen** is the stage at which the hair rests, and lasts for about three to four months. About 14 per cent of hairs will be at this stage. The resting hair will either fall out or be pushed out by a new hair growing beneath it.

**FAST FACT**

The number and distribution of hair follicles are the same in both sexes.

**MEMORY JOGGER**

To help you remember, think of ACT.
A – Anagen: Active stage.
C – Catagen: Changing stage.
T – Telogen: Tired stage.

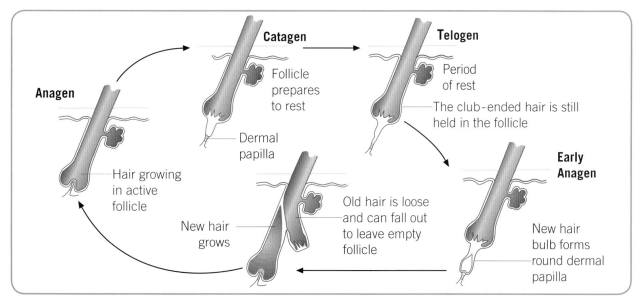

**Figure 2.46** Stages of hair growth

## Conditions associated with the hair

### Factors affecting hair growth
Hair growth can be affected by various factors, including the following.

**Hormones** – varying hormone levels in the body can affect hair growth rates. Male hormones (**androgens**) speed up hair growth (see 'Hirsutism'); female hormones (oestrogens) slow it down.

**Medical treatment** – this can cause significant changes to original hair growth. Chemotherapy causes hair to fall out and regrowth may have a different texture or colour.

**Certain medication** – this may affect hair growth and also have long-terms effects. Drugs that may cause hair loss include acne medications containing vitamin A (retinoids), antidepressants, birth control pills and high blood pressure medications. Chemotherapy and thyroid medication can cause a change in hair colour.

### Medical conditions affecting hair growth

#### Alopecia

**Figure 2.47** Alopecia

Alopecia is the term for loss of hair. **Alopecia totalis** is total hair loss from the scalp. **Alopecia areata** is a form of patchy baldness that usually affects the scalp, causing bald spots. Many women suffer from some degree of alopecia in their lives, especially after the menopause. During pregnancy scalp hair grows thicker than normal, but afterwards a decrease in hormones may cause a sudden loss of hair. Usually the loss is not noticeable because new hairs will be growing. Common reasons for hair loss include hereditary factors (which usually affect men), severe illness and stress.

Other medical conditions that can cause hair loss include diabetes, **anaemia**, lupus and underactive or overactive thyroid.

#### Hirsutism

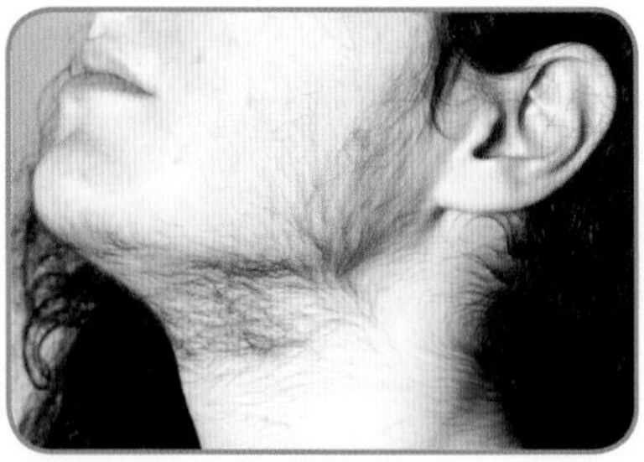

**Figure 2.48** Hirsutism

This is an abnormal growth of excess hair (often thick), which follows a male pattern of hair growth; it grows on parts of the body where hair growth in women is usually minimal or non-existent. It is caused by male hormones called **androgens** (such as testosterone). These hormones are made in larger amounts in men, but small amounts are also produced in women. Hirsutism can be caused by an abnormally high level of androgens, or a normal level of androgens but hair follicles that are oversensitive to them. Levels of androgens can increase at puberty, pregnancy, menopause and at times of stress, so all can lead to hirsutism. Hirsutism can also be caused by medical conditions such as ovarian cysts and anorexia nervosa.

*don't forget*

**The hormone testosterone is a type of androgen.**

# Nails

*don't forget*

**The functions of nails are protection and manual dexterity (they enable us to pick up items).**

Nails are formed from hard, keratinous cells and also contain some water and fat. Nails help to protect the ends of fingers and toes and are also useful for picking up small objects.

## ACTIVITY 2.18

Label the diagram in Figure 2.49, matching the numbers to the numbered terms in the following text. Use this key to colour the diagram.

Red – nail plate
Yellow – lunula
Pink – nail bed
Blue – matrix

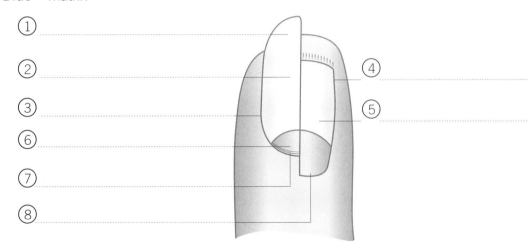

**Figure 2.49** The nail and its structures

## ① Free edge

The free edge is an extension of the nail plate and is the part that we cut and file. If you have long enough nails, look at the palm of your hand and see the nail protruding over the fingertips; this is the free edge.

## ② Nail plate

This is the tough part of the nail that can be seen. It appears pink in colour because of the blood vessels in the nail bed below it. It contains no blood vessels or nerves so can be cut without pain. Its function is to protect the nail bed beneath it.

## ③ Nail walls

These are overlapping folds of skin found at the side of the nails that protect the edges of the nail plate.

## ④ Nail grooves

Grooves at the side of the nails, between the nail plate and nail wall, act as guidelines for growing nails so that they grow in a straight line.

## ⑤ Nail bed

The nail bed is found underneath the nail plate and is rich with nerves and blood vessels. The nail bed and nail plate contain grooves and ridges that enable them to adhere perfectly to each other.

## ⑥ Lunula

The lunula is crescent-shaped and mostly white in colour. It is found at the base of the nail plate. It has no specific function.

## ⑦ Cuticle

The cuticle is the dead, colourless overlapping skin at the base of the nail. It prevents bacteria and any other harmful substances entering the matrix and causing infection.

## ⑧ Matrix

Cell division takes place in the matrix to form the nail plate. It is an area richly supplied with nerves and blood vessels. Injury to this area can mean temporary or permanent damage to the growing nail.

## Hyponychium (hy-poh-nik-eeum)

This is a thickened layer of skin under the free edge of the nail (often known as the 'quick').

## Eponychium (ep-oh-nik-eeum)

The eponychium is the living skin at the base of the nail plate covering the matrix area. It helps to prevent the matrix from becoming infected with germs such as bacteria.

## Paronychium (pa–roh-nik-eeum)

This is the area of the skin that surrounds the side of the nail (the nail border) and can become infected, for example around an ingrowing toenail.

## Nail mantle

The deep fold of skin at the base of the nail, near to the cuticle, that protects the matrix.

**FAST FACT**

The cuticle and eponychium are often thought to be the same, but they are not. The cuticle is dead tissue that adheres to the nail plate; the eponychium is living tissue that grows up to the nail plate.

**Figure 2.50** Healthy nails

**FAST FACT**

The upper layer of the nail plate is hard but thin. This is the layer that often peels away, because of the damage caused by the bonds between it and the middle layer.

**don't forget**

Factors affecting nail growth include poor health, unhealthy diet, certain types of medication, and the ageing process.

## Nail growth cycle

It takes about five to six months for the nail to grow from the matrix to the free edge. Diet, injury, health and age are all factors related to poor nail growth and an unhealthy appearance of the nail.

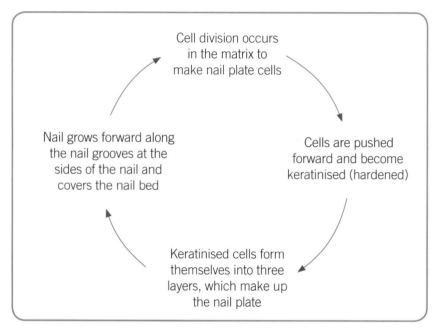

**Figure 2.51** Nail growth cycle

## Conditions associated with the nails

The therapist needs to be aware of nail conditions that are infectious or could cause discomfort for the client during treatment. The colour of the nails is a good indication of any disorder or disease present. Nails that are yellow could indicate psoriasis, especially if there is also pitting in the nail; blue nails indicate poor circulation; if there are patches of green, brown or black, there could be a fungal or bacterial infection present.

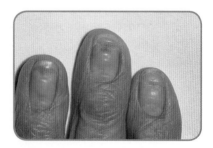

**Figure 2.52** Transverse ridges

### Beau's lines (transverse ridges)

**Description:** Beau's lines are deep grooved lines and ridges that run from side to side on the fingernails. As the nail grows, the Beau's lines may disappear. It is the result of any interruption in the protein formation of the nail plate.

**Causes:** Associated with trauma, illness, poor diet and chemotherapy.

**Advice:** Poor manicure techniques can cause ridges to form. Nail treatment may be given.

### Blue nails

**Description:** Nails show a bluish colour and the hands may feel cool. It is the result of poor circulation of the blood to the fingers.

**Cause:** It may be the sign of a heart condition or a rare condition called Raynaud's disease, which affects the blood vessels, usually of the fingers and toes, so there is poor circulation to the hands and feet.

**Advice:** Complementary therapy treatment can be given and massage will be particularly beneficial to help boost the circulation.

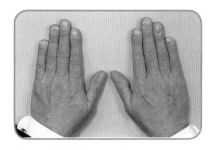
**Figure 2.53** Blue nails

### Brown nail

**Description:** Brown nails can be seen as nails that appear brown coloured.

**Causes:** This may be caused by thyroid disease, pregnancy and poor diet; it often results from occupational hazards. For example, hairdressers, carpenters, photographers and factory workers who come into contact with harmful products containing potassium permanganate, silver nitrate, hair dyes and tobacco.

**Advice:** The nails can be treated providing there is no discomfort to the client.

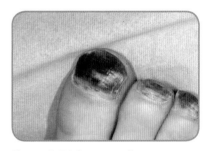
**Figure 2.54** Brown nails

### Bruised nail

**Description:** A bruise on the nail bed, which can vary in colour from maroon to black. If there is severe bruising the nail will fall off.

**Cause:** Trauma to the nail bed.

**Advice:** Do not work on a bruised nail.

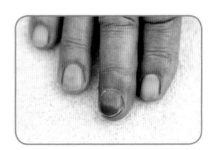
**Figure 2.55** Bruised nail

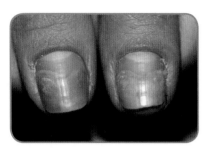

**Figure 2.56** Eggshell nails

### Eggshell nails

**Description:** Thin, white nails that are curved over the free edge.

**Causes**: Poor diet, illness and medication.

**Advice**: Care has to be taken when filing these nails as they are fragile and will easily break. Apply a nail strengthener to help make them stronger.

## ACTIVITY 2.19

Fill in the table below.

| Disorder | Brief description | Should area be avoided during treatment? |
|---|---|---|
| Beau's lines | | |
| Blue nails | | |
| Brown/black nail | | |
| Bruised nail | | |
| Eggshell nails | | |

**Figure 2.57** Hangnail

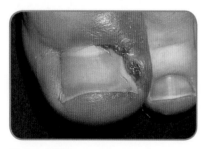

**Figure 2.58** Ingrowing toenail

### Hangnail

**Description:** The cuticle around the nail splits, leaving a dry piece of skin. The area may become infected and painful.

**Causes:** Dry cuticles and skin. The client may also bite the skin around the nail, which results in the formation of hangnails. Regular use of chemicals may cause the skin to become dry.

**Advice:** Regular application of moisturiser and cuticle oil will help prevent them forming. They do not affect treatment.

### Ingrowing toenail (onychocryptosis – on-nik-koh-crip-toe-sis)
**Description:** Inflammation owing to the corner of the nail growing into the skin. There is swelling, redness and it is often painful. It usually affects the big toe.

**Causes**: Pressure from footwear and cutting nails down too far at the sides. There may also be hereditary factors, for example the nails may be too large.

**Advice:** Cutting and filing nails straight across can help prevent it occurring.

### Leuconychia (loo-ko-nee-kee-ah) – white spots

**Description:** A very common condition that shows white spots on the nails that will eventually grow out.

**Cause:** Mostly owning to injury of the nail, which causes air bubbles to form between the nail bed and the nail plate.

**Precautions and advice:** Complementary therapy treatment can be given.

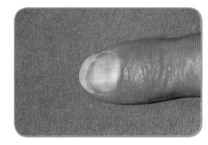

**Figure 2.59** Leuconychia

### Onychauxis (on-ee-kik-sis) – thickened nail

**Description:** Nails with this disorder are abnormally thick and overgrown.

**Causes:** Illness, injury, nail infection or hereditary factors.

**Precautions and advice:** If the client feels no discomfort and the nails are not separating from the nail bed, treatment may be carried out, although it may need to be modified to suit the client's nails.

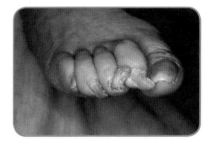

**Figure 2.60** Thickened nail

### Onychia (on-ee-ke-ah) – infection of the nail

**Description:** An infection will cause inflammation of the matrix. There may also be pus. The nail may separate and fall off.

**Causes**: Infection of bacteria through small wounds.

**Precautions and advice:** Do not treat the affected nails.

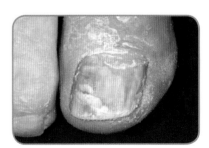

**Figure 2.61** Onychia

### Onycholysis (on-ee-co-lie-sis) – separation of the nail from nail bed

**Description:** Nail separates either partly or fully from the nail bed.

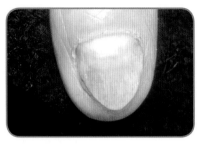

**Figure 2.62** Onycholysis

**Cause:** Mostly caused by physical trauma, such as an injury, but can also be the result of medical conditions such as psoriasis or thyroid disease. Other causes include fungal infections, reactions to certain chemicals, and as a side-effect of medication.

**Precautions and advice:** Avoid the affected area during treatment.

## ACTIVITY 2.20

Fill in the table below.

| Disorder | Brief description | Should area be avoided during treatment? |
|---|---|---|
| Hangnail | | |
| Ingrowing toenail | | |
| Leuconychia | | |
| Onychauxis | | |
| Onychia | | |
| Onycholysis | | |

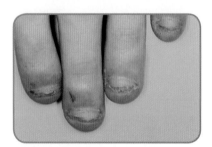

**Figure 2.63** Bitten nails

**Onychophagy (on-ee-co-fa-jee) – bitten nails**
**Description:** Severely bitten nails, which may become deformed and bulbous at the fingertips.

**Cause:** Nail biting.

**Advice:** Complementary therapy treatment can be given.

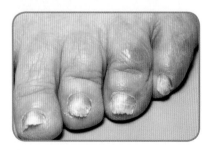

**Figure 2.64** Split nails

**Onychorrhexis (on-ee-co-rex-is) also known as lamella dystrophy – split or brittle nails**
**Description:** Nails that are split or brittle and have lengthwise ridges.

**Causes:** Chemical use, injury, careless filing or poor diet.

**Advice:** Warm oil treatments will help to moisturise and nourish split or brittle nails.

### Overgrown cuticle (pterygium – ter-ridge-e-um)

**Description:** The cuticle grows onto the nail plate and could possibly grow over the nail towards the free edge. This may lead to splitting of the cuticle and infection.

**Causes:** Neglect of nails, very dry cuticles and injury.

**Advice:** A manicure will be very helpful for this condition. Also recommend using a cuticle oil/cream daily and having regular warm oil treatments.

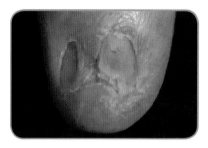

**Figure 2.65** Overgrown cuticle

### Paronychia (par-on-ik-ee-ah)

**Description:** An infected area near to the nail will be quite hard to the touch. It shows itself as a swollen, red and painful area around the nail fold. There may be pus and the infection can spread. The nail may turn brown or black in colour.

**Causes:** Hands continually immersed in water and harsh chemicals, or an ingrown nail that pierces the surrounding skin, allowing bacteria or fungi to get into the opening, resulting in infection. This may be caused by injury, bad manicure and poor cutting technique.

**Advice:** Do not touch the affected area.

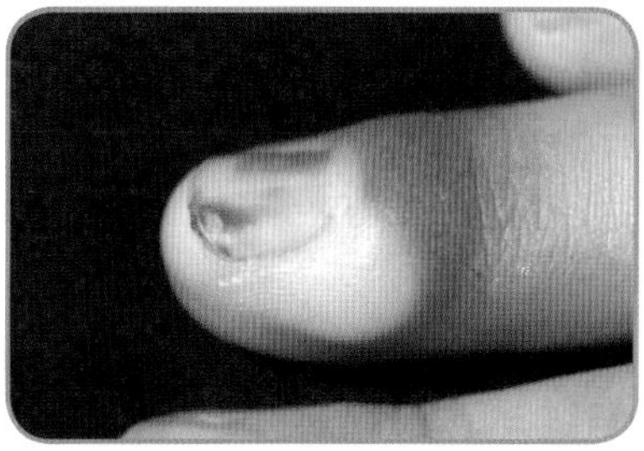

**Figure 2.66** Paronychia

> **FAST FACT**
>
> Untreated paronychia may lead to **sepsis**. Sepsis is the body's response to harmful bacteria or microorganisms that invade the body tissues or bloodstream. The body produces chemicals that cause inflammation throughout the body and can be dangerous.

### Pitting

**Description:** Tiny little circular-shaped dents (pits), the size of pin heads, can be seen in the nail. There may also be a yellowy discolouration of the nail.

**Causes:** Psoriasis, eczema or illness.

**Advice:** If the pitting is minor and the client does not experience any discomfort, normal treatment may be given.

### Ram's horn (club nail) also known as onychogryphosis (on-ee-ko-griff-o-sis)

**Description:** Overproduction of horny cells in the nail, which causes the nail plate to enlarge leading to curvature of the nail, similar in appearance to a ram's horn.

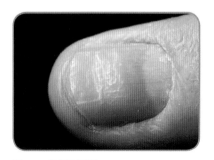

**Figure 2.67** Pitting

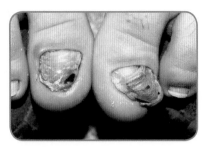

**Figure 2.68** Ram's horn

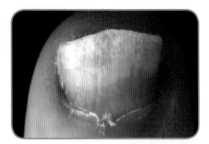

**Figure 2.69** Ringworm of the nail

### don't forget

Advise your client that eating a nutritious, balanced diet will help to improve the condition of the nails.

It is more common in the elderly and the big toe is mostly affected.

**Causes:** Old age, injury, poorly fitting shoes and neglect. This can also be associated with a heart and lung condition.

**Advice:** If severe or painful for the client when touched, do not give treatment.

### Ringworm of the nail – also know as onychomycosis (on-ee-ko-my-ko-sis) or tinea unguium

**Description:** At first, there are white or yellow patches of discolouration. Later, the nail becomes thickened, deformed and has a foul odour (musty smell). It begins at the free edge and spreads downwards. The nail becomes brittle and rough, and may even separate from the nail bed.

**Cause:** Fungal infection. Sweaty shoes and moist socks make ideal living conditions for the fungi. This may also be caused by injury or ingrowing toenail.

**Advice:** Do not touch the infected area as it is contagious.

## ACTIVITY 2.21

Fill in the table below.

| Disorder | Brief description | Should area be avoided during treatment? |
|---|---|---|
| Onychophagy | | |
| Onychorrhexis | | |
| Pterygium | | |
| Paronychia | | |
| Pitting | | |
| Ram's horn | | |
| Ringworm of the nail | | |

# What you should know

## Skin

- [ ] The layers of the epidermis – horny, clear, granular, prickle cell and basal
- [ ] The skin growth cycle – production of new skin cells, keratinisation, desquamtion, healing
- [ ] The layers of the dermis – papillary and reticular, and the structures found within them (collagen and elastin)
- [ ] The subcutaneous layer and its functions
- [ ] The skin structures and their functions – arrector pili muscles, sweat glands (eccrine and apocrine), blood and lymph capillaries, hair, sebaceous gland (sebum), sensory and motor nerves
- [ ] The functions of the skin – sensation, heat regulation, absorption, protection, excretion, secretion, vitamin D production, melanin formation
- [ ] Definition and appearance of skin types – normal/young/balanced, dry, oily, combination, sensitive, dehydrated, mature
- [ ] Factors affecting skin condition including age, diet/nutrition, alcohol, caffeine, smoking, sunlight/UV/environment/climate and stress
- [ ] Skin diseases and disorders (pathologies) – bacterial infections, viral infections, fungal diseases, infestations, pigmentation disorders, skin allergies, sebaceous gland disorders, skin disorders involving abnormal growth, skin cancers (melanoma, carcinoma) and general disorders (sensitive skin, ultraviolet damage, pustules and papules)

## Hair

- [ ] The structure of hair including hair follicle, hair shaft, inner root sheath, outer root sheath, arrector pili muscle, keratin, cuticle, cortex, medulla, dermal papilla
- [ ] Functions of hair – heat regulation and protection
- [ ] Different hair types – lanugo, vellus and terminal
- [ ] Hair growth cycle – anagen, catagen, telogen
- [ ] Factors affecting hair growth – diseases, medication
- [ ] Conditions associated with the hair – alopecia, hirsutism

## Nails

- [ ] The structure of the nail – free edge, nail plate, nail grooves, nail bed, lunula, cuticle, matrix, hyponychium, eponychium, paronychium, mantle, lateral nail fold
- [ ] Functions of nails – to protect and enable manual dexterity (pick up items)
- [ ] Nail growth – nail formation in matrix, which produces layers of keratinised cells
- [ ] Factors affecting nail growth – health, age, diet and medication
- [ ] Conditions and disorders (pathologies) of the nail, including their causes, signs and symptoms

# 3 Skeletal system and common pathologies

**FAST FACT**

99% of calcium is found in the bones and teeth. However, the remaining 1% is very important and its uses include muscle contraction and the passing of nerve messages in the body.

The skeletal system consists of the bones and joints of the body. There are 206 bones in the adult body. However, children are born with over 300 bones. Bones begin to develop before birth and continue to grow up to the age of 18–25. After 25, the bones stop growing, although they can continue to thicken. The bones together make up the skeleton, which has important functions for the body.

## Functions of the skeleton

**FAST FACT**

There are 206 bones in the adult body.

✖ **S – Shape/support.** The skeleton gives the body its shape and supports the weight of all the other tissues.

✖ **A – Attachment for muscles and tendons.** Bones provide the attachment point for the tendons of most skeletal muscles.

✖ **D – Development of blood cells.** Red blood cells, white blood cells and platelets are produced within the red bone marrow of the bone.

**don't forget**

Understanding the skeletal system, including the joints, will help you to work safely and confidently when carrying out treatments.

✖ **P – Protection.** Bones help to protect vital organs from injury. For example, the ribs protect the heart and lungs and the skull protects the brain.

✖ **A – Allows movement of the body.** When skeletal muscles contract, they pull on bones to produce a movement. The bones provide leverage.

**MEMORY JOGGER**

Use the words **SAD PAM** to help you remember the functions of the skeleton.

✖ **M – Mineral store.** Bones store the minerals calcium and phosphorus, which are important for the strength of the bone. If these minerals are required elsewhere in the body, the bones can release them into the bloodstream.

# Bones

Bone is living tissue and is constantly being built up and broken down. It is the hardest of all connective tissue in the body. It is made up of 30 per cent living tissue, such as collagen, and 70 per cent minerals and water. The minerals include mainly calcium and phosphorus. There are various types of bone in the body and these include long bones, short bones, flat bones, irregular bones and sesamoid bones.

## Types of bone

Almost all bones, except the coccyx (tail bone), are designed to meet a particular need in the body. There are five main types of bone.

✖ **Long bones**, such as the humerus in the arm, have a long shaft and two wider ends. They act as levers to enable the body to move. Other examples of long bones include the femur (thigh bone), tibia, fibula (both found in the lower leg), radius, ulna (both found in the lower arm), metacarpals (in the hand) and phalanges (found in fingers and toes).

✖ **Short bones** are roughly cube-shaped. They are found where strength, rather than mobility, is required. Bones of the wrists (carpals) and ankles (tarsals) are examples of short bones.

✖ **Flat bones** help to protect vital organs in the body. Flat bones, such as the skull, protect the brain, and the ribs protect the heart and lungs. Other flat bones include the scapulae (shoulder blades) and the sternum (breast bone).

✖ **Irregular bones**, such as the vertebrae of the spine (backbone), are found in places where extra strength is needed and also make good attachment points for muscles.

✖ **Sesamoid bones** are small, rounded bones that develop in the tendons. They enable the tendon to move smoothly over certain bones. An example is the patella (kneecap), which prevents wear and tear on the tendon of the front thigh muscle, which is attached to the tibia. It keeps the tendon in place when the knee is bent. Sesamoid bones are also found in the palms of the hands and soles of the feet. For example, these bones can be found in tendons lying over the joint, under the head of the first metatarsal in the foot. Their purpose is to protect the tendon as it moves over the joint. They may vary in number from person to person and mostly measure only a few millimetres.

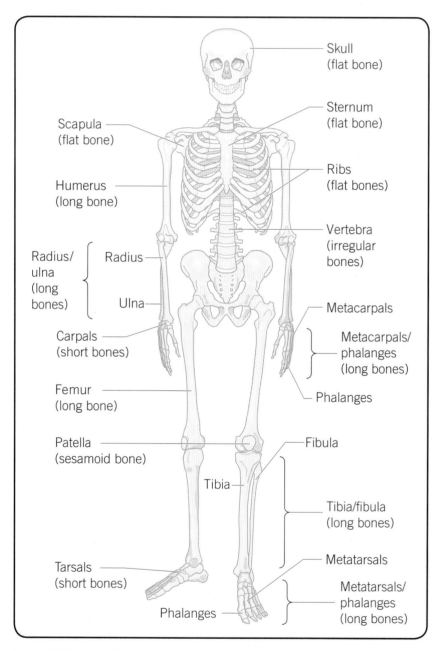

**Figure 3.1** Types of bone

## ACTIVITY 3.1

Which types of bone are the following, and what are their functions?

| Type of bone | Function |
| --- | --- |
| Carpals | |
| Vertebrae | |
| Humerus | |
| Skull | |
| Patella | |

## Formation of bone

The formation of bone is known as **ossification** and continually happens throughout human life. It is more active during the period of body growth and following the **fracture** of a bone.

In the developing **embryo**, rods of cartilage covered by a membrane can be seen and will eventually become the long bones. After birth, calcium is added to the cartilage. This is known as calcification. Bone-making cells, called osteoblasts, make collagen and lay down calcium phosphate to form new bone. They produce bone in the middle of the cartilage, which eventually becomes the shaft of the long bone. Ossification then occurs at the ends of the bones.

The membrane surrounding the bone becomes the **periosteum**, and bone and mineral salts are laid down. This results in an increase of thickness and length of the bone. Cells known as **osteoclasts** break down areas within the bone. A cavity is formed that will become filled with red bone marrow. A thin layer of cartilage will remain to cover each end of the bone.

At birth, all bone marrow is red. As we get older, more of it is turned into yellow marrow because of the addition of fat cells. This fills the cavities of many bones, especially long bones. By adolescence a lot of the bone marrow is yellow.

*don't forget*

Red and white blood cells, and also platelets, are made within the bone marrow.

*don't forget*

Bone is a living structure. As bone cells die, others will be made to replace them.

## A long bone

A long bone has a shaft and two rounded ends, such as the bone in the thigh (femur). The shaft contains yellow bone marrow and the ends have red bone marrow. Compact bone covers them and helps provide strength. Spongy (cancellous) bone is found at each end.

## ACTIVITY 3.2

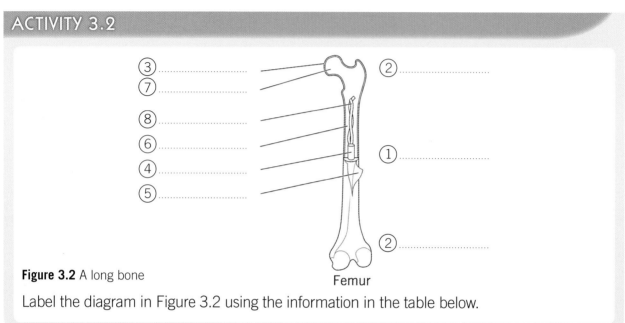

**Figure 3.2** A long bone

Femur

Label the diagram in Figure 3.2 using the information in the table below.

**Table 3.1** Showing bone structures and their function

| Bone Structure | Function |
|---|---|
| ① **Diaphysis (dye-ah-fis-sis)** | The shaft of a long bone, which contains yellow bone marrow. |
| ② **Epiphysis (eh-pif-fi-sis)** | The rounded end of a long bone. |
| ③ **Articular** (hyaline) **cartilage** | Covers the ends of the bones to stop them rubbing together and also helps to absorb shock. |
| ④ **Medullary cavity**/marrow cavity | Contains the yellow bone marrow. This is where white blood cells are made. |
| ⑤ **Periosteum** (pear-ree-oss-tee-um) | A layer that surrounds the bone. Ligaments and tendons attach to the periosteum. |
| ⑥ **Compact bone** tissue | Helps give strength to the bone. |
| ⑦ **Spongy** (cancellous) bone tissue | Contains red bone marrow. This is where blood cells are made. |
| ⑧ **Artery** | Carries oxygen and nutrients to the bone. |

## Bone tissue

There are two types of bone tissue: compact and cancellous (spongy).

### Compact bone tissue

Compact bone tissue is hard and dense. It provides strength, support and protection. It forms the outer layer of all bones and most of the shaft of long bones, such as the thigh bone (femur).

Under a microscope, compact bone looks like honeycomb and many circles can be seen, known as **Haversian** (ha-ver-shan) **systems**. In the centre of these circles are channels running lengthways through the bone, called the **Haversian canals**. The Haversian canals contain nerves, lymph capillaries and blood vessels.

The **lamellae** are rings of bone consisting of mineral salts (mostly calcium phosphates), which gives the bone its hardness. Rope-like collagen fibres give the bone its strength. The **lacunae** are the small spaces between the lamellae and contain cells called **osteocytes** (fully grown osteoblasts), which help to maintain bone tissue. Narrow canals, called canaliculi, radiate from the lacunae. The **canaliculi** are filled with tissue fluid containing oxygen and nutrients for the bone tissue.

### Cancellous bone tissue

Cancellous bone has a spongy appearance and so is often called **spongy bone**. The spongy bone helps to give great strength but also keeps the skeleton light. Spongy bone is found in the end of long bones and in short, flat and irregularly shaped bones. The cancellous bone is filled with red bone marrow. Red bone marrow produces billions of red blood cells every day in adults.

# Ligaments

Ligaments consist of bands of strong, fibrous connective tissue that are silvery in appearance. They prevent dislocation by holding the bones together across joints, rather like straps, but

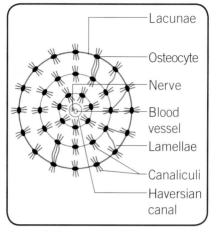

**Figure 3.3** Haversian system in compact bone

**FAST FACT**

Red bone marrow produces billions of red blood cells every day in adults.

**FAST FACT**

Osteocytes account for 90% of all cells in the skeleton.

**ASK FRAN...**

**Q.** How does exercise help to ensure the health of bones?
**A.** Regular exercise is essential – not only does it prevent loss of bone but it also stimulates the formation of new, stronger bone tissue. Bones adapt to the stress of exercise by laying down more calcium and other minerals, and also by increasing the amount of collagen fibres, which helps to strengthen bones. The best exercises for the bones are ones that involve weight-bearing, such as weight training, walking and tennis, so that the body works against gravity.

stretch slightly to allow movement. When excess strain is put on a joint, especially the ankle or knee, the ligaments can become sprained or torn. Injuries to ligaments can be minor or severe, and result in bruising, tenderness and swelling. Minor injury can be treated with ice packs, to reduce the swelling, and then bandaged to support the joint. As ligaments have a relatively poor blood supply when damaged, they can take a long time to heal.

## don't forget

**Ligaments attach bone to bone.**
**Tendons attach muscle to bone.**

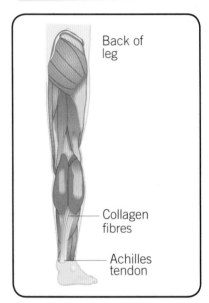

Back of leg

Collagen fibres

Achilles tendon

**Figure 3.4** Achilles tendon

# Tendons

Tendons consist of white, strong, almost inelastic, fibrous bands. Most muscles are attached to bones by tendons. They vary in length and thickness. When a muscle contracts, the force transmitted through the tendon creates movement at the bone. An example of a tendon is the Achilles tendon that attaches the calf muscle to the back of the foot.

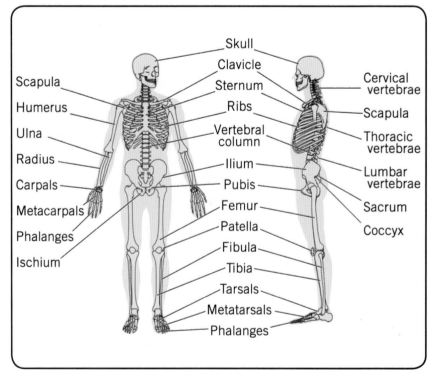

Skull
Clavicle
Sternum
Ribs
Vertebral column
Ilium
Pubis
Femur
Patella
Fibula
Tibia
Tarsals
Metatarsals
Phalanges

Scapula
Humerus
Ulna
Radius
Carpals
Metacarpals
Phalanges
Ischium

Cervical vertebrae
Scapula
Thoracic vertebrae
Lumbar vertebrae
Sacrum
Coccyx

**Figure 3.5** Bones of the skeleton

A tendon can become injured if stretched beyond its limit. This happens in twisted ankles and sprained wrists as the bodyweight is suddenly concentrated in one small area, putting strain on the tendon. The tendon may partially tear when some fibres are torn. The remaining intact fibres hold the torn ends in contact so, with rest, the ends reunite and the area heals. There can also be a complete tearing, in which the tendon is severed. The tendon can tear away from the bone or muscle and this is extremely painful.

MEMORY JOGGER

Memorise the following sentence to remember the bones of the skull:
Orange Tree Provides Edible Sweet Fruit (occipital, temporal, parietal, ethmoid, sphenoid, frontal)

# The bones of the skeleton

## ACTIVITY 3.3

Label the bones of the skull in Figure 3.6.

Use this key to colour the diagram.
Blue – frontal and occipital bones
Yellow – parietal and temporal bones
Green – sphenoid and ethmoid

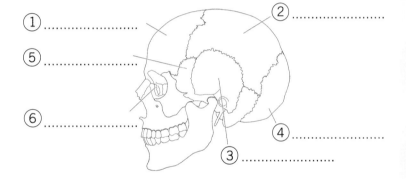

**Figure 3.6** Bones of the skull

① **Frontal** (fron-tall) **bone**. One frontal bone forms the forehead.

② **Parietal** (pa-rye-eh-tal) **bone**. Two parietal bones form the sides and top of the skull.

③ **Temporal** (tem-por-all) **bone**. Two temporal bones are found at the sides of the skull, under the parietals.

④ **Occipital** (ox-sip-pee-tal) **bone**. One occipital bone forms the back of the skull.

⑤ **Sphenoid** (sfee-noid). One sphenoid bone helps to form the base of the skull.

⑥ **Ethmoid** (eth-moid). One ethmoid bone helps to form the eye socket and nasal cavities.

## ACTIVITY 3.4

Label the bones of the face in Figure 3.7.
Use this key to colour the diagram.

Green – turbinate and zygomatic bones
Red – mandible and vomer
Orange – maxilla and nasal

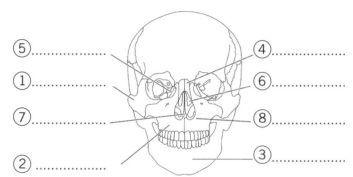

**Figure 3.7** Bones of the face

① **Zygomatic** (zy-go-mah-tic) **bone**. Two zygomatic bones form the cheekbones.

② **Maxilla** (mak-sil-ah). The maxilla forms the upper part of the jaw.

③ **Mandible** (man-dee-ball). The mandible forms the lower part of the jaw. It is the only movable bone of the skull.

④ **Nasal** (nayz-al). Two nasal bones form the bridge of the nose.

⑤ **Lacrimal** (lah-kruh-mul) **bone**. Two lacrimal bones make up part of each eye socket.

⑥ **Turbinates** (tur-bin-nuts). Two turbinate bones make up part of the nasal cavity.

⑦ **Vomer** (voh-mer). One vomer extends upwards from the hard palate to make the nasal septum.

⑧ **Palatine** (pa-la-tyne). Two palatine bones help make up the roof of the mouth, wall of the nasal cavity and floor of the eye sockets.

*don't forget*

**There is a bone in the neck called the <u>hyoid</u> (hi-oyd). It is horseshoe-shaped and is not joined to any other bone. However, it is attached to the temporal bone by ligaments.**

## Bones of the shoulder girdle

① **Clavicle**. This is a long, slender bone also known as the collar bone.

(2) **Scapula** (plural: scapulae). This is a large, triangular, flat bone also known as the shoulder blade.

## Bones of the thorax

The thoracic cavity contains organs such as the heart and lungs, which are protected by the ribcage.

(3) **Ribs**. There are 12 pairs of ribs.

(4) **Sternum**. This is also known as the breast bone.

## Bones of the upper limbs

(5) **Humerus**. This is the long bone of the upper arm.

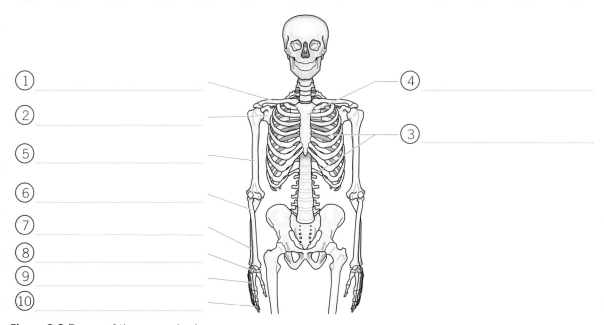

**MEMORY JOGGER**

To help you remember the bones of the skull, try blowing up a balloon, tying its end, and using a thick, black felt-tip to draw on the bones of the skull and face (but not the names). You can use the balloon to practise remembering the bone names.

### ACTIVITY 3.5

(1) _____
(2) _____
(5) _____
(6) _____
(7) _____
(8) _____
(9) _____
(10) _____

(4) _____
(3) _____

**Figure 3.8** Bones of the upper body

Label the diagram in Figure 3.8 using the information on pages 86–88. Use this key to colour the diagram.

Yellow – clavicle          Green – radius
Blue – scapula             Orange – carpals, metacarpals and phalanges
Pink – humerus             Brown – sternum
Red – ulna                 Purple – ribs

**don't forget**

**The axial skeleton is made up of the skull, spine, ribs and sternum.**
**The appendicular skeleton is made up of the shoulder girdle, arms and hands, the pelvic bones and the legs and feet.**

(6) **Radius**. This bone is situated on the thumb side of the forearm.

(7) **Ulna**. This bone is situated on the little-finger side of the forearm.

(8) The **carpals** consist of eight small bones in each wrist (see Figure 3.9).

(9) The **metacarpals** consist of five metacarpal bones (long bones), which form the palm of each hand.

(10) There are 14 **phalanges** in each hand, three in each finger and two in the thumb.

## Bones of the hand and wrist

### ACTIVITY 3.6

Label the diagram in Figure 3.9 using the information below. Use this key to colour the diagram.

Blue – scaphoid and trapezium
Red – lunate and trapezoid
Brown – hamate and triquetral
Green – pisiform and capitate
Yellow – phalanges
Orange – metacarpals

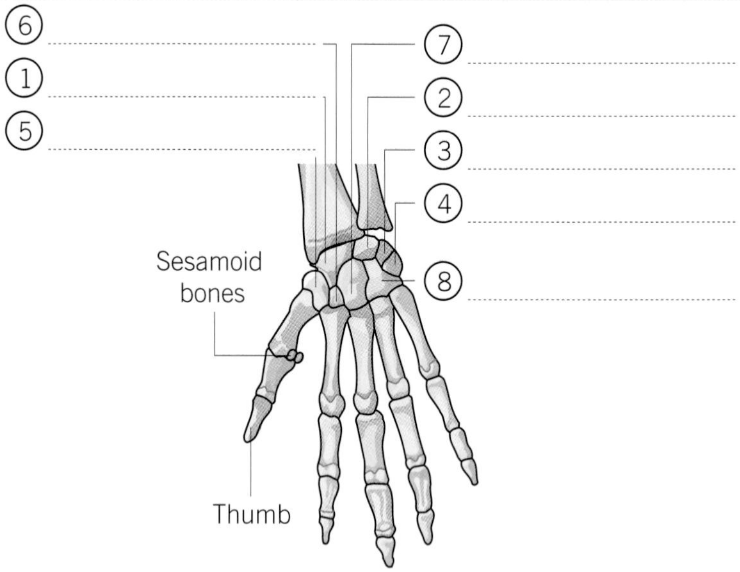


**Figure 3.9** Bones of the hand and wrist

The carpals are: (1) scaphoid (scaf-oid), (2) lunate (lune-ate), (3) triquetral (tri-kwee-tral), (4) pisiform (pie-see-form), (5) trapezium (trap-ee-zee-um), (6) trapezoid (trap-ee-zoid), (7) capitates (cap-ee-tates), (8) hamate (hay-mate).

They are closely fitted together and held in position by ligaments. Tendons of muscles in the forearm cross over the wrist joint and are held close to these bones by strong fibrous bands called **retinacula**.

## MEMORY JOGGER

To help you remember the bones of the hand, make up a memorable sentence, such as: 'Sally Likes To Play The Tiny Chocolate Harmonica' (scaphoid, lunate, triquetral, pisiform, trapezium, trapezoid, capitate, hamate).

## Bones of the pelvic girdle

The pelvic girdle consists of three bones fused together (innominate bones).

1. The **ilium** (ill-lee-um) is the largest of the three bones. The iliac crest can be felt by placing the hand on the hip.
2. The **ischium** (iss-kee-um) forms the posterior aspect of the pelvis.
3. The **pubis** is situated on the anterior aspect of the pelvis. The female's pelvis is wider and shallower, and so has more space than the male's. This is because of the requirements of pregnancy and childbirth.

## Bones of the lower limbs

## ACTIVITY 3.7

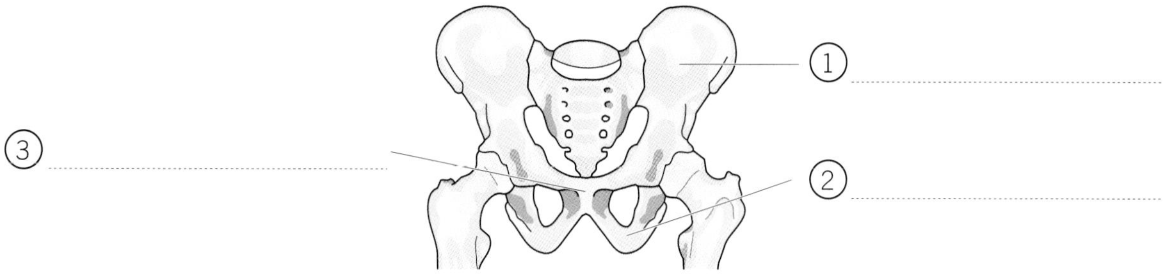


**Figure 3.10** The pelvic girdle

Label the diagram in Figure 3.10 using the information above. Use this key to colour the diagram.

Red – ilium
Orange – ischium
Brown – pubis

## MEMORY JOGGER

Creating flashcards can help you to remember bone names. Using cards, write a bone name on one side, and on the other side write a clue, for example: 'A bone found in the arm that begins with the letter "r".'
You may like to draw a diagram that shows the specific bone or bones you are referring to. Use the cards regularly to test yourself.

## MEMORY JOGGER

To remember that carpals are found in the wrist and tarsals are below, in the ankle, think of <u>CAR on the TAR</u>.

## ACTIVITY 3.8

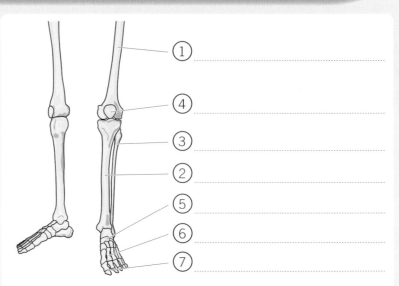

**Figure 3.11** Bones of the lower limbs

Label the diagram in Figure 3.11 using the information below. Use this key to colour the diagram.

Red – femur
Orange – patella
Blue – tibia
Yellow – fibula
Green – tarsals, metatarsals and phalanges

(1) **Femur**. The thigh bone; this is the longest bone in the body.

(2) **Tibia**. The bone situated on the anterior aspect of the lower leg, also known as the shin bone.

(3) **Fibula**. The bone situated on the lateral side of the tibia; it is thinner than the tibia.

(4) **Patella**. This is the kneecap, which articulates with the femur.

(5) **Tarsals**. These are the seven bones of the ankle.

(6) **Metatarsals**. There are five metatarsal bones in each foot.

(7) **Phalanges**. There are 14 phalanges in each foot; these form the toes.

# Bones of the vertebral column (spine)

## ACTIVITY 3.9

Label the diagram in Figure 3.12 using the information below.
Use this key to colour the diagram.

Yellow – cervical spine
Green – thoracic spine
Blue – lumbar region
Orange – sacrum
Red – coccyx

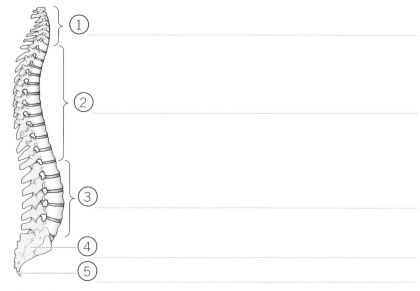

**Figure 3.12** Bones of the vertebral column

The vertebral column supports the upper body and encloses and protects the spinal cord. It consists of 33 bones, which are divided into five groups: cervical, thoracic, lumbar, sacral and coccygeal.

① The **cervical spine** consists of seven vertebrae.

② The **thoracic spine** consists of twelve vertebrae.

③ The **lumbar spine** consists of five bones; these are the largest vertebrae.

④ The **sacrum** consists of five vertebrae fused together, known as sacral bones.

⑤ The **coccyx** consists of four bones fused together, known as coccygeal bones.

In total: 33 bones.

### FAST FACT

The **sacroiliac joint** is the joint found between the sacrum and the ilium (hip bone).

### MEMORY JOGGER

To remember the bones of the vertebrae, think of the following sentence.
'Serve four lumps from the sack of coal.'
Serve is similar to **cer**vical.
Four sounds like **tho**racic.
Lump is similar to **lum**bar.
Sack is similar to **sac**rum.
Coal has the first two letters of **co**ccyx.

### Intervertebral discs

Between the bones of the spine are pads of white fibrocartilage known as **intervertebral discs**. The intervertebral discs are thicker in the lumbar region than in the cervical region and are kept in place by ligaments. Their functions are to act as shock absorbers and to give the spine some flexibility so movement can take place.

## Bones and arches of the feet

The foot is made up of seven tarsals (the ankle bones), which are irregular bones and glide over each other to provide movement. There are five metatarsals (sole bones) and 14 phalanges (bones in toes).

## ACTIVITY 3.10

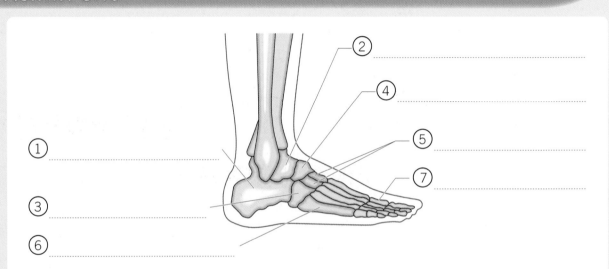

**Figure 3.13** Bones of the feet

Label the diagram in Figure 3.13 using the information on page 93. Use this key to colour the diagram.

Green – calcaneus
Red – talus
Blue – cuboid
Brown – navicular

Orange – cuneiforms
Pink – metatarsals
Yellow – phalanges

The bones of the feet make up a bridge-like structure. There are seven tarsal (ankle) bones, which form the posterior part of the foot:

① **calcaneus** (kal-kay-nee-us) – one bone.

② **talus** (ta-lus) – one bone.

③ **cuboid** (cue-boyd) – one bone.

④ **navicular** (na-vik-cue-ler) – one bone.

⑤ **cuneiforms** (cue-nee-forms) – three bones (medial, intermediate, lateral).

⑥ **metatarsals** – five bones.

⑦ **phalanges** (fah-lan-jez) – 14 bones, which form the toes.

### Arches of the foot

The bones of the feet fit together to make **arches**. The arches help to support the weight of the body and provide leverage when walking. Strong ligaments and tendons support the bones that form the arches.

**MEMORY JOGGER**

To help you remember the number of bones in each group, use the following memory aid.
'Steven's unattractive shoes smell damp.'
Steven's – letters for the seven cervical vertebrae.
Unattractive – 12 letters for the twelve thoracic vertebrae.
Shoes – 5 letters (five lumbar bones).
Smell – 5 letters (five sacral bones).
Damp – 4 letters (four coccygeal bones).

**ACTIVITY 3.11**

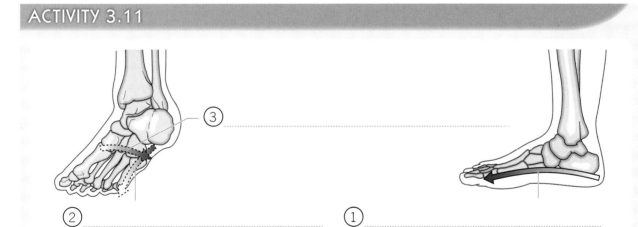

**Figure 3.14** Arches of the foot

Label the diagram in Figure 3.14 using the information on page 94. Use this key to colour the diagram.

Red – medial longitudinal arch
Green – transverse arch
Blue – lateral longitudinal arch

There are arches of the foot.

(1) The **medial longitudinal arch** is the highest arch on the big-toe side of the foot. It begins at the calcaneus, rises to the talus and descends through the navicular, the three cuneiforms and the three medial metatarsals.

(2) The **lateral longitudinal arch** is on the little-toe side of the foot and begins at the calcaneus. It rises at the cuboid and descends to the two outer metatarsal bones.

(3) The **transverse arch** runs between the medial and lateral aspect of the foot and is formed by the navicular, the cuneiform bones and the bases of the five metatarsals.

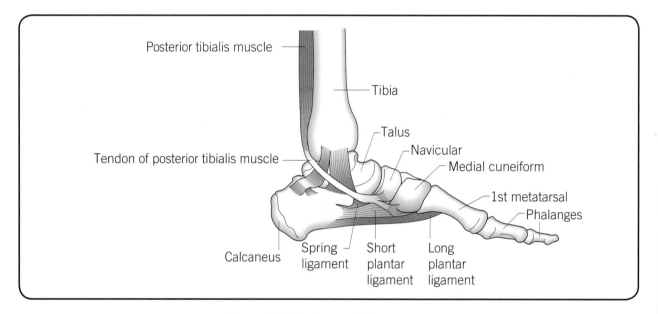

**Figure 3.15** Tendons and ligaments supporting the arches of the foot

# Joints of the body

A 'joint' describes the joining (articulation) of two or more bones of the body. All of the bones, except the hyoid in the neck, form a joint with another bone. Joints hold bones together and allow movement.

There are three main types of joint.

✖ **Fibrous or immovable joints** are fixed joints in which no movement between the joints is possible. Examples are the sutures, or joints, between the skull bones.

✖ **Cartilaginous joints** are slightly movable joints in which only limited movement is possible. Examples are the joints between the bones of the vertebral column, with their intervertebral discs of fibrocartilage.

✖ **Synovial joints** are freely movable joints, of which there are several types, all having similar characteristics. An example is the joint of the knee.

MEMORY JOGGER

To remember the three types of main joints, think of the following sentence. 'Carol told a fib which is a syn' (cartilaginous, fibrous and synovial).

## Synovial joints

ACTIVITY 3.12

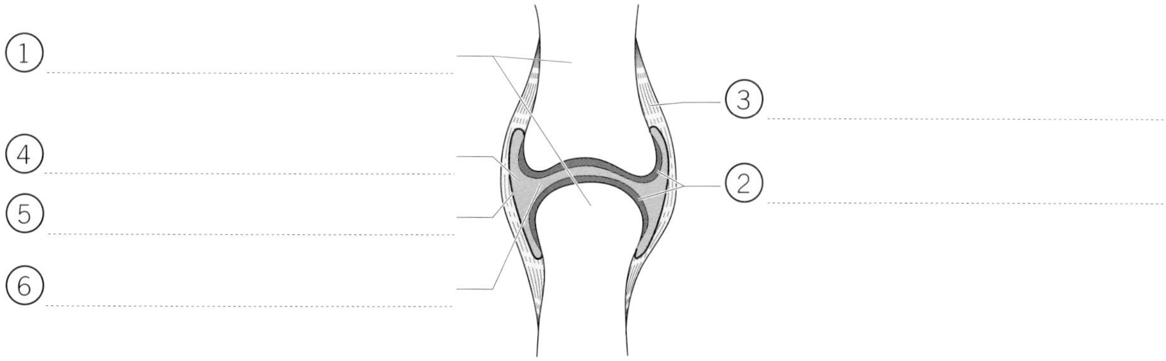

**Figure 3.16** Structure of a synovial joint

Label the diagram in Figure 3.16 using the information on page 96 . Use this key to colour the diagram.

Yellow – bones
Blue – articular cartilage, joint capsule

Green – ligaments
Orange – joint cavity and synovial fluid

## MEMORY JOGGER

The following sentence will help you to remember the synovial joint structures.

**Hy** (Hi) **Symen** (Simon), **Jo's li** (lie) is a **syn** (sin).

Hy – hyaline
Symen – synovial membrane
Jo – joint
li – ligament
syn – synovial fluid

If you make up your own sentence you will find it easier to remember.

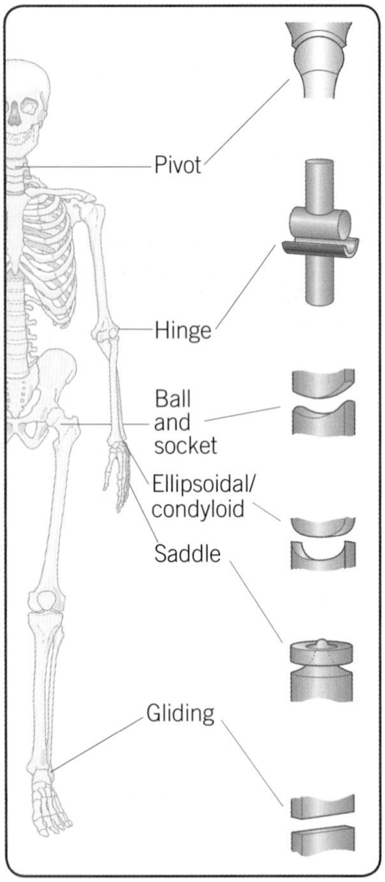

In a freely movable joint, ends of the ① **bones** are mostly covered by ② **articular cartilage**. The cartilage helps to reduce friction and acts as a shock absorber during movement. ③ **Ligaments** are needed to bind the bones together and help prevent dislocation. The space between the bones is called the ④ **joint cavity** and is enclosed by a capsule of fibrous tissue, the joint capsule, which is made of two layers. The inner layer is the ⑤ **synovial membrane** which produces ⑥ **synovial fluid** to lubricate the joint and provide the hyaline cartilage with nutrients.

### Ball and socket joint

A rounded head of a bone fits into a cup-shaped cavity that allows a lot of movement. Movements possible are flexion, extension, adduction, abduction, rotation and circumduction.

Examples are the shoulder and hip joints.

### Hinge joint

A round surface fits into the hollow surface of another bone and allows movement similar to the opening and closing of a hinged door.

Examples are the elbow and knee joints.

### Saddle joint

Similar to a hinge joint, a saddle joint allows more movement. Movements possible are flexion, extension, abduction, adduction and slight circumduction.

Examples include the joint between the thumb and carpals and the joint between the skull and lower jaw.

Pivot
Hinge
Ball and socket
Ellipsoidal/condyloid
Saddle
Gliding

**Figure 3.17** Types of synovial joint

### Ellipsoidal/condyloid joint

Ellipsoid/condyloid joints allow flexion, extension, abduction and adduction, but rotation is limited. This joint is at the metacarpals and phalanges.

### Pivot joint

A socket in one bone rotates around a peg on another so a rotation movement is possible.

An example is the first cervical vertebra, which rotates around the second to turn the head (atlas/axis).

### Gliding joint

Two flat surfaces of bone glide over each other to allow adduction and abduction movements. Examples are the joints between the carpals (wrist) and tarsals (ankle).

> **don't forget**
>
> See Chapter 1 for more information regarding joint movements.

## ACTIVITY 3.13

State whether the following synovial joints are ball and socket, hinge, saddle, ellipsoidal/condyloid pivot or gliding joints.

| Joint | Type |
|---|---|
| Hip | |
| First and second vertebrae | |
| Elbow | |
| Between tarsals | |
| Knee | |
| Shoulder | |
| Between carpals | |
| Between bones of thumb and carpal | |
| Between metacarpals and phalanges | |

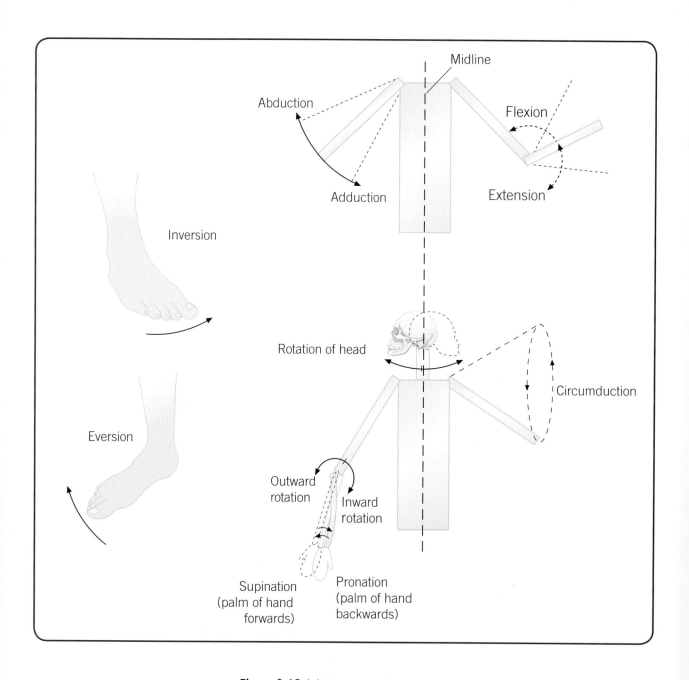

**Figure 3.18** Joint movements

## Conditions associated with bones and joints

### Ankylosing spondylitis

Ankylosing spondylitis (AS) is a type of arthritis that affects the spine, including the muscles and ligaments around the spine. Many people will suffer back pain and stiffness, but some cases can be severe and result in disability. AS mostly affects men, but rarely starts in old age. There is no cure, but most sufferers can be treated with medication and physiotherapy. The cause is unknown, but there appears to be a genetic link and it can run in families.

### Arthritis

The term 'arthritis' refers to many different diseases, most of which are characterised by inflammation of one or more joints. Pain and stiffness may also be present in muscles near the joint. The two main kinds are osteoarthritis and rheumatoid arthritis.

- **Osteoarthritis** is the most common form of arthritis and is caused by wear and tear on the joint. It causes the cartilage to become damaged and so it wears away. Osteoarthritis is more common in people who regularly take part in vigorous exercise. It causes pain and restricted movement, and particularly affects movable joints that tend to be weight-bearing, such as the knees and hips.
- **Rheumatoid arthritis** is less common but is a more severe type of arthritis. It is more common in females and can affect all ages. It is a condition where the body attacks its own tissues and is therefore known as an **autoimmune disease**. The membrane that lines the joint becomes completely swollen. The cause may be viral infection or hereditary factors. There will be inflammation and swelling around the joints. There may also be pain and loss of function. It mostly affects the joints of the hands and feet.

### Artificial joints

An artificial joint usually consists of plastic and metal parts, which are used to replace a natural joint, often the hip or knee joint. Reasons for replacing a joint can include damage caused by osteoarthritis, injury or infection, which can cause pain and stiffness and make joint movement difficult.

### Bone cancer

Bone cancer destroys healthy bone tissue, which can cause

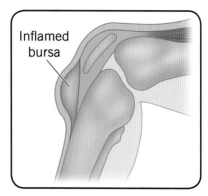

**Figure 3.19** Bursitis

pain to the sufferer. Secondary bone cancer is more common than primary bone cancer. The cause of this type of cancer is unclear; however, some people may be more susceptible owing to hereditary factors and previous cancer treatment involving radiation therapy.

### Bursitis

Some synovial joints contain a sac-like structure called a bursa, which helps to provide padding where tendons rub against bones or other tendons. Bursitis is inflammation of the bursa, which may be caused by injury or repetitive stress. Examples include tennis elbow and housemaid's knee.

### Fractures

When a bone breaks it is called a fracture. There are different types of fracture.

✖ A **simple fracture** occurs if the bone breaks but the skin remains intact and the tissue around it is not broken.

✖ A **compound fracture** means the broken ends of the bone protrude through the skin.

✖ A **comminuted fracture** occurs if the bone breaks in two or more places.

✖ A **greenstick fracture** is a partial fracture, occurring only in children since their bones are soft; when stress is placed on the bone, one side of it may bend enough to cause the other side to splinter.

✖ An **impacted fracture** is when part of a broken bone impacts into another.

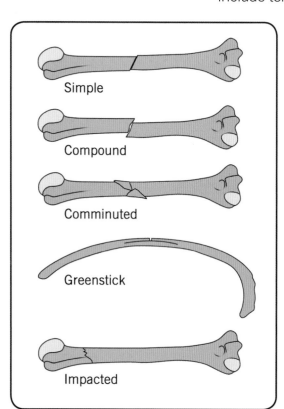

**Figure 3.20** Types of fracture

### Frozen shoulder

This is inflammation of the shoulder joint, which may be a result of muscle injury. There is inflammation and thickening of the lining of the joint capsule in which the shoulder is held. It causes pain and stiffness around the shoulder and movement becomes increasingly difficult.

## Gout

Gout is a common type of arthritis and involves the build up of uric acid crystals around joints, tendons and other tissues of the body. Crystals form when the levels of uric acid in the body are abnormally high. Gout usually begins with pain and inflammation in the joint of the big toe, but it can develop in any joint of the body. Risk factors for gout include drinking alcohol (especially beer) and also consuming a diet rich in purines, which are chemicals found in foods such as red meat and seafood.

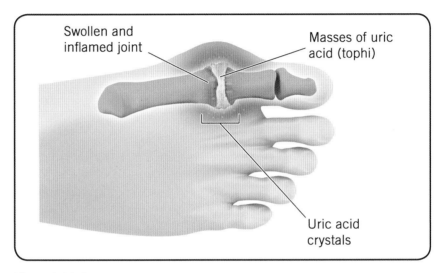

**Figure 3.21** Gout

## Osteoporosis

Bones contain living tissue and so are constantly changing, losing and gaining protein and calcium to and from the bloodstream. Bones are naturally being built up and broken down. **Osteoporosis** causes the bone to break down faster than it is being formed. This causes the bones to become porous, weak and thin and so there is an increased risk of fracture.

It mainly affects middle-aged and older people and is more common in women than men. Hormones, such as oestrogen in women and testosterone in men, help stimulate the bone-forming cells, osteoblasts, to produce new bone tissue. Women produce smaller amounts of oestrogen after the menopause, and men produce smaller amounts of testosterone as they age. As a result, the osteoblasts become less active, and there is a decrease in bone mass.

A well-balanced diet, which includes plenty of vitamin D and calcium, as well as exercise, can help protect against osteoporosis later in life.

### Paget's disease

Paget's disease is a condition that causes bone to be broken down more quickly than it can rebuilt. The body responds by quickly trying to build new bone, which causes the bone to become softer and weaker than ordinary bone. Over time, the affected bones may become weak and misshapen. It is more common in older people, and sufferers may experience pain and tingling and weakness. In most cases, the disease can be managed effectively with painkillers and medications that help to control bone growth. The cause is unknown; however, hereditary factors seem to play a role.

### Postural defects

Postural defects include lordosis, kyphosis and scoliosis. A small amount of kyphotic and lordotic curving of the spine is normal, but too much leads to the conditions lordosis and kyphosis. For further information see Chapter 4 on muscles.

**MEMORY JOGGER**

To remember the difference between lordosis and kyphosis think of the following.
Lordosis – Lumbar (hollow lumbar region)
KYphosis – HY up on the spine (shoulders are hunched forward)

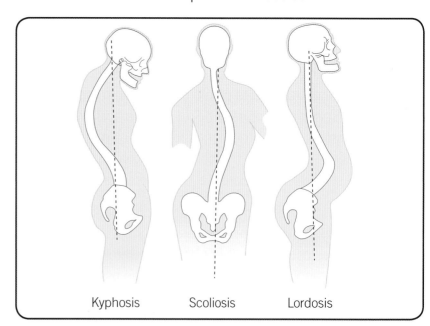

Kyphosis     Scoliosis     Lordosis

**Figure 3.22** Postural defects

Kyphosis is a condition involving an outward curve of the thoracic spine, which leads to rounded shoulders.

Scoliosis is a sideways curving of the spine and is always abnormal.

Lordosis is a condition involving an inward curving of the spine, which affects the lumbar region. This causes the abdomen and buttocks to stick out.

## Repetitive strain injury

Repetitive strain injury (RSI) includes conditions caused by the constant repetition of particular movements. It often affects typists, and there may be pain, aching, weakness or tingling when the fingers are moved. It is caused by irritation of the flexor and extensor tendons in the wrist and hand. RSI can lead to another condition called **carpal tunnel syndrome (CTS)**. This is the result of pressure and a build-up of fluid in the tissue (**oedema**) that affects the median nerve as it passes through a gap under a ligament at the front of the wrist. It causes pain, numbness and tingling sensations in the fingers and hands.

## Rickets

This is a rare disease that affects the bone growth in children, and often results in bowed legs and curvature of the spine. Rickets causes weak and softened bones, which can be painful. It is commonly caused by a lack of vitamin D or calcium in the diet, as these minerals are required to produce strong and healthy bones. Rickets in adults is called osteomalacia.

## Slipped disc

Discs are pads of fibro-cartilage that have a tough casing and are found between the vertebrae. They help to absorb shock, such as when jumping. A slipped disc is one that splits causing the gel-like substance inside it to leak, creating a bulge. The bulge creates pressure on the nerves and causes back pain, as well as pain in other areas of the body. A slipped disc is often caused by the breaking down of the connective tissue surrounding the disc; however, it is unclear why this happens. The likelihood of suffering with a slipped disc increases with age.

## Sprain
A sprain can be caused by wrenching or twisting a joint, causing injury to its ligaments. It occurs when ligaments are stressed beyond their normal capacity.

## Spondylosis
Spondylosis is spinal arthritis and occurs as we age owing to wear and tear of joints and bones of the spine. Most people over the age of 60 will have spondylosis, but will not have any symptoms. However, in some people it can cause stiffness and pain. Occasionally, it can cause nerves to be pinched and so lead to pain and pins and needles in the arms, and also loss of feeling in the hands and legs.

## Systemic lupus erythematosus
Systemic lupus erythematosus (SLE), often known as lupus, is an uncommon condition affecting most of the body's tissues and organs. It mostly affects women and causes symptoms such as chronic fatigue, skin rash and pain and swelling in joints. It is an autoimmune disorder, which means the body attacks its own tissues. The cause is unknown, but genetic and environmental factors are believed to be involved.

## Synovitis
This is inflammation of the synovial membrane, which is the membrane that lines joints. It causes pain in the affected joint. Causes include injury and arthritis.

## Tendonitits
Tendonitis is inflammation of a tendon, which results in swelling. It is caused by injury, such as a sports injury, and is also a result of tendon overuse (repetitive strain injury). The affected area may be stiff and painful.

### Tennis elbow

Tennis elbow is a painful condition in which there is inflammation of the tendon that attaches the muscle of the forearm to the bone of the upper arm. The sufferer will feel discomfort if the elbow is straightened. It can be caused by wrenching, or the overuse of muscles, such as when playing tennis or weightlifting. It also affects people whose work involves activities such as lifting or using heavy tools.

### Whiplash

Any sudden and vigorous movement involving the head may cause a neck injury (whiplash). This is owing to injury of the tendons and ligaments in the neck, and overstretching of the neck muscles. There may stiffness and pain in the neck, and movement involving the neck may be difficult. Road accidents, in which the head is jolted, are a common cause of whiplash.

## Conditions associated with the foot

### Bunions (hallux valgus)

A bunion is a bone deformity of the joint at the base of the big toe, which causes pain, tenderness and swelling. The big toe points towards the smaller toes. Causes include ill-fitting shoes (the condition is more common in women) and hereditary factors. It may also be the result of arthritis, injury or weak ligaments. It can be painful, so the foot should be handled carefully.

### Flatfoot

Weakening of the ligaments and tendons that hold the arches in place can cause the medial longitudinal arch to flatten and the result is flatfoot. Some sufferers find their foot 'rolls' to the inner side, and there may also be discomfort. The causes include injuries to the foot and ankle, excessive weight, hereditary factors or a postural abnormality.

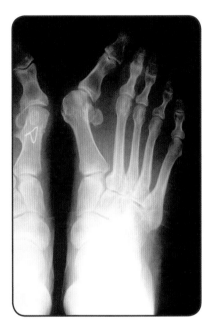

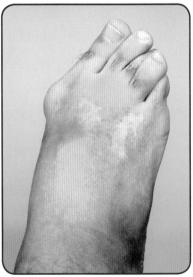

**Figure 3.23** Bunion

### Hammer toes

This is a deformity of the toes in which the middle joints are bent, resulting in bent toes. Corns will often develop on the joints of the toes because of rubbing against footwear, and the condition can be painful. The causes include arthritis, bunions, ill-fitting shoes or hereditary factors.

### Plantar fasciitis

This is inflammation of a ligament, called the plantar fascia, that runs from the heel to the ball of the foot. There is pain at the heel or arch when standing. Causes include conditions in which the feet are not aligned correctly, such as fallen arches, and it may also be caused by injury.

## ACTIVITY 3.14

Which condition is being described?

Read each description and decide which condition is being discussed.

1. A disease that affects children's bone growth and can be caused by a lack of vitamin D and calcium in the diet. ........................................

2. Outward curve of the thoracic spine leading to rounded shoulders. ........................................

3. Constant repetition of a particular movement can lead to pain and tingling.

   ........................................

4. Breakage of bone. ........................................

5. Vigorous movement to the head that causes injury to the tendons and ligaments in the neck. ........................................

6. Inflammation of one or more joints, causing pain and stiffness. ........................................

7. Wrenching or twisting of a joint that causes injury to its ligaments. ........................................

8. Bones become porous, weak and thin and so there is an increased risk of fracture.

   ........................................

# What you should know

## Functions of the skeleton

☐ Shape and support
☐ Attachment for muscles and tendons; leverage
☐ Development of blood cells
☐ Protection
☐ Allows movement of the body
☐ Mineral store

## Location, structure and function of bones

☐ Skeletal system – axial, appendicular
☐ Bones of the head – frontal, parietal, temporal, occipital, sphenoid, ethmoid, nasal, turbinates, palatine, zygomatic, maxilla, mandible
☐ Bones of the neck – cervical, vertebrae, atlas, axis, hyoid
☐ Bones of the spine – thoracic vertebrae, lumbar vertebrae, sacrum, coccyx, intervertebral discs
☐ Bones of the torso – ribs, sternum, clavicle, scapula, pelvic girdle
☐ Bones of the pelvic girdle – ilium, ischium, pubis
☐ Bones of the upper limbs – humerus, radius, ulna
☐ Bones of the hands – carpals, metacarpals, phalanges
☐ Bones of the lower limbs – femur, patella, tibia, fibula
☐ Bones of the feet – tarsals, metatarsals, phalanges
☐ Bones of the arches of the foot – medial longitudinal, lateral longitudinal, transverse arch
☐ Types of bones – compact, cancellous, long, short, flat, irregular, sesamoid
☐ Components of long bone – diaphysis, epiphysis, cartilage, articular cartilage, medullary cavity, periosteum

## Location, structure and function of joints

☐ Classifications – fibrous/immovable, cartilaginous/slightly moveable, synovial/freely movable
☐ Synovial joint – joint capsule, ligaments, synovial fluid, articular cartilage, bone
☐ Types of synovial joint – gliding, ellipsoidal/condyloid, hinge, saddle, pivot, ball and socket
☐ Range of movement associated with joint types (see Chapter 1) – flexion, extension, circumduction, rotation, adduction, abduction, pronation, supination, dorsiflexion, plantar flexion, eversion, inversion

## Growth and repair

☐ Definition and function – osteoblasts, osteocytes, osteoclasts
☐ Process of ossification

## Pathologies

☐ Conditions (pathologies) associated with the bones, joints and foot, including their causes, signs and symptoms – fractures, breaks, osteoarthritis, rheumatoid arthritis, gout, osteoporosis, repetitive strain injuries (for example, tendonitis, bursitis, carpal tunnel syndrome), spinal injuries (for example, whiplash, slipped disc), postural defects (for example, lordosis, kyphosis, scoliosis), foot problems (for example, bunion, hammer toes, plantar fasciitis), artificial joints, systemic lupus erythematosus, synovitis, rickets, bone cancer, ankylosing spondilitis, spondylosis, Paget's disease

# 4 Muscular system and common pathologies

There are over 600 muscles in the human body, which make up 40–50 per cent of the body weight. Muscles generate the force needed to create body movement, help maintain posture and provide heat for the body. They also help pump blood and move lymph around the body, and push food through the digestive tract.

The muscular system consists of three types of muscle.

✖ **Involuntary muscle** is known as **smooth muscle**. Smooth muscle makes up the walls of the blood and lymph vessels, along with other vessels. The muscles allow the walls to relax and constrict. Such muscles are involuntary because they are not under the body's conscious control. The cells of these muscles are spindle-shaped.

✖ The **cardiac muscle** is specialised tissue found only in the heart. This muscle never tires; if it did we would have serious problems! Even if the heart is separated from the body, it will continue to beat for a while.

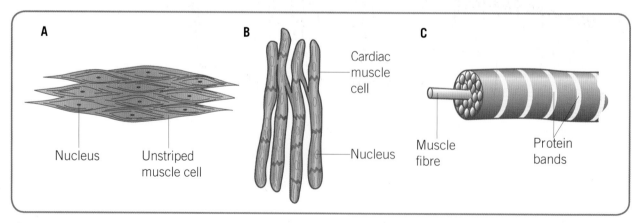

**Figure 4.1** Types of muscle: **A** Involuntary (smooth) muscle; **B** Cardiac muscle; **C** Voluntary (skeletal) muscle

✻ Therapists are mostly concerned with **voluntary muscles**, which are under the body's conscious control so can be moved at will. These are also known as the **skeletal muscles**. Skeletal muscles consist of bundles of muscle fibres, striped in appearance and enclosed in a sheath (**fascia**). They allow movement of the body.

Muscle tissue has various characteristics that help muscle to carry out its functions.

The characteristics of muscles include:

✻ contractibility – the muscle tissue has the ability to shorten and thicken

✻ elasticity – the muscle tissues can return to their normal shape and length after contraction or extension

✻ excitability/irritability – the muscle fibres are stimulated into action by nerve impulses

✻ extensibility – the muscle is able to stretch when the muscle fibres relax.

## Muscle structure

The muscle contains three layers of connective tissue: epimysium, perimysium and an endomysium.

The **epimysium** (ep-ee-miss-ee-um) is a layer of connective tissue containing collagen fibres that covers the entire muscle. It separates the muscle from surrounding tissue and organs.

The **perimysium** (peri-miss-ee-um) is a sheath of connective tissue that groups muscle fibres into bundles.

The **endomysium** (endo-miss-ee-um) is a thin layer of areolar connective tissue that covers each individual muscle fibre.

Fascicles are bundles of muscle fibres. Muscle fibres are long, thin structures, and inside each fibre are thread-like **myofibrils**, which extend the entire length of the muscle fibre.

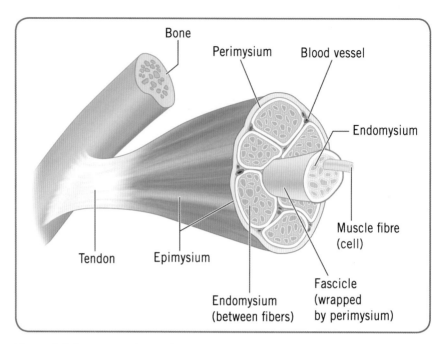

**Figure 4.2** Structure of muscle

**Myofibrils** contain two types of overlapping protein called filaments (actin and myosin), which lie side by side. They do not extend the whole length of the muscle fibre but are arranged into sections called **sarcomeres**. A sarcomere is the segment between two neighbouring Z lines or discs. Each sarcomere is made of overlapping thick and thin filaments. The thinner filaments are called **actin** and the thicker filaments are known as **myosin**. In the zone of overlap, thin filaments are located between the thick filaments, this gives muscle fibres their striped appearance. However, in the H zone there are thick filaments but no thin filaments.

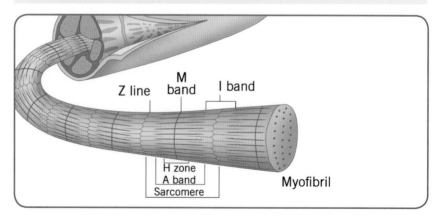

**Figure 4.3** Structure of muscle fibre

## Process of muscle contraction

Muscles are believed to contract by a process called the sliding filament theory. When a muscle contracts, it shortens and thickens, and the Z lines move closer together. This is because the thinner filaments (actin) slide in between the thicker filaments (myosin), which causes the sarcomeres to shorten.

Myosin molecules have little pegs, called cross bridges, which act like levers to pull the filaments past each during the muscle contraction (**cross bridge cycling**). The actin climbs across these bridges (pegs) during contraction. In a fully contracted muscle, the ends of the actin filaments overlap, the H zones disappear and the I bands become very narrow. However, the A band remains unchanged.

Scattered among the myofibrils are mitochondria and granules of glycogen (the storage form of glucose – sugar). The mitochondria provide the **adenosine triphosphate (ATP)** molecules that are needed to produce energy to carry out muscle contractions. The myofibrils are surrounded by **sarcoplasmic reticulum** that stores and releases calcium, which is also required for muscle contraction.

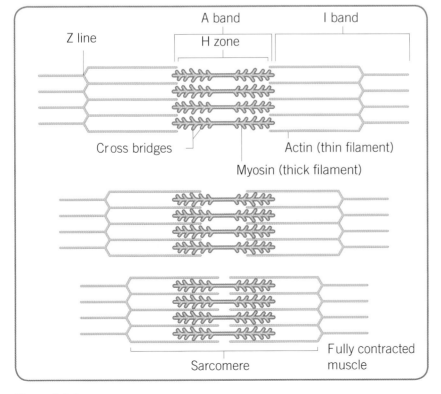

**Figure 4.4** Sarcomere

**don't forget**

Muscles are covered in fibrous tissue called <u>fascia</u> (fash-ee-ah). Fascia covers the entire muscle and is located over the layer of epimysium. It extends to become <u>tendons</u> and attaches the muscle to bone. Fascia allows the muscles to glide smoothly past each other but they sometimes adhere to one another. When this happens the affected muscles do not function as well, so there may be restricted movement and some discomfort.

When the muscle relaxes, the thinner filaments slide back out again and the actin and myosin filaments lie side by side. The H zones and I bands are now at their maximum length.

Skeletal muscles are richly supplied with blood vessels and nerves. Before movement of a muscle can occur, a message must be sent from the brain through a motor nerve, which in turn stimulates the muscle to contract. The point at which a motor nerve enters a muscle is called the **motor point**. A motor nerve branches out, the ends of which are called **motor end plates**, and rest on muscle fibres. Each muscle fibre has its own nerve ending. Branches of one motor nerve can stimulate up to 150 muscle fibres at any one time.

Skeletal muscles bring about movement by exerting a pull on tendons, which cause the bones to move at the joints.

## Types of muscle contraction during movement

Activity involving lifting requires **isotonic** contractions, which involves the muscle shortening as it contracts. For example, an isotonic contraction can be seen when the arm is bent, causing the biceps to contract. Movement of a body part occurs.

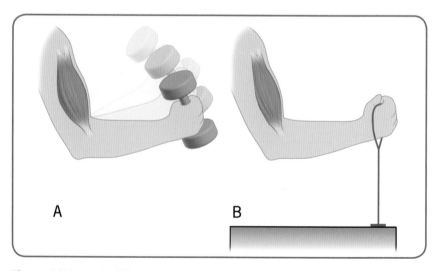

**Figure 4.5** Isotonic (A) and isometric (B) contraction

There are two types of isotonic contraction.

1.  Concentric muscle contraction is when the muscle shortens as it contracts.

2.  Eccentric muscle contraction is when the muscle lengthens while it contracts.

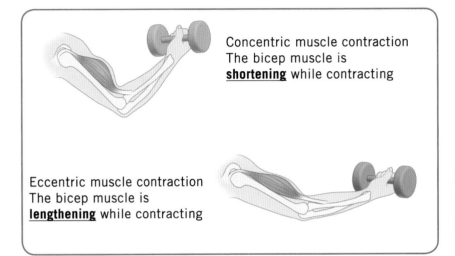

Concentric muscle contraction
The bicep muscle is
**shortening** while contracting

Eccentric muscle contraction
The bicep muscle is
**lengthening** while contracting

**Figure 4.6** Concentric and eccentric muscle contraction

Isometric contraction is contraction of a muscle without changing the length of the muscle. It is a static position rather than a movement (see Figure 4.5).

## Muscle fibre types and characteristics

There are two different types of muscle fibres in muscle: slow and fast twitch.

Slow twitch (type 1) muscle fibres contract slowly but keep going for a long time and so are very slow to fatigue; they are useful for endurance activities such as long distance running or cycling. These types of muscle fibres contain more mitochondria than fast twitch fibres and so can produce more energy. The dark meat found in chicken legs is mostly made up of slow twitch fibres, as chickens generally use their legs for long periods of standing or walking. The meat is dark as it contains lots of blood vessels.

**don't forget**

When an activity such as a bicep curl using a weight is carried out, concentric contraction happens when the user pushes the dumbbell up, against gravity; eccentric contraction occurs when the dumbbell is lowered.

**FAST FACT**

Genetics determines the number of slow and fast twitch fibres a person will have. People who do well at endurance sports tend to have a higher number of slow twitch muscles. However, people who are able to run quickly tend to have higher numbers of fast twitch fibres. Both of these types of muscle fibres can be developed with specific training.

Fast twitch (type 2) muscle fibres contract rapidly, but quickly become tired. There are two types: type 2A muscle fibres fatigue at an intermediate rate, and type 2B fibres fatigue at a very quick rate. They are useful for quick movements such as jumping or a rapid sprint. When a muscle contracts, type 1 fibres are activated first, then type 2A, and then type 2B. The white meat found in chicken wings and breasts is mostly made up of fast twitch muscle fibres, as these fibres contract rapidly to help it carry out periods of rapid movement, such as flying.

Most muscles are made of a mixture of both slow (type 1) and fast twitch (types 2A and 2B) muscle fibres. Muscles in the back, which help to maintain posture, contain mainly slow twitch muscle fibres, as does the heart. However, muscles that move the eyes are made up of fast twitch muscles fibres.

## Muscle tone

Muscle is never completely at rest but is in a state of partial contraction. The partial contraction is not enough to move the muscle but will cause some tension. All skeletal muscles must be slightly contracted if the body is to remain upright. If all of the muscles relaxed, the body would fall to the floor. This continuous slight tension is involuntary and is known as **muscle tone**. Different groups of muscle fibres contract at different times; this prevents the muscle from becoming fatigued.

Each person's degree of muscle tone varies depending on the amount of activity or exercise taken. People who are sedentary and do not exercise usually have poor muscle tone as the muscle fibres do not contract as far as they should. This results in a lowering of muscle tone and muscles becoming flaccid. Regular exercise and massage can help to maintain the elasticity of the muscle fibres, which will improve the tone of the muscle.

**FAST FACT**

**Atony** refers to a low amount of, or lack of, muscle tone.

**FAST FACT**

Poor diet or lack of use can cause muscles to **atrophy** (waste away).

### don't forget

Oxygen debt is when oxygen supplies have been used up, such as during vigorous exercise, and oxygen cannot be supplied fast enough to the muscle fibres. Breathing is increased to help repay the oxygen debt.

**FAST FACT**

Vigorous exercise can cause minor tearing of muscle fibres and is thought to be a major reason why muscles become sore and stiff 12–48 hours afterwards.

## Muscle fatigue

Muscles require fuel in the form of glucose, and oxygen is needed to burn the glucose to make energy. When muscles become overworked, for example during vigorous exercise, the oxygen and glucose supplies are used up. If there is insufficient oxygen and glucose, the muscles cannot produce enough energy to contract. The contractions will become weaker until they eventually stop. This is known as **muscle fatigue**.

As a result, an accumulation of harmful waste products, such as lactic acid and carbon dioxide, starts to build up in the affected muscle, causing stiffness and pain. Muscle fatigue is common among athletes who compete in endurance sports such as marathon races. Resting and gentle massage of the muscle will ensure that the blood brings oxygen and glucose and removes the waste products so that the muscles can work properly again.

## Growth and repair of muscle

When muscles undergo strenuous exercise, such as weightlifting, there is injury (tearing) to the muscle fibres. The body cannot produce new muscle fibres but repairs damaged ones, which causes increased strength and muscle size. Muscle growth occurs because of **hypertrophy**, which is an increase in the size of muscle owing to an increase in the size of muscle fibres. Lifting heavy weights results in muscle fibres developing more myofibrils than do muscle fibres that are less used; each myofibril contains more thick and thin filaments. Muscle fibres will also develop more mitochondria as a result of strenuous exercise, as more energy is required to move them.

## Effects of temperature

Exercise is an effective way of increasing body temperature because when muscles are working they produce heat. When muscle tissue is warm, the muscle fibres contract more easily as the blood circulation is increased. Therefore, the chemical reactions that naturally take place in the muscle cells are

> **FAST FACT**
>
> People are unable to grow new muscle fibres, so genetic factors are believed to determine the quantity that a person has. Therefore, an individual with more muscle fibres can grow larger muscles than someone with less muscle fibres.

## ASK FRAN...

**Q.** What are the effects of massage on muscles?
**A.** Massage is very beneficial for muscle tissue and includes the following effects.

- The blood supply to the muscle is increased during massage, bringing fresh oxygen and nutrients and removing waste products such as lactic acid. Massage can help to alleviate muscle fatigue. The muscle is warmed because of the increased blood flow and, because warm muscles contract more efficiently than when cold, the likelihood of injury is reduced.
- Massage helps to relieve pain, stiffness and fatigue in muscles as the waste products are removed and normal functioning is quickly restored. The increased oxygen and nutrients aid tissue repair and recovery of the muscle.
- Massage can help the breakdown of muscles' **knots**, which are areas of muscle contraction that develop within a muscle because of tension, injuries or poor posture. Knots are commonly found in the shoulder area.
- Massage helps to increase the tone of the muscles and delays wasting away of muscles through lack of use.

speeded up. When muscle tissue is cold, the opposite happens – the chemical reactions slow down and so contraction will be slower. You may have noticed this when your hands are in a cold environment and it is difficult to quickly bend the fingers.

### ACTIVITY 4.1

Fill in the gaps in the following text.

- There are over ............................ muscles in the body.
- The three types of muscle are ........................, ........................ and ........................ .
- Skeletal muscles are an example of ............................ muscles.
- When a muscle contracts the thinner filaments, ........................, slide in between thicker filaments, called ........................ .
- A ........................ nerve stimulates the muscle to contract.
- Muscle ........................ is the slight tension in which the muscles are continually held.
- Muscle fatigue occurs when there is insufficient ............... ........... and ........................ .
- Stiffness and pain results when the waste products ........................ and ........................ accumulate in the muscle.
- Injury to a muscle can cause complete or partial ........................ of the muscle fibres.
- Knots can develop as a result of ........................, ........................ or ........................ .

# Muscles of the body

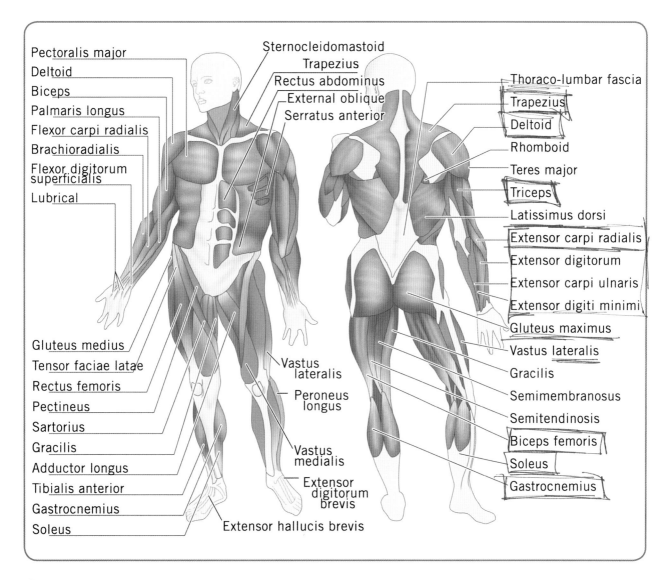

Pectoralis major
Deltoid
Biceps
Palmaris longus
Flexor carpi radialis
Brachioradialis
Flexor digitorum superficialis
Lubrical

Sternocleidomastoid
Trapezius
Rectus abdominus
External oblique
Serratus anterior

Thoraco-lumbar fascia
Trapezius
Deltoid
Rhomboid
Teres major
Triceps
Latissimus dorsi
Extensor carpi radialis
Extensor digitorum
Extensor carpi ulnaris
Extensor digiti minimi
Gluteus maximus
Vastus lateralis
Gracilis
Semimembranosus
Semitendinosis
Biceps femoris
Soleus
Gastrocnemius

Gluteus medius
Tensor faciae latae
Rectus femoris
Pectineus
Sartorius
Gracilis
Adductor longus
Tibialis anterior
Gastrocnemius
Soleus

Vastus lateralis
Peroneus longus
Vastus medialis
Extensor digitorum brevis
Extensor hallucis brevis

**Figure 4.7** The muscles of the body

## don't forget

Almost every muscle in the body uses factors such as its shape, size, location and function in its name. For example, biceps femoris contains both its location and shape in its name. 'Biceps' tells us it has two heads and 'femoris' means it is on the femur.

# Muscles of the head, face and neck

## ACTIVITY 4.2

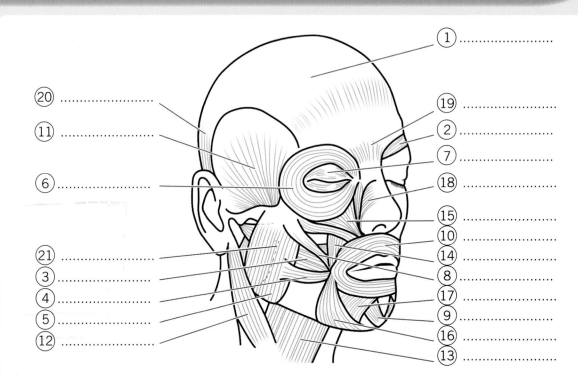

**Figure 4.8** Muscles of the face and neck

Label the diagram in Figure 4.8 using the information in Table 4.1 on pages 119–121. Use the information below to colour in each muscle.

(1) Frontalis (Use a red colour to shade this muscle.)

(2) Corrugator (Use a blue colour to shade this muscle.)

(3) Buccinator (Use a yellow colour to shade this muscle.)

(4) Risorius (Use an orange colour to shade this muscle.)

(5) Masseter (Use a red colour to shade this muscle.)

(6) Orbicularis oculi (Use an orange colour to shade this muscle.)

(7) Levator palpebrae superioris (Use a blue colour to shade this muscle.)

(8) Zygomaticus major (Use a brown colour to shade this muscle.)

(9) Mentalis (Use a brown colour to shade this muscle.)

(10) Orbicularis oris (Use an orange colour to shade this muscle.)

## ACTIVITY 4.2 (cont.)

(11) Temporalis (Use a red colour to shade this muscle.)

(12) Sternocleidomastoid (Use a red colour to shade this muscle.)

(13) Platysma (Use a blue colour to shade this muscle.)

(14) Levator anguli oris (Use a red colour to shade this muscle.)

(15) Levator labii superioris (Use a green colour to shade this muscle.)

(16) Depressor anguli oris (Use a red colour to shade this muscle.)

(17) Depressor labii inferioris (Use a blue colour to shade this muscle.)

(18) Nasalis (Use a yellow colour to shade this muscle.)

(19) Procerus (Use a green colour to shade this muscle.)

(20) Occipitalis (Use a brown colour to shade this muscle.)

(21) Pterygoids (Use a blue colour to shade this muscle.)

**FAST FACT**

Aponeurosis is a flat sheet of tendon-like connective tissue that contains collagen. It helps to bind muscles together and also connect muscle to bone. An example of an aponeurosis is the galea aponeurotica on the top of the head that covers the upper part of the skull.

**Table 4.1** Muscles of the head, face and neck

| Muscle | Position | Action |
| --- | --- | --- |
| (1) Frontalis (fron-tal-lis) | Across the forehead | Draws scalp forward and raises eyebrows. |
| (2) Corrugator (cor-oo-gater) | Between the eyebrows | Lowers eyebrows and wrinkles skin of forehead, as in frowning. |
| (3) Buccinator (bux-sin-ay-ter) (supercilii) | In each cheek, to the side of the mouth | Compresses cheeks, as in whistling and blowing, and draws the corners of the mouth in, as in sucking. |
| (4) Risorius (ree-so-re-us) | Extends diagonally from either side of the mouth | Draws the corner of the mouth outwards, as in grinning. |
| (5) Masseter (ma-see-ter) | The cheeks | The muscle of chewing: it closes the mouth and clenches the teeth. |

| Muscle | Position | Action |
|---|---|---|
| ⑥ Orbicularis oculi (or-bik-cue-la-riss ok-you-lie) | Around the eyes | Closes the eye. |
| ⑦ Levator palpebrae superioris (le-vay-tor pal-per-bree su-peer-ree-aw-ris) | Around the eyes | Lifts the eyelid. |
| ⑧ Zygomaticus major (zy-go-mat-ti-kus) | Extends diagonally from the corners of the mouth | Lifts the corners of the mouth upwards and outwards, as in smiling or laughing. |
| ⑨ Mentalis (men-ta-lis) | On the chin | Raises and protrudes lower lip, wrinkles skin on the chin. |
| ⑩ Orbicularis oris (or-bik-cue-la-riss aw-riss) | Surrounds the mouth | Closure and protrusion of the lips; changes shape of lips for speech. |
| ⑪ Temporalis (temp-po-rah-lis) | Extends from the temple region to the upper jaw bone | Raises the lower jaw and draws it backwards, as in chewing. |
| ⑫ Sternocleidomastoid (sterno-cly-doh-mas-toyd) | A pair of muscles running from the top of the sternum to the clavicle and temporal bones | Both together bend the head forward; one muscle only rotates the head and draws it towards the opposite shoulder. |
| ⑬ Platysma (pla-tis-ma) | Extends from the lower jaw to the chest and covers the front of the neck | Depresses lower jaw and draws lower lip outwards, and draws up the skin of the chest. |
| ⑭ Levator anguli oris (le-vay-tor an-goo-lie aw-riss) | On the cheek | Raises the corner of the mouth, as in smiling. |
| ⑮ Levator labii superioris (le-vay-tor lay-bee su-peer-ree-aw-riss) | On the cheek | Lifts the upper lip, as in smiling. |
| ⑯ Depressor anguli oris (de-press-or an-goo-lie aw-riss) | On the chin | Draws the corners of the mouth down, as in frowning. |
| ⑰ Depressor labii inferioris (de-press-or lay-be in-fear-ree-aw-riss) | On the chin | Lowers the bottom lip. |

| Muscle | Position | Action |
|---|---|---|
| (18) Nasalis (nay-sah-lis) | Sides of the nose | Opens the nostrils, as when angry. |
| (19) Procerus (pro-seer-rus) | On the nasal bone | Causes the small horizontal lines between the eyebrows when angry. |
| (20) Occipitalis (ox-sip-pee-tah-lis) | At the back of the head | Draws the scalp backwards. |
| (21) Pterygoids (lateral and medial) (terry-goyds) | Outer part of the cheek | Moves the mandible from side to side, as in chewing. |

## Origin and insertion

The **origin** of a muscle is the bone to which it is attached that does not move. The **insertion** is the bone to which the muscle is attached that does move. For example, the biceps of the upper arm has its point of origin at the shoulder, while the point of insertion is the radius of the lower arm. The insertion is the part farthest away from the spine. Muscles always move towards their origins.

## Muscle roles during movement

Muscles in the body normally work in pairs to produce movement. During movement, one muscle will contract while another relaxes.

- **Agonist or prime mover** – the muscle or muscles that move and contract.
- **Antagonist** – the muscle or muscles that relax while the prime mover is contracting.
- **Synergist** – a muscle that assists another muscle to produce a movement. An example of a synergist is the deltoid muscle, which assists the pectoral major muscle while carrying out a press-up.

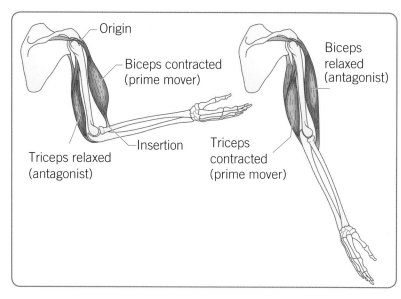

**Figure 4.9** How muscles act to bend the elbow

✖ **Fixator** – a muscle that acts to 'fix' or stabilise the origin of the agonist. For example, fixator groups of muscles at the ankles keep the joints stable when we stand up, otherwise the ankles would bend, making balance difficult.

When the forearm is bent, the muscle at the front of the arm (the biceps) contracts, so it is called the prime mover. The muscle at the back of the arm (the triceps) relaxes, so it is called the antagonist (Figure 4.9).

## Muscles of the shoulders and neck

### ACTIVITY 4.3

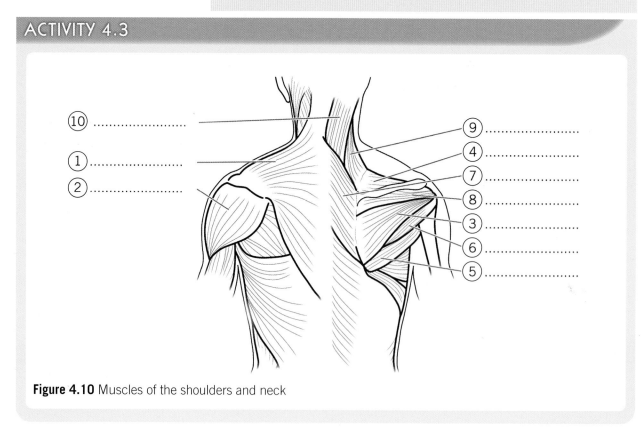

**Figure 4.10** Muscles of the shoulders and neck

# ACTIVITY 4.3 (cont.)

Label the diagram in Figure 4.10 using the information in Table 4.2 on pages 123–124. Use the information below to colour each muscle.

① Trapezius (Use a red colour to shade this muscle.)

② Deltoid (Use a blue colour to shade this muscle.)

③ Infraspinatus (Use a green colour to shade this muscle.)

④ Supraspinatus (Use a yellow colour to shade this muscle.)

⑤ Teres major (Use a blue colour to shade this muscle.)

⑥ Teres minor (Use a red colour to shade this muscle.)

⑦ Rhomboids (Use an orange colour to shade this muscle.)

⑧ Subscapularis – this muscle is found underneath the scapula so does not need to be coloured.

⑨ Levator scapulae (Use a blue colour to shade this muscle.)

⑩ Splenius capitis (Use a red colour to shade this muscle.)

**Table 4.2** Muscles of the shoulders and neck

| Muscle | Position | Origin | Insertion | Action |
|---|---|---|---|---|
| ① Trapezius (tra-pee-zee-us) | Forms a large, kite-shaped muscle across the top of the back and neck. | Occipital bone and vertebrae | Scapula and clavicle | Lifts the clavicle, as in shrugging, and also draws the head backwards. |
| ② Deltoid (del-toyd) | A thick, triangular muscle that caps the shoulder. | Clavicle and scapula | Humerus | Abducts the arm and draws it backwards and forwards. |
| ③ Infraspinatus (in-fra-spin-na-tus) | Deep muscle that covers the lower part of the scapula. | Scapula | Humerus | Laterally rotates and adducts the arm. |

| Muscle | Position | Origin | Insertion | Action |
|---|---|---|---|---|
| ④ Supraspinatus (su-pra-spin-na-tus) | Deep muscle that covers the upper part of the scapula. | Scapula | Humerus | Helps the deltoid muscle to abduct the arm. |
| ⑤ Teres major (terrys) | Deep muscle across the back of the shoulders. | Scapula | Humerus | Helps medially rotate and adduct the arm. |
| ⑥ Teres minor (terrys) | Deep muscle across the back of the shoulders. | Scapula | Humerus | Laterally rotates and adducts the arm. |
| ⑦ Rhomboids (rom-boyds) | Between the vertebral column and the scapula. | Thoracic vertebrae | Scapula | Rotate and adduct (pull) the scapula towards the spine. |
| ⑧ Subscapularis (sub-scap-you-la-ris) | Large, triangular muscle found beneath the scapula. | Scapula | Humerus | Medially rotates the arm. |
| ⑨ Levator scapulae (le-vay-tor skap-you-lee) | At the back and side of the neck, onto the scapula. | Cervical vertebrae | Scapula | Lifts the shoulder and scapula. |
| ⑩ Splenius capitis (splee-knee-us cap-pee-tiss) | Found under the trapezius in the neck. | Thoracic/cervical vertebrae | Occipital bone | Helps to hold neck and head in an upright position and aids rotation of the head. |

### Rotator cuff

The rotator cuff is a group of muscles and tendons that provide stability and strength to the shoulder joint.

The muscles of the rotator cuff include the subscapularis, supraspinatus, infraspinatus and teres minor. These muscles join the scapula to the humerus. Their flat tendons join together to form a whole circle around the shoulder joint, like the cuff on a shirt sleeve.

# Muscles of the posterior aspect of the trunk

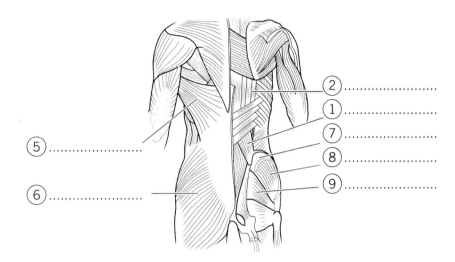

**Figure 4.11** Muscles of the posterior aspect of the trunk

Label the diagrams in Figures 4.11 and 4.12 using the information in Table 4.3. Use the information below to colour each muscle.

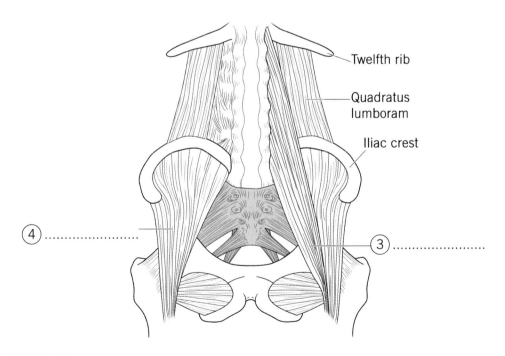

Twelfth rib

Quadratus lumboram

Iliac crest

**Figure 4.12** The iliopsoas

## ACTIVITY 4.4 (cont.)

(1) Quadratus lumborum (Use a blue colour to shade this muscle.)

(2) Erector spinae (Use a red colour to shade this muscle.)

(3) Psoas (Use a green colour to shade this muscle.)

(4) Iliacus (Use a yellow colour to shade this muscle.)

(5) Latissimus dorsi (Use a red colour to shade this muscle.)

(6) Gluteus maximus (Use a blue colour to shade this muscle.)

(7) Gluteus medius (Use a yellow colour to shade this muscle.)

(8) Gluteus minimus (Use a green colour to shade this muscle.)

(9) Piriformis (Use an orange colour to shade this muscle.)

**Table 4.3** Muscles of the posterior aspect of the trunk

| Muscle | Position | Origin | Insertion | Action |
|---|---|---|---|---|
| (1) Quadratus lumborum (qua-dra-tus lum-bor-rum) | Deep muscle. Found medially on the lower part of the back. | Iliac crest | Ribs | Lateral flexion (side bending) of lumbar vertebrae; assists diaphragm when breathing in. |
| (2) Erector spinae (ee-rek-tor spee-ny) | Three groups of deep muscles found on either side of the vertebrae. | Vertebrae, ribs, iliac crest | Cervical and lumbar vertebrae, ribs | Extends the spine and so helps to hold the body in an upright position. |
| (3) Psoas (so-as) | In the lumbar region of the spine and across the hip joint. | Lumbar vertebrae/ sacrum | Femur | Flexes the thigh and helps to laterally rotate the thigh. |

| Muscle | Position | Origin | Insertion | Action |
|---|---|---|---|---|
| (4) Iliacus (ee-lee-ak-us) | Deep muscle of the pelvis that crosses the hip joint. | Ilium | Femur | Flexes the thigh and helps to laterally rotate the thigh. |
| (5) Latissimus dorsi (lah-tis-i-mus dor-se) | A large sheet of muscle down the back of the lower thorax and lumbar region. | Vertebrae | Humerus | Draws the arm back and inwards towards the body; helps to pull the body upwards when climbing. |
| (6) Gluteus maximus (glue-tee-us max-ee-mus) | Lower part of the back forming the buttocks. | Ilium, sacrum, coccyx | Femur | Extends the hip and rotates the thigh laterally; used in running and jumping. |
| (7) Gluteus medius (glue-tee-us me-dee-us) | Lateral part of the buttocks, deep to gluteus maximus. | Ilium | Femur | Abducts and medially rotates the thigh; used in walking and running. |
| (8) Gluteus minimus (glue-tee-us min-knee-mus) | Lateral area of the buttocks, beneath gluteus medius. | Ilium | Femur | Abducts and rotates the thigh; used in walking and running. |
| (9) Piriformis (peer-ree-form-miss) | Found in the gluteal region and lies almost parallel to gluteus medius. | Anterior of sacrum | Top of femur | Lateral rotation and abduction of the hip. |

# Muscles of the arms and hands

## ACTIVITY 4.5

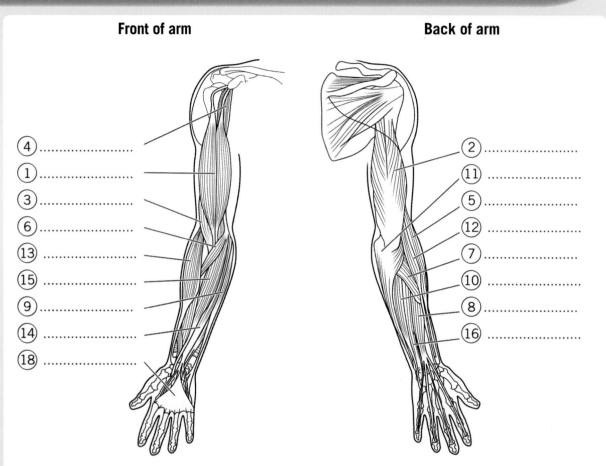

**Front of arm**

**Back of arm**

**Figure 4.13** Muscles of the front of the arm

**Figure 4.14** Muscles of the back of the arm

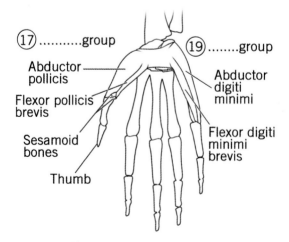

(17)..........group

(19)........group

Abductor pollicis

Abductor digiti minimi

Flexor pollicis brevis

Sesamoid bones

Flexor digiti minimi brevis

Thumb

**Figure 4.15** Muscles of the hand

# ACTIVITY 4.5 (cont.)

Label the diagams in Figures 4.13, 4.14 and 4.15 using the information in Table 4.4 on pages 130–132. Use the information below to colour each muscle.

(1) Biceps brachii (Use a red colour to shade this muscle.)

(2) Triceps (Use a red colour to shade this muscle.)

(3) Brachialis (Use a blue colour to shade this muscle.)

(4) Coracobrachialis (Use a yellow colour to shade this muscle.)

(5) Brachioradialis (Use an orange colour to shade this muscle.)

(6) Pronator teres (Use a blue colour to shade this muscle.)

(7) Supinator (Use a yellow colour to shade this muscle.)

(8) Extensor carpi digitorum (Use a red colour to shade this muscle.)

(9) Flexor digitorum superficialis (Use a brown colour to shade this muscle.)

(10) Extensor carpi ulnaris (Use an orange colour to shade this muscle.)

(11) Flexor carpi ulnaris (Use a green colour to shade this muscle.)

(12) Extensor carpi radialis (Use a blue colour to shade this muscle.)

(13) Flexor carpi radialis (Use a purple colour to shade this muscle.)

(14) Palmaris longus (Use a yellow colour to shade this muscle.)

(15) Flexor digitorum profundus (Use a red colour to shade this muscle.)

(16) Extensor pollicis longus (Use a blue colour to shade this muscle.)

(17) Thenar muscles (Use a red colour to shade these muscles.)

(18) Palmar aponeurosis (Use a green colour to shade this muscle.)

(19) Hypothenar muscles (Use a blue colour to shade these muscles.)

**Table 4.4** Muscles of the arms and hands

| Muscle | Position | Origin | Insertion | Action |
|---|---|---|---|---|
| ① Biceps brachii (by-seps brah-key) | Down anterior surface of the humerus | Scapula | Radius and flexor muscles in the forearm | Flexes and supinates the forearm. |
| ② Triceps (tri-seps) | Posterior surface of the humerus | Humerus and scapula | Ulna | Extends the forearm. |
| ③ Brachialis (bray-key-ah-liss) | On the anterior aspect of the humerus, beneath the biceps | Humerus | Ulna | Flexes the forearm. |
| ④ Coracobrachialis (coh-rah-co-bray-key-ah-liss) | Upper arm | Scapula | Humerus | Flexes and adducts the arm at the shoulder joint. |
| ⑤ Brachioradialis (bray-key-oh-ray-dee-ah-liss) | On the same side as the radius bone of the forearm | Humerus | Radius | Flexes supinates and pronates forearm. |
| ⑥ Pronator teres (pro-nay-ter terrys) | Anterior side of the forearm, across the elbow joint | Humerus and ulna | Radius | Pronates and flexes forearm. |
| ⑦ Supinator (su-pin-nay-ter) (deep muscle) | Forearm | Humerus | Radius | Supinates forearm. |
| ⑧ Extensor carpi digitorum (ex-ten-sore car-pee diji-tor-rum) (superficial muscle) | Forearm | Humerus | Phalanges | Extends phalanges. |
| ⑨ Flexor digitorum superficialis (flex-or diji-tor-rum super-fish-ee-ah-liss) (superficial muscle) | Forearm | Humerus | Phalanges | Flexes phalanges. |
| ⑩ Extensor carpi ulnaris (ex-sten-sore car-pee ul-nar-riss) (superficial muscle) | Forearm | Humerus | Fifth metacarpal | Extends and adducts the hand at the wrist joint. |

| Muscle | Position | Origin | Insertion | Action |
|---|---|---|---|---|
| (11) Flexor carpi ulnaris (flex-or car-pee ul-nar-riss) (superficial muscle) | Forearm | Humerus | Carpals and fifth metacarpal | Flexes and adducts the hand at the wrist joint. |
| (12) Extensor carpi radialis (ex-sten-sore car-pee ray-dee-ah-liss) (deep muscle) | Forearm | Humerus | Second metacarpal | Extends and abducts the hand at the wrist joint. |
| (13) Flexor carpi radialis (flex-or car-pee ray-dee-ah-liss) (superficial muscle) | Forearm | Humerus | Metacarpals | Flexes and abducts the hand at the wrist joint. |
| (14) Palmaris longus (pal-mar-ris long-us) | Forearm | Humerus | Flexor retinaculum and palmar aponeurosis | Flexes the hand. |
| (15) Flexor digitorum profundus (flex-or diji-tor-rum pro-fun-dus) | Forearm | Ulna | Phalanges of the fingers | Flexes the fingers. |
| (16) Extensor pollicis longus (ex-sten-sor pol-lis-sis lon-gus) | Forearm | Ulna | Phalanx of the thumb | Extends the thumb. |
| (17) Muscles of thenar eminence (superficial muscle) | On the palm of the hand. Consists of three muscles: abductor pollicis brevis, flexor pollicis brevis and opponens pollicis | Carpals and metacarpals | Phalanx of the thumb | The four thenar muscles act on the thumb. Movements include adduction, abduction and flexion of the thumb. |
| (18) Palmar aponeurosis (pal-mar ap-pon-ner-row-sis) | Strong, triangular membrane on the palm of the hand | Flexor retinaculum | Skin of the palm | Helps with gripping action of the hand and protects the tendons. |

| Muscle | Position | Origin | Insertion | Action |
|--------|----------|--------|-----------|--------|
| ⑲ Muscles of hypothenar eminence (superficial muscle) | On the palm of the hand | Carpals | Phalanx of the little finger and the metacarpal near to the little finger | The three hypothenar muscles act on the little fingers. Movements include abduction and flexion of the little finger. |

## Muscles of the anterior aspect of the trunk

### ACTIVITY 4.6

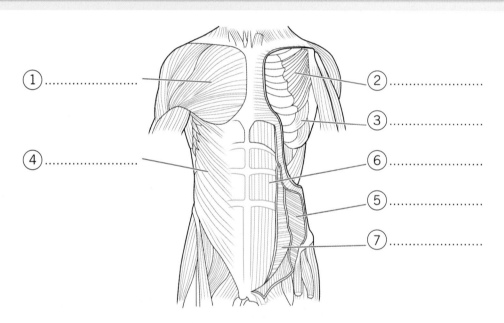

**Figure 4.16** Muscles of the anterior trunk

Label the diagram in Figure 4.16 using the information in Table 4.5 on page 133.

Use this key to colour the muscles.

① Pectoralis major (Use a red colour to shade this muscle.)

② Pectoralis minor (Use a brown colour to shade this muscle.)

③ Serratus anterior (Use a blue colour to shade this muscle.)

## ACTIVITY 4.6 (cont.)

④ External obliques (Use a yellow colour to shade this muscle.)

⑤ Internal obliques (Use an orange colour to shade this muscle.)

⑥ Rectus abdominis (Use a blue colour to shade this muscle.)

⑦ Transversus abdominis (Use a yellow colour to shade this muscle.)

**Table 4.5** Muscles of the anterior aspect of the trunk

| Muscle | Position | Origin | Insertion | Action |
|---|---|---|---|---|
| ① Pectoralis major (peck-tor-rah-lismay-jur) | Covers the upper part of the thorax. | Sternum, ribs and clavicle | Humerus | Adducts and medially rotates the arm. |
| ② Pectoralis minor (peck-top-rah-lis my-nor) | Small muscle found beneath pectoralis major. | Ribs | Scapula | Draws the shoulder downwards and forwards. |
| ③ Serratus (ser-a-tis) anterior | Sides of the ribcage below the armpits. | Ribs | Scapula | Draws the scapula forward, as in pushing movements. |
| ④ External obliques | Found laterally from side of the waist to anterior of the abdomen. | Ribs | Iliac crest and linea alba | Twists trunk to opposite side. |
| ⑤ Internal obliques | Found laterally on anterior of the abdomen. | Iliac crest | Ribs and linea alba | Twists trunk to opposite side. |
| ⑥ Rectus abdominis | Extends the whole length of the abdomen. | Pubic bone | Sternum and lower ribs | Supports abdominal organs and flexes vertebral column, as in bending forwards. |
| ⑦ Transversus abdominis | Found laterally on the front of abdomen, beneath internal oblique muscle. | Iliac crest, ribcage and vertebrae | The pubis, sternum and linea alba | Supports abdominal organs and flexes vertebral column. |

# Muscles of the legs and feet

## ACTIVITY 4.7

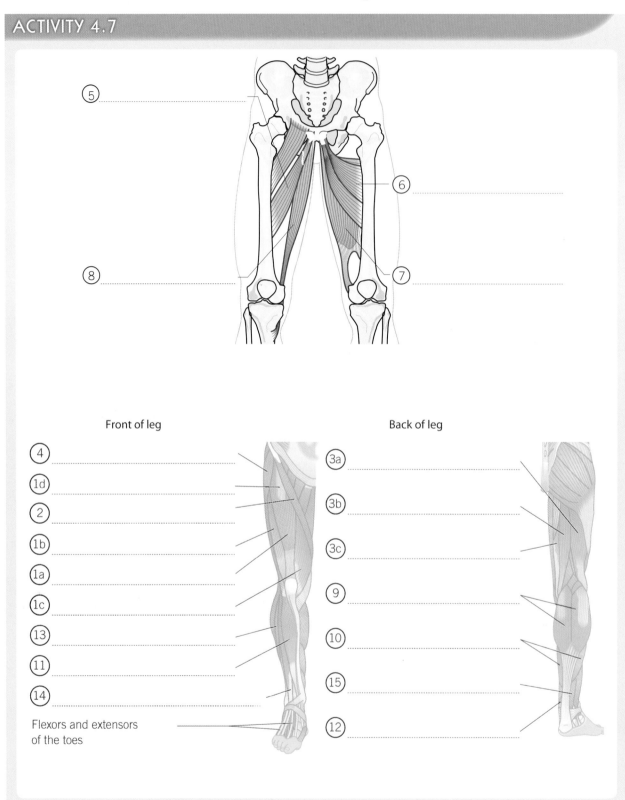

Front of leg

⑤
⑥
⑦
⑧

④
①d
②
①b
①a
①c
⑬
⑪
⑭

Flexors and extensors of the toes

Back of leg

③a
③b
③c
⑨
⑩
⑮
⑫

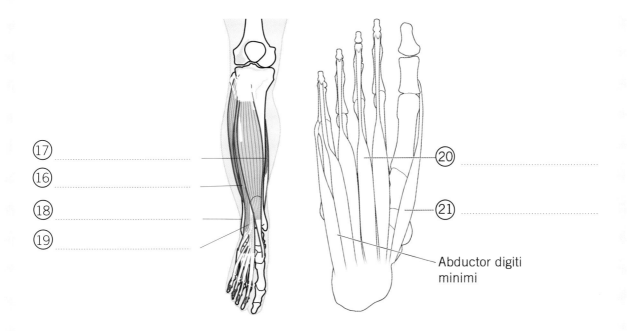

**Figure 4.17** Muscles of the legs and feet

Label the diagrams in Figure 4.17 using the information in Table 4.6 on pages 136–139. Use the information below to colour each muscle.

(1a) (1b) (1c) (1d) Quadriceps femoris (Use a red colour to shade these muscles.)

(2) Sartorius (Use a blue colour to shade this muscle.)

(3a) (3b) (3c) Hamstrings (Use a green colour to shade these muscles.)

(4) Tensor fasciae latae (Use a yellow colour to shade this muscle.)

(5) Adductor longus (Use a red colour to shade this muscle.)

(6) Adductor brevis (Use an orange colour to shade this muscle.)

(7) Adductor magnus (Use a green colour to shade this muscle.)

(8) Gracilis (Use a blue colour to shade this muscle.)

(9) Gastrocnemius (Use a yellow colour to shade this muscle.)

(10) Soleus (Use a green colour to shade this muscle.)

(11) Tibialis anterior (Use a brown colour to shade this muscle.)

## ACTIVITY 4.7 (cont.)

⑫ Tibialis posterior (Use a yellow colour to shade this muscle.)

⑬ Peroneus longus (Use an orange colour to shade this muscle.)

⑭ Extensor hallucis longus (Use a blue colour to shade this muscle.)

⑮ Flexor hallucis longus (Use a green colour to shade this muscle.)

⑯ Extensor digitorum longus (Use a brown colour to shade this muscle.)

⑰ Flexor digitorum longus (Use a yellow colour to shade this muscle.)

⑱ Peroneus brevis (Use a red colour to shade this muscle.)

⑲ Peroneus tertius (Use a blue colour to shade this muscle.)

⑳ Digitorum brevis (Use a green colour to shade this muscle.)

㉑ Abductor hallucis (Use a purple colour to shade this muscle.)

**Table 4.6** Muscles of the legs and feet

| Muscle | Position | Origin | Insertion | Action |
|---|---|---|---|---|
| ① Quadriceps femoris (quad-dree-seps fem-mor-riss) | Group of four muscles located on the front of the thigh:<br>a) rectus femoris<br>b) vastus lateralis<br>c) vastus medialis<br>d) vastus intermedius. | Ilium and femur | Patella and tibia | Extends the leg and the rectus femoris, also flexes the thigh. |
| ② Sartorius (sar-tor-ee-us) | Crosses diagonally on the anterior aspect of the thigh. | Ilium | Tibia | Flexes the knee and hip, and rotates the thigh laterally. |
| ③ Hamstrings (ham-strings) | Group of three muscles situated on the back of the thigh:<br>a) biceps femoris<br>b) semitendinosus<br>c) semimembranosus. | Ischium | Tibia | Flexes the knee and extends the hip. |

| Muscle | Position | Origin | Insertion | Action |
|---|---|---|---|---|
| ④ Tensor fasciae latae (ten-sore fash-ee-a la-tee) | Along the lateral side of the thigh. | Ilium | Tibia | Abducts and flexes the thigh. |
| ⑤ Adductor longus (ad-duk-tor long-us) | Medial side of the thigh. | Pubis and ischium | Femur | Adducts and flexes the thigh at the hip; medially rotates thigh. |
| ⑥ Adductor brevis (ad-duk-tor bray-viss) | Medial side of the thigh. | Pubis | Femur | Adducts and flexes the thigh at the hip; medially rotates the thigh. |
| ⑦ Adductor magnus (ad-duk-tor mag-nus) | Medial side of the thigh. | Pubis and ischium | Femur | Adducts the thigh; anterior part flexes the thigh and posterior part extends the thigh. |
| ⑧ Gracilis (gra-sil-lis) (adductor muscle) | Medial side of the thigh. | Pubic bone | Tibia | Adducts the thigh and flexes the leg at the knee joint. |
| ⑨ Gastro-cnemius (gas-troc-nee-me-us) | Back of the lower leg. | Femur | Calcaneum in the foot via the Achilles tendon | Plantar flexes the foot (draws the foot downwards). |
| ⑩ Soleus (so-lee-us) | At the back of the lower leg, deep to gastrocnemius. | Tibia and fibula | Calcaneum via the Achilles tendon | Plantar flexes the foot. |
| ⑪ Tibialis anterior (tib-ee-ah-liss an-tear-rhee-er) | Down the shin bone. | Tibia | Tarsal and metatarsal bones | Dorsiflexes the foot (draws the foot upwards). |
| ⑫ Tibialis posterior (tib-ee-ah-liss pos-tear-rhee-er) | Deepest muscle on the back of the lower leg. | Tibia and fibula | Metatarsals, navicular, cuneiforms and cuboid | Plantar flexes and inverts the foot (turns the foot inwards). |

| Muscle | Position | Origin | Insertion | Action |
|---|---|---|---|---|
| (13) Peroneus longus (per-row-knee-us long-us) | Down the outside of the lower leg. | Fibula | First metatarsal and cuneiform bone | Plantar flexes and inverts the foot (turns the foot outwards); supports the transverse and lateral longitudinal arches of the feet. |
| (14) Extensor hallucis longus (ex-ten-sore ha-loo-sis long-gus) | Down the front of the lower leg. | Fibula | Phalanx of the big toe | Extends the big toe. |
| (15) Flexor hallucis longus (flex-er ha-loo-sis long-us) | Outer side and towards the back of the lower leg. | Fibula | Phalanx of the big toe | Flexes the big toe, inverts and plantar flexes the foot, also supports medial longitudinal arch of the foot. |
| (16) Extensor digitorum longus (ex-ten-sore diji tor-rum long-us) | Lateral to tibialis anterior muscle. | Tibia and fibula | Phalanges | Dorsiflexes the foot. |
| (17) Flexor digitorum longus (flex-er diji-tor-rum long-us) | Medial to tibialis anterior muscle. | Tibia | Phalanges | Plantar flexes the foot. |
| (18) Peroneus brevis (per-ron-knee-us bray-viss) | Lies under the peroneus longus muscle. | Tibia | Fifth metatarsal | Everts and plantar flexes the foot. |
| (19) Peroneus tertius (per-ron-knee-us ter-shus) | Outer side of the lower leg. | Fibula | Fifth metatarsal | Dorsiflexes and everts the foot. |

| Muscle | Position | Origin | Insertion | Action |
|--------|----------|--------|-----------|--------|
| ⑳ Digitorum brevis (dij-gee-tor-rum bray-viss) | In the middle of the sole of the foot. | Calcaneus | Splits to become four tendons, which attach from the second to fifth toes | Flexes and extends the phalanges of the second to fifth toes. |
| ㉑ Abductor hallucis (ab-duct-tor ha-loo-sis) | Medial border of the foot. | Calcaneus | Phalanx of the big toe | Flexes and abducts the big toe, and also supports the medial longitudinal arch. |

## ACTIVITY 4.8

Use the information in Table 4.7 to label Figure 4.18 which shows the muscles of respiration.

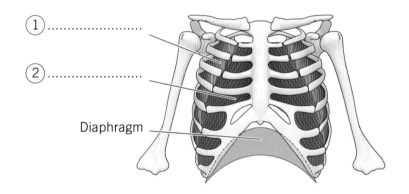

① .....................

② .....................

Diaphragm

**Figure 4.18** Muscles of respiration

## ACTIVITY 4.9

Copy Tables 4.1 to 4.7. Mix up the names, positions, origins, insertions and actions and try to match them back together.

**Table 4.7** Muscles of respiration

| Muscle | Position | Origin | Insertion | Action |
|---|---|---|---|---|
| External intercostal (ex-ster-nal in-ter-cos-tal) muscles. | Found between the ribs and help to form and move the chest wall. | Ribs | Ribs | Helps to lift and expand the ribcage while breathing in (inspiration). |
| Internal intercostal (in-ter-nal in-ter-cos-tal) muscles. | Found between the ribs and help to form and move the chest wall. | Ribs | Ribs | Aid in forced expiration (breathing out), such as coughing. They are responsible for the depression of the ribs, which helps air to move out of the lungs when breathing out. |

## ACTIVITY 4.10

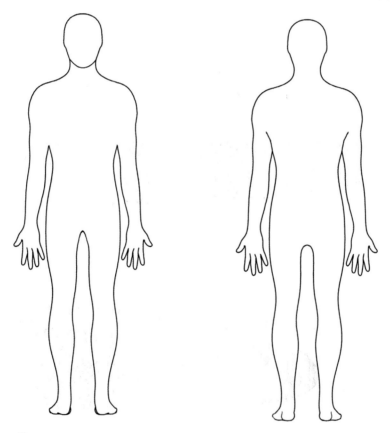

**Figure 4.19** Body outlines

Use the body outlines in Figure 4.19 to draw and shade the following muscles.

1. Trapezius
2. Gastrocnemius
3. Rectus abdominis
4. Triceps
5. Biceps
6. Pectoralis major
7. Deltoid
8. Frontalis
9. Soleus
10. Sartorius
11. Obliques
12. Biceps femoris
13. Rectus femoris
14. Achilles tendon
15. Latissimus dorsi
16. Gluteus maximus

# Posture

A good posture means that the body is aligned and balanced so that the work carried out by muscles to maintain it is kept to a minimum. It will ensure that muscles and joints are working efficiently so that the body remains free from muscular tension, strains, stiffness and pain. A poor posture means that the body is out of balance causing certain muscles to contract strongly to maintain it. Over a period of time, these muscles will tighten and shorten, while others will stretch and weaken. Three main postural faults are lordosis, kyphosis and scoliosis (Figure 4.20).

## Lordosis

Lordosis is a condition that shows itself as an inward exaggeration of the lumbar region of the spine. The client will appear to have a hollow back and there will be protrusion of the abdomen and buttocks. Gymnasts often acquire this posture.

✸ **Weak muscles** – the hamstrings, gluteus maximus, rectus abdominis, internal and external oblique muscles are stretched and lengthened.

✸ **Tight muscles** – the muscles of the lumbar region are shortened and the gluteal muscles weakened.

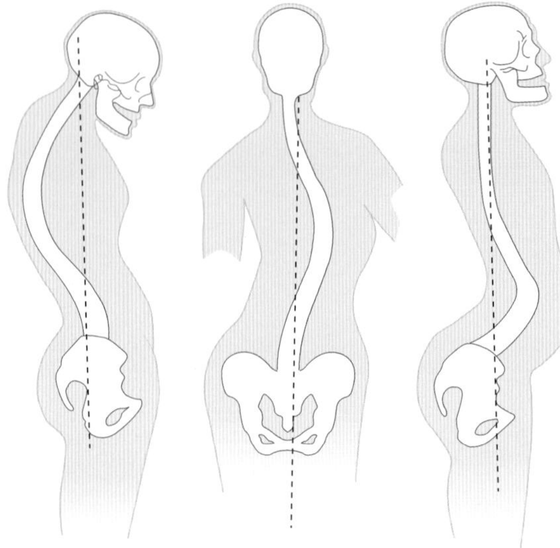


**Figure 4.20** Postural faults

## Kyphosis

Kyphosis is a condition where there is an exaggeration of the thoracic curve of the spine. The client will have rounded shoulders and the chin will poke forwards. Adopting a poor posture often causes kyphosis.

- **Weak muscles** – the upper back muscles are weakened and overstretched.
- **Tight muscles** – the pectoral muscles are tightened and shortened.

## Scoliosis

A feature of scoliosis is a lateral curvature of the spine, which may be C- or S-shaped. It can result in the level of the shoulders and pelvic girdle being slightly uneven. An individual may be born with this condition; the continual carrying of heavy bags on one particular shoulder over a period of time can also cause it. The muscles that are shortened are found on the inside of the curve and the muscles that are overstretched will be found on the outside of the curve. Shortened and tight muscles can be relaxed and stretched with massage, which can help to correct posture faults.

# Conditions associated with muscles

## Adhesions and fibrous tissue

Injury and damage to the muscle may cause scar tissue to form owing to insufficient healing by collagen fibres. This may be because the muscles remained tense while healing took place. The scar tissue creates adhesions and fibrous tissue. Muscle fibres need to be able to glide smoothly past each other but cannot do this when the fibres are stuck together (**adhesions**). After a while the fibres will knit together and form a hard lump or knot (**fibrous tissue**).

## Cramp (leg muscles)

Cramp is a painful muscle spasm caused by contraction of the affected muscle, and may arise following exercise. Muscle spasms occur when excessive strain is placed on leg muscles, or when excessive sweating causes water and salt loss. Lightly massaging and gradually stretching the affected muscle can relieve the spasm and pain. Sometimes cramp can occur for no reason, for example during sleep, and is believed to be the result of abnormal nerve activity.

## Fibromyalgia

Fibromyalgia is a condition that causes pain and stiffness in muscles, ligaments and tendons. The pain can be mild or severe and is usually more severe in the parts of the body that are used most, such as the hands and hips. Other symptoms include tiredness, irritability, forgetfulness, sleeping difficulties, headaches, depression and anxiety. The exact cause of fibromyalgia is unknown.

## Fibrositis

This is inflammation of fibrous connective tissue, particularly around muscles, tendons and joints. The affected area is stiff, painful and tender. The causes include injury, infection and repetitive use of a body part.

## Lumbago

Lumbago is a term used to describe lower back pain (in the lumbar region of the spine). Stiffness and muscle spasms may also be experienced by the sufferer. Causes include injury and disease.

## Medial epicondylitis (golfer's elbow) and lateral epicondylitis (tennis elbow)

Golfer's elbow features pain in the inner elbow and may be felt in the forearm too. Tennis elbow involves pain on the outer part of the elbow. Both of these conditions are a form of tendonitis and are caused by an overuse of the muscles and tendons of the forearm, which leads to inflammation around the elbow joint.

## Muscular dystrophy (MD)

don't forget

'Atrophy' means to waste away

This is a group of inherited diseases that weaken muscles. People with MD do not make the necessary proteins for healthy muscles, so the muscles progressively become weaker and atrophy (waste away). Symptoms include muscle weakness, lack of coordination and loss of mobility.

## Myasthenia gravis

A rare autoimmune disorder (where the body attacks its own tissues) in which there is weakness and rapid fatigue of muscles that are under voluntary control. Symptoms include eye problems, such as drooping of one or both eyes and double vision. Other signs include weakness of neck, arm or leg muscles, swallowing, chewing and breathing difficulties. The cause is a breakdown of communication between the nerves and muscles (the muscle does not receive the signal from the nerves). Symptoms can be controlled effectively with medical treatment.

## Myopathy

'Myopathy' means muscle disease, and refers to any disease that affects the muscle tissue. This results in muscle weakness, stiffness or rapid fatigue in muscles. Myopathy in later years may be linked to thyroid disease.

## Rheumatism

This is used to describe various painful conditions affecting the muscles, tendons, bones and joints. Examples include bursitis and fibromyalgia.

## Shin splints

Shin splints may occur during or following vigorous exercise, and pain will be felt in the front lower leg (shin). The exact cause is unknown but it may be the result of tiny fractures developing in the shin bone. The sufferer should not continue exercising and is encouraged to rest for around two weeks.

## Sprain and strain

A sprain is the stretching or tearing of ligaments, which commonly occurs at the ankle. A strain is stretching or tearing of muscle or tendon. Overwork or overstretching of the muscles can cause strain and may result in muscle fibres being torn. It can normally be felt as hardness in the muscle, usually running in the same direction as the muscle fibres. Strains are common in the lower back and hamstrings. Treatment for both sprains and strains includes rest, ice, compression and elevation (RICE method). Severe sprains and strains sometimes require surgery.

## Tearing of muscle fibres

Injury to a muscle can cause complete or partial tearing of the muscle fibres. Partial tears result in the tearing of some muscle fibres and will feel very tender and painful, especially when contracting the muscle. Complete tearing involves tearing all of the muscle fibres, which causes the two ends of the muscle to contract away from each other. It is extremely painful and there is complete loss of function.

**Myositis** is inflammation of a muscle.

**Rupture** is a tearing or bursting of the fascia that surround the muscle.

**Spasticity** refers to a spasm within one or more muscles. This is a problem associated with the nervous system.

Overworking a muscle or a tendon can lead to a **strain**. There may be pain, swelling and stiffness.

## Tetanus

Tetanus is a bacterial infection that enters a deep flesh wound and affects the nervous system, resulting in painful muscle contraction, especially of the jaw and neck muscles. It can make breathing difficult so can be life threatening.

## Torticollis

Torticollis happens when muscle spasm in the neck causes the head to twist and be pulled over to one side. The neck will feel painful and stiff, although recovery usually occurs within a few days. Sleeping awkwardly and injury to the neck muscles are common causes. It can also be caused by certain medications and recreational drugs.

# What you should know

## Functions of the muscular system
- [ ] Movement of skeleton
- [ ] Maintenance of posture
- [ ] Generation of heat

## Structure and function
- [ ] Muscle types – involuntary/smooth, voluntary/skeletal, cardiac
- [ ] Characteristics of muscle – contractibility, elasticity, excitability, extensibility
- [ ] Structure of skeletal muscle – origin, insertion, tendon, aponeurosis, epimysium, endomysium, perimysium, fascicles, muscle fibres, myofibrils, actin and myosin, sarcoplasmic reticulum
- [ ] Muscle fibre types and characteristics (slow type 1, fast type 2A and 2B)
- [ ] Process of muscle contraction – sarcomere, actin, myosin, cross bridge cycling, zones, discs, role of ATP
- [ ] Types of muscle contraction during movement – isotonic concentric, isotonic eccentric, isometric
- [ ] Muscle roles during movement – agonist, antagonist, synergist, fixator

## Location and action of skeletal muscles
- [ ] Muscles of the scalp and face – frontalis, occipitalis, orbicularis oculi, corrugators (supercilii), nasalis, orbicularis oris, zygomaticus, risorius, mentalis
- [ ] Facial muscles of mastication (chewing) – buccinators, masseter, temporalis
- [ ] Neck muscles – platysma, sternocleidomastoid

- [ ] Muscles of anterior thorax – pectoralis major and minor, external and internal intercostals, diaphragm, serratus anterior
- [ ] Muscles of posterior thorax – erector spinae, trapezius, latissimus dorsi, levator scapulae, rhomboids major and minor, rotator cuff, supraspinatus, infraspinatus, teres minor, subscapularis, teres major
- [ ] Muscles of upper arm – deltoid, biceps brachii, coraco – brachialis, brachialis, triceps brachii
- [ ] Muscles of lower arm and hand – pronator teres, brachioradialis, flexor carpi radialis, flexor carpi ulnaris, flexor carpi digitorum, longus, brevis, extensor carpi ulnaris, extensor carpi digitorum, abductor pollicis brevis, flexor pollicis brevis, thenar and hypothenar eminence
- [ ] Muscles of abdominal region – external and internal obliques, rectus abdominis, transverseus abdominis, quadratus lumborum
- [ ] Muscles of the hip – iliopsoas, piriformis, gluteus maximus, gluteus medius, gluteus minimus, tensor fasciae latae
- [ ] Muscles of the thigh – sartorius, rectus femoris, vastus lateralis, vastus intermedius, vastus medialis, biceps femoris, semitendinosus, semimembranosus, gracilis, adductors longus, brevis, magnus
- [ ] Muscles of the lower leg and foot – gastrocnemius, soleus, tibialis anterior, peroneus longus, extensor digitorum longus, flexor digitorum longus, extensor hallucis longus
- [ ] Growth and repair – process of muscular hypertrophy
- [ ] Conditions associated with muscles, including their causes, signs and symptoms – for example cramp, spasm, fatigue, inflammatory conditions, sprains, muscle strains, rheumatism, atrophy, tetanus, torticollis, fibrositis, fibromyalgia

# Nervous system and common pathologies

The nervous and endocrine systems work together to maintain a stable internal environment (**homeostasis**) within the body. The nervous system consists of the brain, spinal cord, nerves and sense organs. It controls all the bodily systems and provides the most rapid means of communication in the body.

Millions of nerve impulses (messages) are continually reaching the brain from receptors in, for instance, the skin. Just as many leave the brain to stimulate muscles to move and organs to carry out their work. In the body, the messages are in the form of electrical impulses that pass from **neurone** (nerve cell) to neurone. There are billions of neurones within the body, and their function is to transmit nerve impulses.

# Neurones

## Structure of a motor neurone

The cell body contains a nucleus and branches of nerve fibres called **dendrites** (see Figure 5.1). Dendrites bring information (carry the impulses) to the cell body and the axon, which is a long fibre of a nerve cell, takes information away from the cell body. Therefore, impulses only move in one direction. Neurones generally only have one axon, but this can be anything from 1 mm long to over 1 m long.

The axon is covered in a fatty **myelin sheath**. The myelin sheath insulates the neurone to prevent loss of the electrical impulses, and also increases the speed at which the impulse is conducted. Some (**unmyelinated**) nerve cells do not have a myelin sheath.

Nerve cells with a sheath are able to transmit impulses 200 times faster than unmyelinated ones. The myelin sheath consists of a series of **Schwann cells** arranged along the length of the axon. The outer layer of the Schwann cell membrane is sometimes called the **neurilemma**. Gaps occur in the myelin sheath and are called **nodes of Ranvier**, which help to ensure the impulses (messages) are carried quickly from neurone to neurone. An axon terminal is a club-shaped structure found at the end of an axon and is the point at which messages are passed to other neurones.

FAST FACT

Types of neurones include motor, efferent and afferent.

don't forget

Neurones come in many different shapes and sizes.

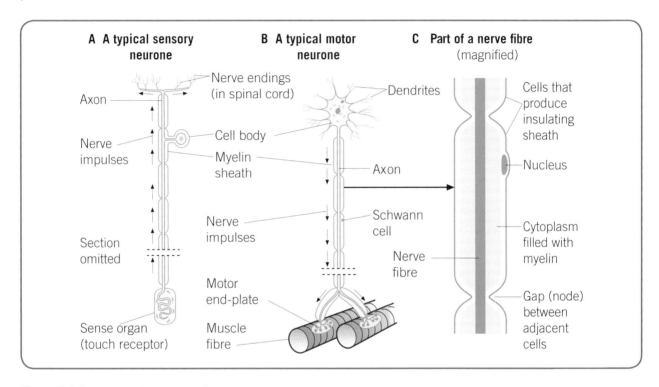

**Figure 5.1** Structure of a nerve cell

## Types of neurones (nerve cells)

Neurones can be classified by the direction that they send information.

Afferent (or sensory) neurones send information from sensory receptors, such as those found in the skin, eyes and ears.

Efferent (or motor) neurones send information away from the central nervous system to muscles or glands.

Interneurones send information between sensory and motor neurones, and are mostly found in the central nervous system.

## ACTIVITY 5.1

Match the terms in the bubbles with the correct description in the list.

- Gap between two nerve cells ...............

- Fatty insulating material ...............

- Branch from the cell body ...............

- Carries impulses away from cell body ...............

- Nerve cell ...............

> 1.
> dendrite

> 2.
> neurone

> 3.
> myelin sheath

> 4.
> axon

> 5.
> synapse

# How impulses are transmitted

Neurones transmit nerve impulses to other neurones or organs such as muscles. When two neurones meet, there is a gap between them called a **synapse** (see Figure 5.2). The nerve impulse is transferred to the next neurone by the release of chemicals, called neurotransmitters, which diffuse across the

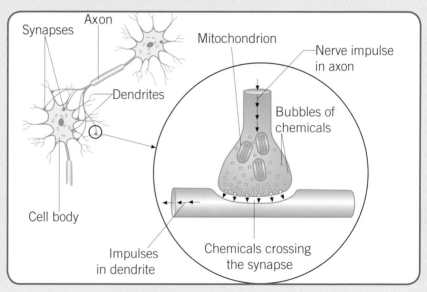

**Figure 5.2** Structure of a synapse

synapse. The chemicals then set off a new electrical signal in the next neurone. The signal passes from the dendrite to the cell body and through the axon. Salt and potassium ions are vital for the transmission of the nerve impulse through a nerve cell.

## ACTIVITY 5.2

Decide the order of sequence for the passing of an impulse through a nerve cell. Place the correct letter in each box.

A. The impulse reaches the axon terminal.

B. The impulse travels along the axon.

C. The impulse reaches the cell body.

D. The impulse is transferred to the next neurone by the release of chemicals.

E. The impulse reaches the dendrite.

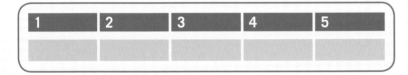

| 1 | 2 | 3 | 4 | 5 |
|---|---|---|---|---|
|   |   |   |   |   |

# Nerves

The axons from a large number of neurones are arranged in bundles and form **nerves** (Figure 5.3). Nerves are rather like electrical wires surrounded by cable. A **ganglion** (plural: ganglia) is a group of nerve cell bodies that are located outside the brain and spinal cord.

## Growth and repair of nerves

Unlike other cells, most neurones cannot divide and reproduce themselves. If neurones die, many of them cannot be replaced, although they can be repaired if damaged.

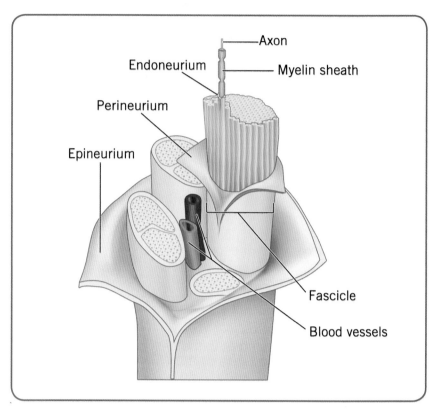

**Figure 5.3** Structure of a nerve

# Divisions of the nervous system

The nervous system can be divided into the central, peripheral and autonomic nervous systems.

## Central nervous system (CNS)

The central nervous system consists of the brain and spinal cord. The brain is the most important part of the system and contains 100 billion neurones. The brain receives and stores messages, as well as transmitting them to all parts of the body to stimulate organs to do their work.

# ACTIVITY 5.3

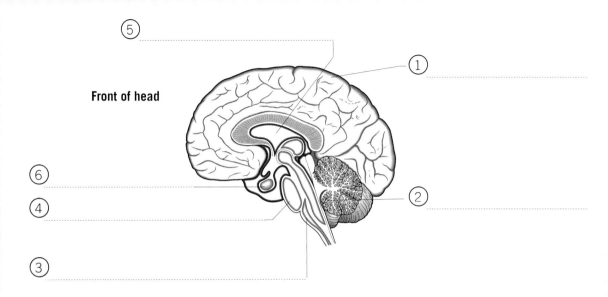

**Figure 5.4** Structures in the brain

Label the diagram in Figure 5.4 matching the numbers to the numbered terms in the following text. Use this key to colour the diagram.

Yellow – cerebrum
Blue – pons varolii
Pink – cerebellum

Green – thalamus
Orange – medulla oblongata
Red – hypothalamus

## ① Cerebrum

The cerebrum is the largest portion of the brain. It is a dome-shaped area of nervous tissue split into two halves:

✸ the **left hemisphere**, which controls the right side of the body. In most people, the left hemisphere is more important for language, numerical and scientific skills.

✸ the **right hemisphere**, which controls the left side of body. The right side is the creative side and is important for musical and artistic ability.

Within the cerebral hemispheres and brain stem are spaces called ventricles, which are filled with **cerebrospinal fluid** (CSF). Cerebrospinal fluid is a clear, colourless fluid that covers the whole surface of the central nervous system.

**FAST FACT ❯**

Some pathological conditions involve the build-up of CSF within the ventricles. This is known as hydrocephalus. This extra fluid results in increased pressure on the brain, which can cause damage to its tissue.

The **grey matter** on the surface of the brain is made up of nerve cell bodies and is where the main functions of the cerebrum are carried out. These include all conscious activities, such as touch, taste, smell, hearing, vision, and all voluntary muscular movement. The cerebrum also controls the powers of reasoning, learning, emotion and memory.

The **white matter** of the brain and spinal cord consists of nerve fibres (axons) in white myelinated sheaths.

FAST FACT ❯

The medulla oblongata is responsible for vomiting, which basically involves squeezing the stomach between the diaphragm and abdominal muscles.

② Cerebellum

The cerebellum deals with movement. It helps to control balance and posture. It maintains muscle tone and coordinates muscles during activities such as walking and running. It is also responsible for learning skills, such as playing the piano or riding a bike.

③ Medulla oblongata

The **medulla oblongata** is a mass of grey matter. It regulates the heart and breathing rates, constriction and dilation of the blood vessels, body temperature and the reflex actions of sneezing, coughing, vomiting and swallowing.

④ Pons varolii

The **pons varolii** forms a bridge (*pons* is Latin for bridge) that transmits messages between the spinal cord, cerebellum and cerebrum.

⑤ Thalamus

The thalamus coordinates impulses from sense organs, such as the skin, eyes, nose and taste buds, before they reach the cerebrum.

**don't forget**

The brain stem is made up of three parts: the medulla oblongata, the pons varolii and the <u>mid-brain</u>. The mid-brain is found between the cerebrum and cerebellum.

⑥ Hypothalamus

The hypothalamus controls the activities of the autonomic nervous system (see page 163) and an endocrine gland called the **pituitary gland**. The hypothalamus is one of the main regulators of homeostasis, helping to maintain a constant internal environment in the body.

The hypothalamus controls many body functions.

- Through the autonomic nervous system, it controls blood pressure, heart rate, contraction of the bladder and the movement of food through the alimentary canal.
- With the help of the kidneys, it controls the salt and water balance of the body.
- It controls hunger and thirst to ensure sufficient intake of water and nutrients into the body.
- It controls the body temperature by acting like a thermostat. If the temperature of the blood flowing through the hypothalamus is above normal, the hypothalamus instructs the autonomic nervous system to promote heat loss by means of, for example, sweating and vasodilation. If the blood temperature is below normal, the hypothalamus causes the body to shiver to produce heat.
- Together with the **limbic system**, it controls the feelings associated with aggression, pain, pleasure and sexual arousal.
- It helps to maintain waking and sleeping patterns.

### Neuroglia

The spaces between neurones are filled with cells called **neuroglia**, which support the neurones, provide nutrients and help them to conduct nerve impulses. Two types of neuroglia are:

- **Astrocytes**. Many of these star-shaped cells are found in the brain, lying next to blood vessels. Astrocytes only allow certain substances to pass from the blood into the brain. This is known as the **blood–brain barrier** and protects the brain cells from most harmful substances. Certain substances, such as oxygen, glucose and also carbon dioxide, alcohol and nicotine, pass quickly across this barrier into the brain. It is thought that essential oils can also pass through the blood–brain barrier.

### ASK FRAN...

**Q.** What is the best way to learn and retain new information?

**A.** Most of us have to work hard at remembering facts, such as long muscle names! It has been discovered that we lose about 75% of what we learn after 48 hours if good learning methods aren't employed. A good way to help transfer information into the long-term memory is to repeat it over and over. You should use as many senses as possible to learn new facts, such as looking at pictures, listening to, and writing, information. Different methods of learning, such as labelling diagrams, colouring pictures and making flashcards (these activities can all be found throughout this book) are effective ways to help you both learn and remember new facts.

✂ **Oligodendrocytes**. These cells form a supporting network around the nerve cells of the central nervous system. They also produce the myelin sheath for these nerve cells.

### Spinal cord

The spinal cord is continuous with the medulla oblongata, extending downwards through the vertebral column and ending level with the lumbar vertebrae. It contains about 100 million neurones. As in the brain, coverings called **meninges**, made up of three connective tissue layers, protect it. The layers are called **pia mater**, **arachnoid** and **dura mater**.

*don't forget*

Meningitis is inflammation of the meninges.

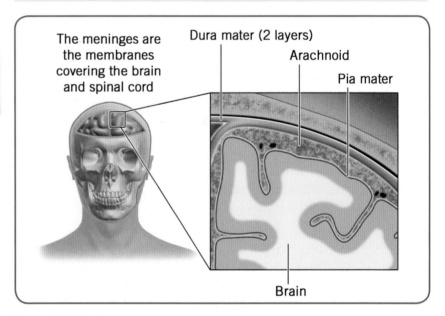

The meninges are the membranes covering the brain and spinal cord

Dura mater (2 layers)

Arachnoid

Pia mater

Brain

**Figure 5.5** Meninges

The spinal cord contains white and grey matter. Grey matter appears as a butterfly shape in the middle of the spinal cord and is surrounded by white matter.

The **cerebrospinal fluid** (CSF) is similar to blood plasma in composition. It protects the brain and spinal cord by acting as a cushion and shock absorber between the brain and the cranial bones. It also keeps the brain and spinal cord moist and provides nutrients for the nerve cells.

The function of the spinal cord is to provide communication between the brain and all parts of the body. It is also involved with reflex actions.

# Peripheral nervous system

The peripheral nervous system is concerned with all nerves situated outside the central nervous system, which include:

✂ **efferent/motor nerves**, which carry nerve impulses from the brain, through the spinal cord to the skeletal muscles, glands and smooth muscular tissue to stimulate them into carrying out their work

✂ **afferent/sensory nerves**, which carry nerve impulses from sensory nerve endings in organs, such as the skin, and transmit the impulse to the brain and spinal cord

✂ **mixed nerves**, which consist of motor and sensory nerves

✂ **interneurones**, which carry nerve impulses from sensory neurones to motor neurones. They are only found in the brain and spinal cord.

## Cranial nerves

There are 12 pairs of cranial nerves that originate from the brain inside the skull. They supply the muscles and sensory organs (such as the eyes and skin) of the head and neck.

Cranial nerves include ① **abducent**, ② **auditory**, ③ **facial**, ④ **glosso-pharyngeal**, ⑤ **hypoglossal**, ⑥ **oculomotor**, ⑦ **olfactory**, ⑧ **optic**, ⑨ **trochlear**, ⑩ **trigeminal**, ⑪ **accessory**, ⑫ **vagus.**

## ACTIVITY 5.4

Jayne has slightly burned her finger. Which types of nerve are responsible for informing her brain of this injury?

Andy has spotted some money on the floor. He bends down to pick it up. Which types of nerve are responsible for the action of picking up the money?

# ACTIVITY 5.5

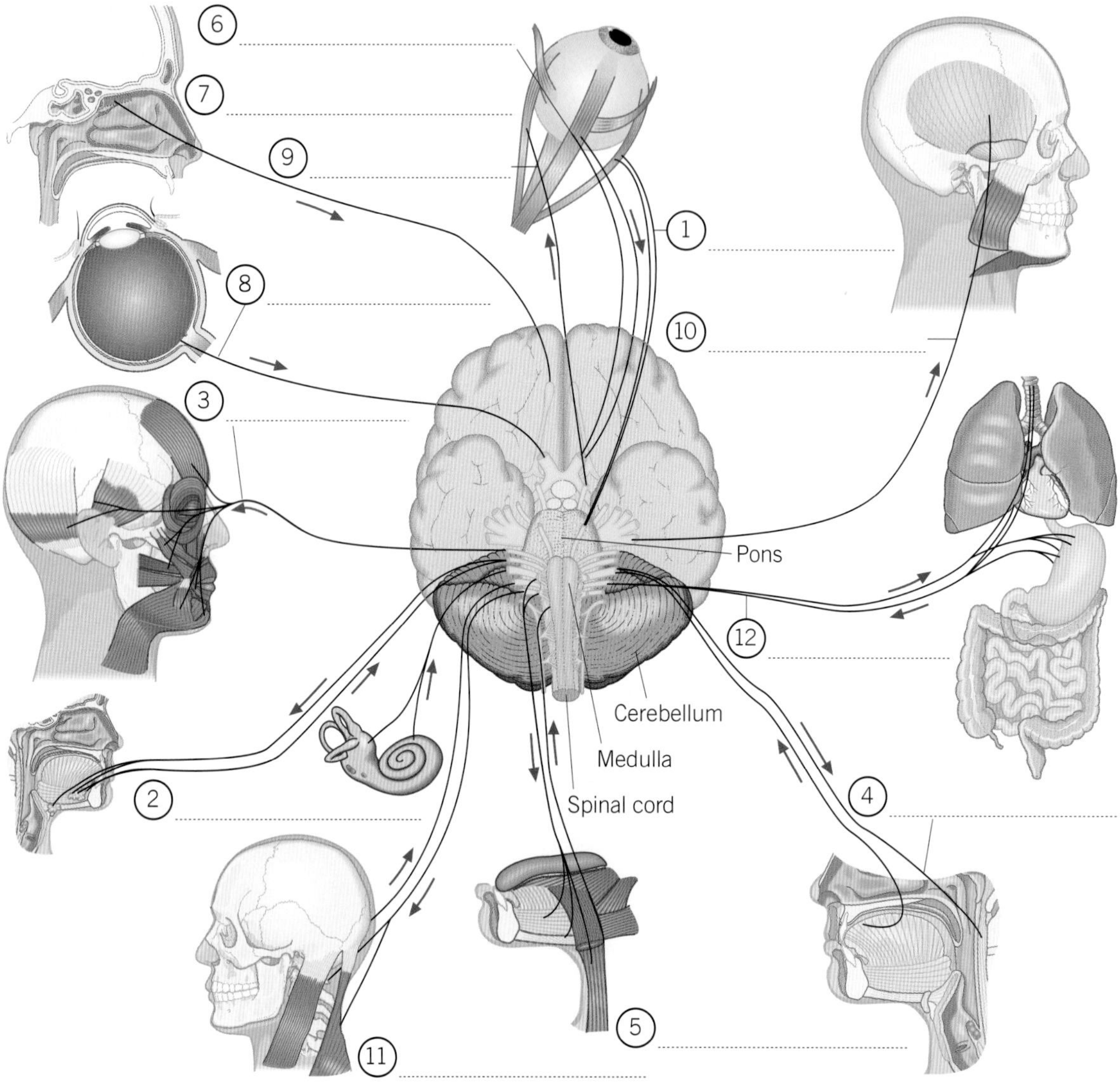

**Figure 5.6** Cranial nerves

Label the diagram in Figure 5.6 using the information above.

# Sense organs and receptors

The five sense organs are the eyes, ears, nose, skin and tongue. Each sense organ contains a **receptor**, which is a group of cells that is sensitive to a stimulus, such as sound or cold. Information is received by the brain from the stimulus in the form of electrical impulses.

**don't forget**

The Eustachian tube connects the middle ear with the upper part of the throat. Harmful substances, such as bacteria, can travel through this tube to cause infection in the middle ear.

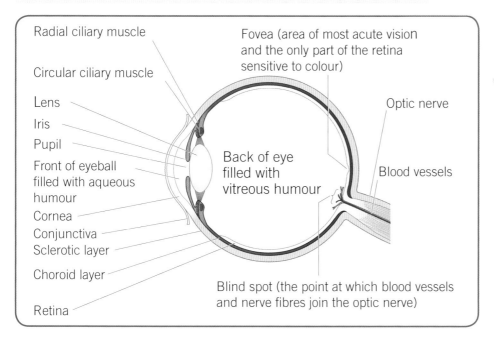

Radial ciliary muscle
Circular ciliary muscle
Lens
Iris
Pupil
Front of eyeball filled with aqueous humour
Cornea
Conjunctiva
Sclerotic layer
Choroid layer
Retina
Fovea (area of most acute vision and the only part of the retina sensitive to colour)
Optic nerve
Blood vessels
Back of eye filled with vitreous humour
Blind spot (the point at which blood vessels and nerve fibres join the optic nerve)

**Figure 5.7** The eye

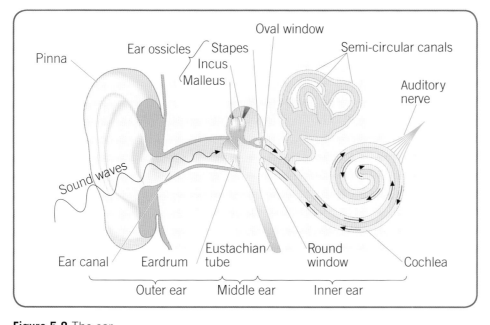

Pinna
Ear ossicles
Stapes
Incus
Malleus
Oval window
Semi-circular canals
Auditory nerve
Sound waves
Ear canal
Eardrum
Eustachian tube
Round window
Cochlea
Outer ear
Middle ear
Inner ear

**Figure 5.8** The ear

* The **eyes** contain light receptors known as rods and cones.

* The **ear** is a sense organ that contains sound receptors.

* The **nose** contains taste and smell receptors.

* The **skin** contains pressure, touch and temperature receptors.

* The **tongue** contains taste buds that are receptors for taste.

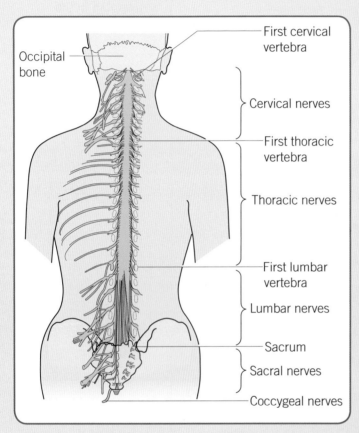

Occipital bone

First cervical vertebra

Cervical nerves

First thoracic vertebra

Thoracic nerves

First lumbar vertebra

Lumbar nerves

Sacrum

Sacral nerves

Coccygeal nerves

**Figure 5.9** The spinal cord and spinal nerves

## Spinal nerves

There are 31 pairs of spinal nerves that originate from the spinal cord and emerge between the vertebrae. The nerves are either sensory, motor or mixed (containing both types). The spinal nerves are named according to the region of the spinal cord from which they emerge

There are:

* eight pairs of cervical nerves

* twelve pairs of thoracic nerves

* five pairs of lumbar nerves

* five pairs of sacral nerves

* one pair of coccygeal nerves.

Each spinal nerve divides into branches, forming groups of nerves called **plexuses**. They are named after the vertebrae to which they connect. The main plexuses are:

* the **cervical plexus**, in the neck, which supplies the skin and muscles of the head, the neck and the upper part of the shoulders and chest

* the **brachial plexus**, at the top of the shoulder, which supplies the whole of the shoulders and arm

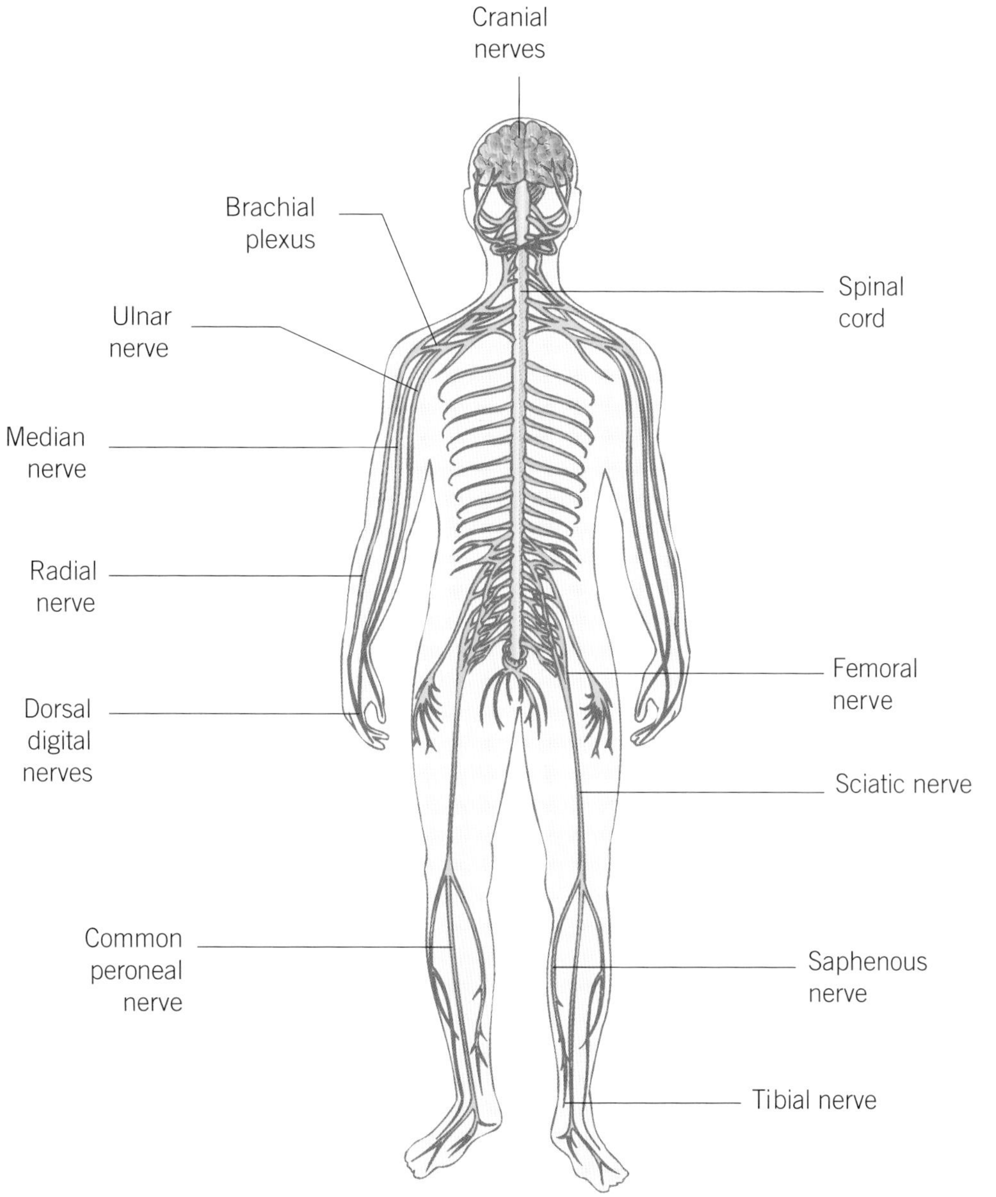
Cranial nerves
Brachial plexus
Spinal cord
Ulnar nerve
Median nerve
Radial nerve
Dorsal digital nerves
Femoral nerve
Sciatic nerve
Common peroneal nerve
Saphenous nerve
Tibial nerve

**Figure 5.10** Nerves of the body

- the **thoracic plexus**, between the upper back and the waist, which supplies the chest muscles and most of the abdominal wall
- the **lumbar plexus**, between the waist and the hip, which supply the lower part of the abdominal wall and part of the leg
- the **sacral plexus**, at the base of the abdomen, which supply the buttock and some leg muscles

✖ the **coccygeal plexus**, on the back of the pelvic cavity, which supplies the muscles and skin of the pelvic area.

## Reflex action

Normally, nerve impulses are sent to the brain and a message is sent back, but this could take long enough for a serious injury to occur. So a **reflex action** protects the body from danger. An example of a reflex action would be the quick removal of the hands from a hot plate to prevent the hands from being burned.

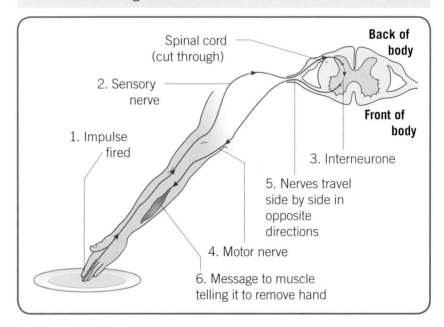

**Figure 5.11** The reflex arc

The **reflex arc** is shown in Figure 5.11 and described below.

1. Reflex actions depend on an impulse being fired from a sensory organ (in this case, pain receptors in the fingers).

2. Impulses are carried from sensory organs through sensory nerves. (Sensory nerves enter the back of the spinal cord, called the **dorsal root**.)

3. Impulses are passed from sensory nerves to interneurones.

4. Impulses pass from interneurones to motor nerves. (Motor nerves emerge from the front of the spinal cord, called the **ventral root**.)

5. Usually, motor and sensory nerves travel side-by-side through the body, although the impulses travel in opposite directions.

6. An impulse passes through the motor nerves to the muscles in the hand that had responded to the stimulus (the hot plate). The hands will then release the plate.

The reflex action ensures that the body can act quickly. Nerve impulses also travel to the brain so that it is aware of what is happening.

# Autonomic nervous system

You can blink or move your fingers at will, but you cannot voluntarily control your heart rate or how fast your stomach digests food. The autonomic nervous system controls the involuntary movements of smooth and cardiac muscle, and of the glands. It is part of the peripheral nervous system.

The autonomic nervous system is connected to the blood vessels and the organs in the body by nerves. It is controlled by the medulla oblongata and hypothalamus, which receive impulses from the central nervous system.

The autonomic nervous system has two parts: the **sympathetic** and **parasympathetic nervous systems**, which have opposite effects. Each organ has a sympathetic and parasympathetic nerve supply:

✖ The **sympathetic nerves** are responsible for actions in time of stress and are made of a network of interlaced nerves or plexuses.

✖ The **parasympathetic nerves** control everyday bodily activities, such as digestion and urination. They are directed towards relaxation and restorative processes. The heart rate slows, blood pressure drops and the digestive system becomes active.

In an emergency, such as when we feel threatened, the sympathetic nervous system has immediate effects on the body.

## don't forget

In reflexology, the solar plexus reflex helps to calm and relax the whole nervous system. The solar plexus is part of the autonomic nervous system and consists of sympathetic and parasympathetic nerve cells. It is a large network of nerves that controls the functioning of many organs. It is found in the abdomen at the level of the last thoracic and first lumbar vertebrae.

**Table 5.1** Sympathetic and parasympathetic responses

| Part of body affected | Sympathetic stimulation | Effect | Parasympathetic stimulation |
|---|---|---|---|
| Heart | Increases heart rate | More oxygen supplied to tissues | Slows heart rate down |
| Coronary blood vessels | Dilates | Heart obtains more oxygen | Constricts |
| Skeletal muscles | Blood vessels in muscles widen | Provides more nutrients and oxygen | No effect |
| Bronchi/bronchioles in lungs | Dilates | More air breathed in, so more oxygen obtained | Constricts |
| Bladder | Relaxes wall and closes sphincter muscles | Hopefully prevents urination | Contracts bladder and opens sphincter to allow urination |
| Digestive system | Reduces peristalsis (wave-like contractions of foodpipe) | Digestion is stopped | Increases peristalsis |
| Adrenal glands | Causes release of adrenalin and noradrenalin | Fight or flight | No effect |
| Liver | Causes conversion of glycogen to glucose | Extra glucose for tissues | Causes conversion of glucose to glycogen |
| Salivary glands | Decreases secretion of saliva | Dry mouth | Stimulates production of saliva |
| Arterioles/skin | Constricts arterioles, so less blood flows near skin surface | Skin may look pale | No effect |
| Sweat glands | Stimulates glands | Increased secretion of sweat | No effect |
| Eye | Dilates pupil | Vision is improved | Constricts pupil |

Sympathetic nerves stimulate the **adrenal glands** to produce the hormone adrenalin. The hormone is distributed quickly by the blood and stimulates organs into greater activity. When the emergency is over, the parasympathetic system returns the body to its normal state (Table 5.1).

## ACTIVITY 5.6

Indicate which nerves, sympathetic or parasympathetic, are responsible for the following effects.

| Effect | Nerve type |
| --- | --- |
| Dilation of pupils | |
| Dilation of bronchi | |
| Stimulation of sweat glands | |
| Slowing of heart rate | |
| Increased peristalsis | |
| Decreased saliva production | |
| Constriction of coronary blood vessels | |
| Raising of glucose levels by promoting conversion of glycogen to glucose in the liver | |

# Conditions associated with the nervous system

## Alzheimer's disease

Alzheimer's disease is the most common form of dementia and mainly affects people over 65. Common symptoms include poor memory, forgetfulness, confusion and speech problems. It is caused by certain areas of the brain wasting away (atrophy), although it is uncertain why this happens in some people.

## Anxiety attack

Usually the parasympathetic nerves balance the action of the sympathetic nerves, but when we are stressed the sympathetic nerves dominate. This results in the excess release of **adrenalin**.

Many symptoms can be experienced by a sufferer during an anxiety or panic attack, including difficulty in breathing, churning stomach, dizziness, nausea and racing heart. It can be so distressing that the sufferer may think they are going to die.

## Bell's palsy

Bell's palsy is the inflammation of the facial nerve, often caused by injury or infection. It causes facial paralysis, although it is usually temporary.

## Cataracts

Cataracts commonly affect older people and are the main cause of blindness in the world. Symptoms of cataracts include clouding of the lens, which lies behind the iris and the pupil. The lens is mainly made of water and protein, but as we age the protein may clump together, resulting in areas of the lens becoming cloudy. If it affects both eyes, the vision may be blurred, misty, and small dots may also be apparent.

## Cerebral palsy

Cerebral palsy can be caused by abnormal brain development or birth-related brain injury. Some children suffer only the slightest of disability; others are almost totally disabled. There is often difficulty in walking, and speech can be affected.

## Deafness (hearing impairment)

Deafness means difficulty hearing noise, and can be caused by an injury, disorder or disease, or even a blob of wax that blocks the ear canal. The most common cause of hearing impairment is age-related, or presbycusis, where there is deterioration of the inner ear. There are different types of deafness, some temporary and some permanent, which range from mild to severe.

## Earache

Earache is more common in children than adults, and is often the result of an ear infection, a blob of earwax stuck in the ear, glue ear, or a throat infection, such as tonsillitis. It can be felt as a sharp, dull or burning sensation and can affect one ear or both.

## Epilepsy

Epilepsy is a disorder of the brain. Sufferers may experience 'absences' or 'seizures'. An absence is when a person experiences momentary lapses of attention and perhaps a little abnormal movement. The seizures, or convulsions, are caused by abnormal electrical activity in the brain. Often there is no obvious cause, but in some cases the seizures are the result of scars on the brain following surgery or injury. Some sufferers find that flickering fluorescent lights or television screens spark off a seizure. Certain essential oils may also provoke seizures in epileptics.

## Glaucoma

Glaucoma, of which there are various types, is a term used to describe a group of eye conditions that affect eyesight. It commonly affects both eyes and, if left untreated, may lead to blindness. Glaucoma occurs when there is a blockage in part of the eye that leads to fluid build-up, which causes pressure to increase. This can lead to damage of the optic nerve (which connects the eye to the brain), therefore affecting the vision. People with diabetes have a greater chance of getting glaucoma.

## Glue ear

This condition mainly affects children and is caused by a build-up of sticky fluid behind the eardrum. It often causes loss of hearing and may also cause earache. The condition generally improves and so treatment is not usually required.

## Meningitis

Meningitis is inflammation of the meninges and can be caused by a bacterial or viral infection. Symptoms include stiffness in the neck, fever and headache. In severe cases, meningitis can also cause paralysis, coma and death.

## Motor neurone disease

Motor neurone disease (MND) is a condition in which spinal nerves and motor neurones are destroyed. The main symptoms are weakness and atrophy (wasting) of all the muscles in the body.

**FAST FACT**

MS may cause the muscles to become stiff, so they will not easily move. This is known as spasticity.

## Multiple sclerosis (MS)

Most nerve fibres are surrounded by myelin, which helps messages to travel quickly through nerves. MS is an autoimmune condition; therefore, the immune system attacks the myelin. The myelin becomes damaged and so affects the passing of these messages. There are many symptoms, which include fatigue, vision problems, muscle weakness and stiffness, pain, mobility problems, numbness and tingling. Most people are diagnosed between the ages of 20 and 40, but it can affect other age groups too, and almost twice as many women have MS as men.  No one knows the exact cause of MS.

## Myalgic encephalomyelitis

Myalgic encephalomyelitis (ME) is a condition also known as chronic fatigue syndrome (CFS). Many cases of ME develop following a viral infection, such as glandular fever or flu. Symptoms include severe fatigue after exercise, muscle weakness and pain. There may also be poor concentration, depression, disturbed sleep and mood swings.

## Neuralgia

Neuralgia causes brief bouts of throbbing or stabbing pain, which is often severe and sometimes shoots along the pathway of affected nerves. It is caused by irritation or damage to a nerve and is a symptom of migraine or shingles.

## Neuritis

Neuritis affects the peripheral nerves after they leave the spinal cord. It can affect one or several nerves. The nerves become inflamed possibly because of infection or injury. It is a painful condition and can cause loss of use of the body parts supplied by the affected nerves.

## Paralysis

Paralysis involves being unable to move one or more muscles, and there may also be loss of sensation. It is mainly due to the nerves that control the affected muscles becoming damaged. Causes of paralysis include injury, stroke and multiple sclerosis.

## Parkinson's disease

This condition results from the loss of dopamine, a chemical messenger, produced in the part of the brain that controls movement. It causes muscular rigidity, tremor and slowness of movement.

## Poliomyelitis

Poliomyelitis, also known as polio, is caused by a viral infection. Following introduction of the polio vaccine in 1955 there have been few cases, and since 1998 there have been no reported cases in the UK. The symptoms of polio are usually similar to those of flu, but for a few sufferers it can cause paralysis and even death. A severe attack causes nerve cells to become damaged and so muscles cannot function, leading to paralysis (paralytic polio).

## Raynaud's disease

The cause is unknown, but there is an overstimulation of the sympathetic nerves, which causes blood vessels to constrict within the fingers and toes. Therefore, blood flow is reduced and the fingers become cold. There is also tingling, burning and numbness in the affected parts.

## Referred pain

Referred pain is pain that can be felt in an area of the body away from the actual source of the pain. For example, when a person suffers a heart attack they may feel pain in the arm, neck and shoulders, rather than in the chest area. Another example is when a person suffers with a gall bladder problem; although the gall bladder is located in the abdomen, sufferers may feel the pain in their right shoulder. The exact cause of referred pain is unknown.

## Sciatica

Irritation or compression of the sciatic nerve may cause sciatica. Pain can commonly be felt in the lower back, travelling down the leg to the calf. Other symptoms include numbness, weakness and tingling. Causes include a slipped disc, injury and infection. However, the cause is often unknown.

## Strokes

A stroke, or a transient ischaemic attack (TIA), involves the blood supply to a certain area of the brain being reduced or interrupted, depriving the brain of oxygen and food. The brain cells can die within minutes. Strokes can often be prevented by making lifestyle changes, such as giving up smoking, maintaining a healthy weight and following government guidelines regarding drinking alcohol.

## Transient ischaemic attack (TIA)

A TIA is often called a mini stroke, and has similar symptoms to a stroke. It usually lasts only a few minutes and causes no permanent damage. Symptoms will often show themselves on one side of the body and include:

✖ weakness, numbness or paralysis in the face, arm or leg

✖ dizziness

✖ slurred speech

✖ double vision or sudden blindness in one or both eyes

✖ poor coordination.

If signs and symptoms last more than 24 hours or cause lasting brain damage, it's considered to be a stroke.

## Tinnitus

Tinnitus is a common condition in which a person hears noise, often ringing, in one ear or both. Other sounds include humming, buzzing and whistling. Tinnitus may be temporary; a person may have a cold, minor injury or have listened to loud noises, such as music. However, for some people it can be a long-term condition. Tinnitus is commonly caused by damage to the nerves inside the inner ear, causing abnormal nerve impulses to be passed to the brain, which interprets it as a sound. Other causes include a build-up of earwax in the ear, infection, anaemia, glue ear or a perforated eardrum. Rarer causes include a head injury or high blood pressure.

## Vertigo

The sufferer of vertigo feels like they are moving or spinning, or that the environment around them is moving. Other symptoms include feeling sick, vomiting and difficulties in standing up and walking. It may be caused by a problem with the balance mechanisms in the inner ear, problems within nerves or the brain, injury, migraines or infection.

# What you should know

## Function of the nervous system

☐ Detection of stimuli, process and interpretation of stimuli, response to stimuli

## Location, structure and function

☐ Central nervous system – brain, spinal cord
☐ Peripheral nervous system – cranial nerves, spinal nerves, brachial plexus, lumbar plexus, sacral plexus
☐ Autonomic nervous system – sympathetic, parasympathetic
☐ Types of neurone – motor, efferent, afferent
☐ Structure of a motor neurone – axon, dendrites, cell body, myelin sheath, neurilemma, axon terminals, synapse, nodes of Ranvier, grey matter, white matter
☐ Brain – meninges, ventricles, cerebrospinal fluid, cerebrum, cerebellum, pons varolii, medulla oblongata, hypothalamus, thalamus, brain stem
☐ Spinal cord – white matter, grey matter, dura mater, arachnoid, pia mater, cerebrospinal fluid
☐ Generation of nerve impulses, growth and repair of nerves

## Pathologies

☐ Conditions associated with the nervous system, including their causes, signs and symptoms
☐ Stress, sciatica, neuralgia, myalgic encephalomyelitis/chronic fatigue syndrome, referred pain, epilepsy, cerebral palsy, Alzheimer's disease and dementia, strokes including transient ischaemic attacks, Bell's palsy, Parkinson's disease, motor neurone disease, multiple sclerosis, myasthenia gravis, meningitis, paralysis, poliomyelitis, deafness, earache, glue ear, tinnitus, vertigo, cataracts, conjunctivitis, glaucoma.

# Endocrine system and common pathologies

The nervous and endocrine systems work together to control the functions of all the body's systems and help to maintain homeostasis. The endocrine system consists of glands situated throughout the body. The endocrine glands are ductless and secrete (release) chemical messengers called **hormones** directly into the bloodstream. Like nerves, they carry messages from one part of the body to another. The hormones are carried in the bloodstream and only affect certain cells, called **target cells**, in which they produce a response.

Exocrine glands secrete their products into ducts and include salivary, eccrine, apocrine, sebaceous and mammary glands.

The trigger needed for the glands to secrete their hormones may be a nerve impulse, a chemical change in the blood or another hormone passing by that influences its release. Although minute amounts of hormones are produced by endocrine glands, they can have powerful effects upon the body.

The endocrine glands consist of the (1) **pituitary gland**, (2) **pineal gland**, (3) **thyroid gland**, (4) **parathyroid gland**, (5) **thymus**, (6) **adrenal glands**, (7) **pancreas**, (8) **ovaries** and (9) **testes**.

> ## don't forget
>
> **All the body systems work together to maintain homeostasis (for example, correct body temperature, pH (acidity), and oxygen levels in the body), which ensures survival of cells.**

## The pituitary gland

The pituitary gland is situated in the middle of the brain, just behind the nose, and is about the size of a pea. It is attached by a stalk to the **hypothalamus**. The hypothalamus is made up of nerve tissue, so this stalk is where the nervous system meets the endocrine system. The hypothalamus controls many bodily activities, such as the heart rate and emptying of the bladder. It also controls the pituitary gland by stimulating, or interfering with, the release of hormones from it. Emotions such as joy and anger, as well as long-term stress, influence the endocrine system through the hypothalamus.

## ACTIVITY 6.1

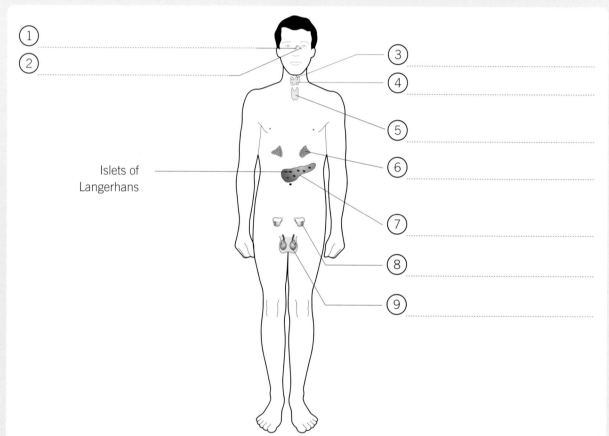

Islets of
Langerhans

**Figure 6.1** The main endocrine glands

Label the diagram in Figure 6.1, matching the numbers to the numbered terms in the text on page 173. Use this key to colour the endocrine glands.

Unshaded – pituitary and pineal glands
Yellow – adrenal glands
Red – thyroid and parathyroid

Brown – pancreas
Green – thymus
Orange – ovaries and testes

The pituitary gland is called the master gland because it releases several hormones that control most of the other endocrine glands, such as the ovaries, testes, thyroid gland and adrenal glands. It secretes hormones that affect growth, kidney function, delivery of babies and milk production.

The pituitary gland consists of two parts: the anterior lobe and posterior lobe.

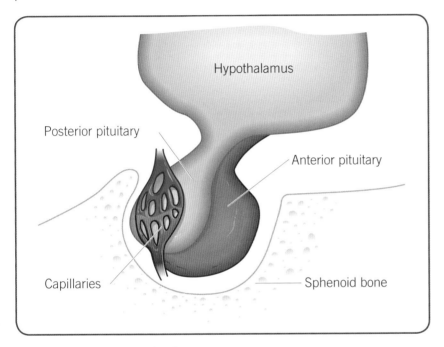

**Figure 6.2** The pituitary gland

## The anterior lobe

The anterior and posterior lobes of the pituitary gland are controlled by the hypothalamus. The following hormones are secreted by the anterior lobe (the numbers refer to Activity 6.2 on page 177).

(1) **Adrenocorticotrophic hormone** (ACTH), which controls the activity of the adrenal cortex of the adrenal gland. The adrenal glands are found above each kidney.

(2) **Thyroid-stimulating hormone** (TSH), which controls the activity of the thyroid gland in the neck.

③ **Growth hormone**, sometimes called somatotropin, which controls the growth of the skeleton, muscles, connective tissues and organs such as the kidneys and liver.

④ **Lactogenic hormone** (prolactin), which is responsible for stimulating milk production in the breasts. It has a direct effect on the breasts after pregnancy.

⑤ **Melanocyte-stimulating hormone** (MSH), which increases skin pigmentation by stimulating the release of melanin granules in melanocytes. However, only a tiny amount is produced in humans and its exact function is uncertain.

Two **gonadotrophic hormones** control the ovaries in females and the testes in males.

⑥ **Follicle-stimulating hormone** (FSH), which:

✖ in women, stimulates the development of ova (eggs) in the ovaries, and stimulates the ovaries to produce the hormone oestrogen

✖ in men, stimulates the testes to produce sperm.

⑦ **Luteinising hormone** (LH), also known as interstitial cell-stimulating hormone (ICSH) which:

✖ in women, stimulates release of the egg from the ovary (**ovulation**) and production of progesterone by the ovary

✖ in men, stimulates the testes to make the hormone testosterone.

## The posterior lobe

The posterior lobe of the pituitary gland is controlled by nervous system stimulation of nerve cells within the hypothalamus. It releases two hormones.

⑧ **Antidiuretic hormone** (ADH) regulates water balance in the body by controlling the amount of water in urine.

The hormone causes water to be returned (through reabsorption) into the blood circulation by the kidneys rather than being lost as urine. On a hot day, sweating increases and

*don't forget*

Alcohol interferes with the release of ADH from the pituitary gland. Therefore, drinking alcohol leads to an increase in the urine produced, so a person will need to urinate more frequently. Drinking a great deal of alcohol can lead to dehydration, which is largely responsible for the headache the following morning.

so water is lost. The body needs to hold on to as much water as it can. ADH is released, causing the kidneys to reabsorb water into the bloodstream rather than passing it to the bladder to be excreted from the body. This results in the production of a decreased amount of urine, which will be more concentrated.

(9) **Oxytocin** is responsible for the release of milk from the breast during suckling and for contracting the **uterus** during labour and after birth. Synthetic oxytocin is often used to induce labour and works in the same way as the natural hormone.

## ACTIVITY 6.2

Complete the table below. The numbers correspond to the numbered terms on pages 175–177.

| Endocrine gland | Hormone released | Target organ affected | Controls or stimulates production of |
| --- | --- | --- | --- |
| Anterior pituitary | (1) | | |
| Anterior pituitary | (2) | | |
| Anterior pituitary | (3) | | |
| Anterior pituitary | (4) | | |
| Anterior pituitary | (5) | | |
| Anterior pituitary | (6) | | |
| Anterior pituitary | (7) | | |
| Posterior pituitary | (8) | | |
| Posterior pituitary | (9) | | |

## Conditions associated with the pituitary gland

### Acromegaly

If too much growth hormone is produced in adulthood, it can lead to a condition called acromegaly (ak-roe-meg-ah-lee), in which there is bone thickening and gradual enlargement of the hands, feet, jaws, ears and nose.

### Diabetes insipidus

Diabetes insipidus is associated with the posterior pituitary gland. It is either due to the gland not being able to release ADH, or the kidneys not being able to respond to it. Symptoms include large quantities of urine, dehydration and thirst.

### Dwarfism

If too little growth hormone is produced in a young person, bone growth will slow down and other organs will also fail to grow. The person may only grow to 1–1.25 m tall. Children can be treated with growth hormone to prevent this.

### Giantism

If too much growth hormone is produced during childhood, an abnormal increase in the length of the bones will result. The long bones continue to grow and the person becomes very tall. Giantism can be caused by a pituitary tumour.

# The pineal gland

The pineal (pin-ee-al) gland is situated in the brain and releases a hormone called **melatonin**. More melatonin is released when a person is in darkness, and this results in sleepiness. In bright sunlight, less melatonin is produced, so there is a lack of sleepiness. During sleep, the melatonin level is high and then decreases to a low level again before awakening. Therefore, melatonin helps to control body rhythms.

## Condition associated with the pineal gland

### Seasonal affective disorder

Seasonal affective disorder (SAD) is a type of depression that affects some people during the winter months when the days are short and the amount of daylight is decreased. The cause is thought to be overproduction of melatonin. Special light boxes that mimic sunlight are used to help sufferers.

# The thyroid

The thyroid is made up of two lobes and is found in front of the throat, just below the voice box. It produces the hormone **thyroxine**, which

- controls the body's metabolism and affects all tissues of the body. **Metabolism** is the sum of all the chemical processes going on inside the body, especially the conversion of glucose into energy by the cells – the burning of calories to provide energy for the body. Thyroxine helps to control how energetic a person is by stimulating cells to burn more or less glucose
- has a major influence on the development of the body mentally and physically after birth.

Another hormone released by the thyroid is called **T3** (triiodothyronin). It is essential for normal growth and metabolism.

**Iodine** is needed by the thyroid to produce its hormones. The body obtains iodine from the food we eat.

## Conditions associated with the thyroid

### Goitre (goy-ter)

This is the result of a lack of iodine and causes the thyroid gland to enlarge, which causes a lump to develop in the throat. Symptoms include coughing, hoarseness and a tight feeling in the throat. Treatment includes taking iodine supplements if the goitre is caused by an iodine deficiency.

**Figure 6.3** Goitre

### Hyperthyroidism (thyrotoxicosis – thigh-roe-toxi-co-sis)

Overproduction of thyroxine can result in hyperthyroidism, also known as **overactive thyroid**. This causes the metabolism to speed up so that the sufferer loses weight, has a fast heartbeat and increased sweating, and also develops bulging eyes because of the swelling of tissues behind them. This is a dangerous condition, which needs medical treatment.

### Hypothyroidism (myxoedema – mix-oh-dee-ma)

Undersecretion of thyroxine causes hypothyroidism, also known as myxoedema or **underactive thyroid**. This causes the metabolism to slow down so that the sufferer puts on weight and becomes lethargic. The hair becomes dry and brittle and there may be some loss of hair. The skin appears thickened, coarse and dry. The circulation may be poor so the sufferer feels the cold more than normal. This condition also needs medical treatment.

# The parathyroid

The four tiny parathyroid glands can be found embedded on the back of the thyroid gland. They produce the hormone parathormone.

The parathyroids are sensitive to the levels of calcium in the blood. Calcium is important as it is needed for muscle contraction, transmission of nerve impulses and blood clotting. The main function of parathormone is to control calcium levels in the blood to maintain normal limits.

If calcium levels become very high, **calcitonin** is released from the thyroid gland. This hormone quickly helps to prevent removal of calcium from the bones.

If calcium levels are low, parathormone will cause calcium to be taken from bones, decrease the rate at which calcium is lost from the urine and increase absorption of calcium from the small intestine to increase levels within the blood.

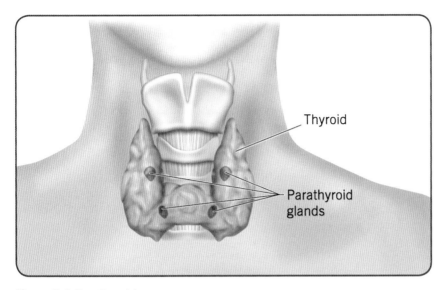

**Figure 6.4** Parathyroid

# Conditions associated with the parathyroid

### Hypersecretion

Overproduction of parathormone causes an increased amount of calcium in the blood. It may cause excess calcium to be lost from the bones, leading to brittle bones that fracture easily (**osteoporosis**).

The hormone **oestrogen,** produced by the ovaries, interferes with the release of parathormone. After the menopause, the oestrogen levels in the body decrease. This means that parathormone is no longer inhibited, so excess calcium may be taken from the bones, which can also lead to osteoporosis.

### Hyposecretion

Undersecretion of parathormone can lead to a deficiency of calcium in the body. As calcium is needed for muscle contraction, it can lead to a condition known as tetany, in which the muscles become stiff and go into spasm.

# The thymus

The thymus gland is situated in the thorax (chest region) behind the sternum. It is made up of lymphoid tissue. In an infant, it is large, but after puberty it begins to waste away. It releases hormones, one of which is called thymosin. Thymosin is involved with the production of **lymphocytes**, which help fight against viruses and other infections in the body.

## ACTIVITY 6.3

Complete the table below.

| Endocrine gland | Hormone released | Effect |
|---|---|---|
| Pineal | | |
| Thyroid | | |
| Parathyroid | | |
| Thymus | | |

# The adrenal glands

Androgen levels rise in women during puberty, pregnancy and the menopause.

The adrenal glands are found on top of each kidney. They are made of two parts: the cortex and the medulla. The cortex is the outside, and the medulla is the inner part of the gland.

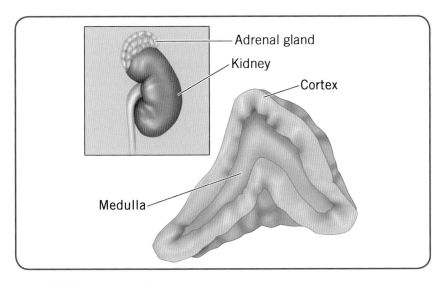

**Figure 6.5** Adrenal gland

## Adrenal cortex

The adrenal cortex is essential to life and plays an important role in states of stress. It is known that the adrenal cortex releases over 50 hormones. All of these hormones are steroids and are produced from a fatty substance called **cholesterol**. They are grouped into three categories: sex corticoids, glucocorticoids and mineral corticoids, according to the type of action in which they are involved.

## ① Sex corticoids

These help control the changes in males and females during puberty. The female sex hormones **oestrogen** and progesterone, and the male hormones, **androgens** (for example, **testosterone**), are produced in small amounts from this gland.

## Conditions associated with sex corticoids

### Gynaecomastia
This is a condition affecting males only and is mostly temporary. It is caused by increased oestrogen levels in the body. The sufferer develops excessive growth of one breast or both.

### Hirsutism

Oestrogen and androgens are produced in both males and females. Men produce more androgens than women. If a woman is particularly sensitive to androgens, excess hair may develop in the male pattern, for example on the chin. This is called hirsutism. Androgen levels rise in women during puberty, pregnancy and the menopause.

### Virilism

Virilism is a condition in which there is an oversecretion of androgens in a female. The increased amount of androgens causes the woman to become masculine. Symptoms develop, such as receding hairline, increased growth of body and facial hair, the voice deepens and the menstrual cycle stops.

## ② Glucocorticoids

Glucocorticoids are a group of steroids that affect the metabolism and have anti-inflammatory effects. They mostly affect the metabolism of carbohydrates and, to a lesser extent, fats and proteins in the body. They help to regulate nutrient levels within the blood and turn food that we eat into energy. One main glucocorticoid is called **cortisol**.

Cortisol has several functions.

- It affects the metabolism by increasing the use of protein and fats as a source of energy in the body. Cortisol causes proteins to be broken down into **amino acids**. The amino acids can be converted into glucose by the liver. Cortisol also acts on fats, which are broken down into fatty acids. The glucose and fatty acids are used by the body as sources of energy, if required.
- **Adrenalin** is quickly released from the adrenal medulla whenever danger threatens. Cortisol is released a little while later and prepares the body for the after-effects of danger. It helps reduce the feelings of pain, which is why people who are severely injured may feel no pain until some time later. Cortisol helps the body to return to a normal state after a high-stress event.

**FAST FACT**

Cortisol helps reduce the feelings of pain, which is why people who are severely injured may feel no pain until some time later.

- It provides more rapid breakdown of glycogen into glucose for extra energy during a highly stressful situation or an increased need. This raises sugar levels in the blood to ensure that cells have sufficient glucose for energy.
- It helps to control body rhythms. Cortisol levels are highest between 6am and 9am and trigger waking from sleep. The levels are at their lowest between midnight and 3am and so promote sleepiness.
- Glucocorticoids have strong anti-inflammatory and immunosuppressive effects, so are often used to treat inflammatory conditions. Synthetic forms of cortisol, such as hydrocortisone, can be used to treat conditions like rheumatoid arthritis, and inflammatory skin disorders.

Stress, anger, fright or rapidly falling sugar levels can cause ACTH (adrenocorticotrophic hormone) to be released from the anterior lobe of the pituitary. This stimulates the release of cortisol by the adrenal glands.

## ③ Mineral corticoids

Mineral corticoids help to maintain the right balance of minerals such as sodium (salt) and potassium in the body. One of the mineral corticoids is called **aldosterone** and is released if sodium levels drop in the body, for example through sweating a lot. Aldosterone ensures that the sodium is passed back into the blood from the kidneys and not excreted in the urine; this helps to increase sodium levels. Oversecretion of aldosterone causes increased levels of sodium, which can lead to fluid retention (**oedema**).

## Conditions associated with glucocorticoids and mineral corticoids

### Addison's disease

This results from abnormally low levels of aldosterone and cortisol. Symptoms include low blood glucose levels, low levels of sodium in the blood, an inability to use fat and protein for energy, low blood pressure and excessive urination. Cortisol can be used to treat Addison's disease.

### Cushing's syndrome

Cushing's syndrome is caused by oversecretion of cortisol and aldosterone. The symptoms include a moon-shaped face, wasting of muscle tissue, high blood levels of glucose, high blood pressure and excess fat tissue on the trunk of the body. A pituitary tumour can cause Cushing's syndrome.

## Adrenal medulla

The adrenal medulla produces hormones called ④ **adrenalin** and ⑤ **noradrenalin**, which together prepare the body for action, known as the **fight or flight response**. In response to a stress situation, where the body is in danger, the hypothalamus sends a message via sympathetic nerves to the adrenal glands. Adrenalin is released and is distributed quickly by the blood.

Adrenalin has the following effects.

✖ The heart beats stronger and faster, which increases blood pressure.

✖ The arteries supplying the skin and internal organs constrict, so blood flow decreases. However, the blood flow increases in skeletal muscle so that the extra oxygen and glucose can help to provide extra energy. This is why we can look pale in an emergency.

✖ Adrenalin also increases the breakdown of glycogen to glucose in the liver. This ensures that there is a ready supply for the muscles.

✖ The airway passages dilate (widen), allowing air to move in and out of the lungs with greater ease.

✖ Adrenalin also stimulates ACTH, so that glucocorticoids are released, and TSH, to increase the metabolism to help prepare the body for action.

## ACTIVITY 6.4

Complete the table below. The numbers correspond to the numbered terms in the text on pages 183–186.

| Endocrine gland | Hormone released | Effect |
|---|---|---|
| Adrenal cortex | ① | |
| Adrenal cortex | ② | |
| Adrenal cortex | ③ | |
| Adrenal medulla | ④ | |
| Adrenal medulla | ⑤ | |

# The pancreas

Carbohydrates are made up of many sugar molecules, mostly glucose. Eating carbohydrate food means a rise of sugar in the blood. Vigorous exercise causes a lot of glucose to be used by muscles, which lowers the sugar levels in the blood.

The **islets of Langerhans** in the pancreas are sensitive to sugar levels in the body. To maintain the balance of sugar in the blood, the islets of Langerhans release hormones.

✖ When blood sugar levels are too high, the hormone ① **insulin** is released. Insulin causes the liver and muscles to store glucose in the form of glycogen (lots of glucose molecules joined together). This helps to bring the blood sugar levels down.

✖ If sugar levels are too low in the blood, the hormone ② **glucagon** is released. It causes the liver and muscles to release glucose into the bloodstream to help restore levels.

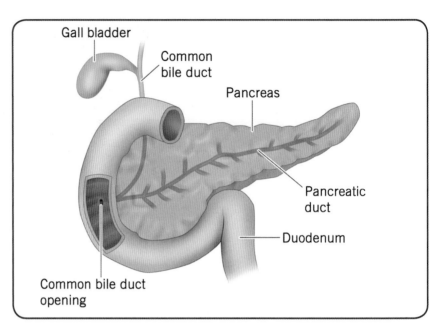

Gall bladder

Common bile duct

Pancreas

Pancreatic duct

Duodenum

Common bile duct opening

**Figure 6.6** Pancreas

## Condition associated with the pancreas

### Diabetes mellitus

Diabetes mellitus is a disease caused *either* by the pancreas producing insufficient amounts of insulin *or* by the tissues not responding to insulin. This results in the sugar (glucose) level in the blood rising too high, which leads to the symptoms and complications of diabetes such as tiredness and thirst.

Insulin is needed by the body to allow glucose to enter into the cells. Without insulin the cells cannot process the glucose to produce energy, which may result in fats being broken down to provide energy instead. The breakdown of fats could result in a build-up of chemicals called ketones in the bloodstream, which are produced by the liver. A build-up of ketones may lead to illness.

There are two types of diabetes mellitus.

✘ **Type 1** is often called **insulin-dependent diabetes** and mostly develops in people under the age of 20. This type is more serious and is often caused by the production of little or no insulin. With this type, it is essential to have insulin treatment to survive. The symptoms develop quickly and include dehydration, excessive thirst, increased urination, weight loss, vomiting, drowsiness, weakness and finally coma.

✖ **Type 2** is more common and often affects people over the age of 35 who are overweight. It is also called **maturity-onset diabetes mellitus**. This type usually develops from the reduced ability of the tissues to respond to insulin, although insulin is still being produced. Type 2 diabetes can often be controlled by diet, exercise and weight loss. The symptoms are similar to type 1, but they develop gradually and are less severe. Diabetic coma does not occur with type 2.

Treatment for diabetes rapidly restores health to normal. However, poorly controlled diabetes over a long period of time can cause the following problems.

✖ The tissues can become damaged and waste away; for example, the skin may become paper thin. There may also be skin infections such as spots and boils.

✖ Eye diseases, such as diabetic retinopathy, can develop and, in a few people, can lead to blindness. Diabetic retinopathy is caused by blood leaking from damaged capillaries.

✖ High blood pressure is more common in diabetics. It can lead to capillary damage in the kidneys, causing swollen ankles, fatigue and the build-up of **urea**, which is a harmful waste product in the blood.

✖ Damage to nerves (neuritis) can lead to a loss of sensation in the legs but mainly affects the feet. An example of this is the diabetic who, while walking, did not realise that there was a golf ball inside one shoe.

✖ Problems arise because the diabetic may be unaware of injury to the feet. The injuries may be further aggravated by poor circulation; therefore, healing is poor, which can lead to ulcers and infection. This can become serious and may even lead to amputation.

✖ Hardening and narrowing of the arteries is more common in diabetics. This can cause poor circulation in the legs and feet. It can also contribute to heart attack and stroke.

Diabetes mellitus can be treated with insulin injections. The insulin passes directly into the bloodstream and so is effective straight away. Occasionally, diabetics can give themselves too much insulin, which results in a condition called **hypoglycaemia** – an abnormally low level of sugar in the blood. The sufferer sweats, trembles, has blurred vision and lacks concentration. The behaviour of someone suffering from hypoglycaemia may be mistaken for drunkenness. A sweet snack, such as fruit juice or a small chocolate bar, is needed to raise the sugar levels in the blood.

# The ovaries

The ovaries are a pair of almond-shaped organs found within the female pelvis, one on either side of the uterus. They produce the female hormones oestrogen and progesterone, which are responsible for all female secondary sexual characteristics such as breasts, a female body shape and ova (egg) production.

③ **Oestrogen** causes the lining of the uterus to thicken and grow during a menstrual cycle. It also stimulates the release of an egg from the ovary.

④ **Progesterone** maintains the lining of the uterus. When the levels of progesterone fall, the lining then breaks down and is shed in the menstrual flow.

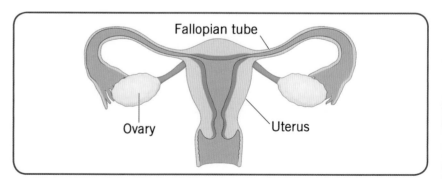

**Figure 6.7** Ovaries

## Effects of hormones at puberty

Puberty in girls normally begins at around 11 years old. When a girl reaches puberty, her ovaries grow up to 10 times larger. As the ovaries grow, they release the hormone oestrogen, which is responsible for the bodily changes at puberty, such as female curves and the growth of the breasts. After an egg is released (**ovulation**), the ovaries release progesterone to prepare the body for possible pregnancy. If the egg is not fertilised, the ovaries stop producing progesterone and the menstrual period follows.

Androgen levels in girls also increase at puberty, causing axillary (under the armpit) and pubic hair growth. Androgens are also a main cause of acne because of inflammation of the sebaceous glands.

## Effect of hormones in pregnancy

During pregnancy, various hormones are produced, including the following (see also Chapter 12).

- After **conception**, human chorionic gonadotropin (HCG) is produced.

  HCG keeps the pregnancy hormones (oestrogen and progesterone) at their ideal levels until the placenta has developed enough to take over this function. During the first trimester, HCG is responsible for increasing the blood supply to the pelvis, which results in an increased need for urination.

  HCG is believed to be responsible for many other symptoms linked to early pregnancy, including nausea (morning sickness) and vomiting.

- Oxytocin, which induces contractions in labour, as well as Braxton Hicks, and stimulates the mammary glands (breasts) to produce milk.
- Endorphins, these 'happy hormones' are released to help the pregnant woman deal with stress and pain.

**FAST FACT**

Large brown patches can appear on the skin during pregnancy, especially the face. These are known as **chloasma** or **melasma**. High levels of oestrogen and progesterone are thought to be the cause.

> **ASK FRAN...**
>
> **Q.** How does hormone replacement therapy work?
>
> **A.** Oestrogen and progesterone levels become low during the menopause and can cause a number of unwanted symptoms. To help with these symptoms, women are often treated with **hormone replacement therapy** (HRT), which consists of oestrogen and progesterone. There are different ways to take HRT, including a cream, gel, tablets, a patch on the skin, and an implant that can be inserted under the skin. HRT can give relief from menopausal symptoms, including hot flushes, vaginal dryness and mood swings, and can help with the laying down of new bone to protect against the development of osteoporosis. The oestrogen also helps to keep the skin and hair in good condition.
>
> A healthy diet, exercise and lifestyle factors have been shown to offer identical benefits to HRT but without the risks. HRT slightly increases the risk of certain types of cancer. There is also a small risk of stroke and heart attack. Fat produces oestrogen and, as the oestrogen levels decrease during the menopause, body fat becomes an alternative manufacturing plant for making oestrogen. Oestrogen can help protect the older woman from osteoporosis so it is advisable to have a diet that includes some fat.

- Relaxin, which causes softening of ligaments and tissues to help increase flexibility in the pelvic joints and lower back in preparation for birth.

Sometimes, excess androgens can be produced, resulting in excess hair growth. It is usually only temporary and returns to normal after the baby is born.

Most pregnancy symptoms are due, or partly due, to increased levels of oestrogen and progesterone during pregnancy, and include:

- fatigue
- increased heartburn and acid reflux
- breast soreness
- increased sensitivity of the sense of smell
- feeling emotional and mood swings.

## Effect of hormones at the menopause

The menopause usually begins between the ages of 45 and 55. The ovaries decrease in size and no longer respond to the gonadotrophic hormones of the anterior pituitary gland. Oestrogen levels therefore decrease. Oestrogen helps to protect the bones and so the decrease in oestrogen levels may lead to osteoporosis, a condition in which the bones become brittle and fracture easily.

The low levels of oestrogen also cause the menstrual cycle to become irregular and gradually stop. The breasts start to shrink and there is thinning of the axillary and pubic hair. During the menopause, increased levels of androgens can cause excess facial and body hair.

### Symptoms of the menopause

Symptoms of the menopause include hot flushes, headaches, depression, insomnia, fatigue and inability to concentrate, and the skin and hair can become dry. Many of the symptoms of the menopause, especially hot flushes, appear to be a result of altered function of the hypothalamus.

# The testes

The testes are found in the groin area of the male in a sac called the scrotum. The testes produce the hormone (5) **testosterone**, which is responsible for all male secondary sexual characteristics at puberty, such as body hair, deep voice and muscle development.

The testes also contain fine tubes in which sperm are produced when stimulated by follicle-stimulating hormone.

The production of testosterone from the testes decreases with age, although many older men still produce active sperm in normal numbers.

# Relationship of the endocrine system to other body systems

## Nervous system

The nervous and endocrine systems work together to control the functions of all the body's systems and maintain homeostasis.

## Circulatory system

The endocrine system releases hormones that are carried in the bloodstream.

## Digestive system

The pancreas produces insulin and glucagon that help to control blood sugar levels in the body. Glucocorticoids, produced by the adrenal glands, help to control nutrient levels within the blood.

## ACTIVITY 6.5

Complete the table below. The numbers correspond to the numbered terms in the text on pages 187, 190 and 193.

| Endocrine gland | Hormone released | Effect |
|---|---|---|
| Pancreas | ① | |
| Pancreas | ② | |
| Ovaries | ③ | |
| Ovaries | ④ | |
| Testes | ⑤ | |

## Reproductive system

The pituitary gland produces lactogenic hormone, which is responsible for milk production in the breasts. Oxytocin is responsible for the release of milk from the breasts. Follicle-stimulating hormone and luteinising hormone control the ovaries and testes. Sex corticoids help to control changes in males and females during puberty. Ovaries produce oestrogen and progesterone, and the testes produce testosterone.

## Integumentary system

The pituitary gland releases melanocyte-stimulating hormone, which stimulates the release of melanin.

# What you should know

## Functions of the endocrine system

☐ Hormone secretion into the bloodstream

☐ Maintenance of homeostasis

☐ Control of body's functions – stimulation/ inhibition of growth, induction/suppression of cell death, inhibition of immune system, regulation of metabolism, preparation for new activity, preparation for new phase in life, controlling reproductive cycle

## Location, structure and function

☐ Endocrine glands – hypothalamus, pituitary, pineal, thyroid, parathyroid, thymus, adrenal, pancreas, ovaries, testes

☐ Associated hormones and hormone actions – thyroid-stimulating hormone, adrenocorticotrophic hormone, human growth hormone, follicle-stimulating hormone, luteinising hormone, lactogenic hormone, antidiuretic hormone, oxytocin, melatonin, thyroxine, T3, calcitonin, parathormone, insulin, glucagon, aldosterone, cortisone, testosterone, oestrogen, progesterone, adrenalin, noradrenalin

☐ Relationship of endocrine system with other body systems – nervous, circulatory, digestive, reproductive, integumentary

☐ Growth and repair (see Chapter 1)

## Pathologies

☐ Conditions associated with the following including their causes, signs and symptoms – pituitary gland, pineal gland, thyroid, parathyroid, sex corticoids, glucocorticoids and mineral corticoids, pancreas

# 7

# Respiratory system and common pathologies

Every living cell in the body needs oxygen. We obtain the oxygen we require from the air that we breathe. **Inspiration** is the movement of air into the lungs and **expiration** is the movement of air out of the lungs. The respiratory system is concerned with the exchange of gases between the lungs and the blood, and consists of a number of organs.

## ACTIVITY 7.1

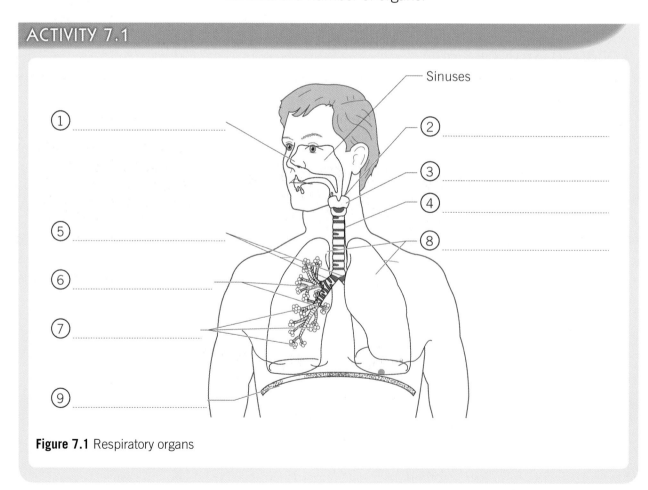

**Figure 7.1** Respiratory organs

Label the diagram in Figure 7.1, matching the numbers to the numbered terms in the text on pages 197–199. Use this key to colour the respiratory organs.

Red – nose, sinuses, pharynx, larynx, trachea, bronchi and bronchioles
Yellow – alveoli
Brown – the lungs
Blue – diaphragm

# The respiratory system

## ① Nose

Air is breathed in through the nose and becomes moistened and warmed. Coarse hairs filter out large dust particles. In the nasal cavity, there are tiny, hair-like structures called **cilia**. A sticky substance called **mucus** is produced by **goblet cells** and helps to trap dust particles. The cilia transport the mucus with the trapped dust particles towards the pharynx (throat) where they are swallowed and destroyed by acid in the stomach.

The **sinuses** are hollow spaces within the bones of the skull that open into the nasal cavity. These spaces are filled with air and are lined with a mucous membrane. Infection or allergy causes these membranes to become swollen, leading to excessive mucus production and a watery discharge.

*don't forget*

The functions of the respiratory system include providing an oxygen supply to body tissues and removal of carbon dioxide from body tissues.

*don't forget*

The closing of the epiglottis while swallowing ensures (most of the time) that the food will enter the foodpipe rather than the windpipe, otherwise choking will result.

## ② Pharynx (throat)

The pharynx is a tube and acts as an air and food passage. It allows air to enter the larynx and food to enter the foodpipe. The larynx is anterior to the foodpipe. The **tonsils** are found at the back of the pharynx. They are made up of lymphoid tissue and their job is to filter bacteria in the same way as lymph nodes.

The throat is connected to an area of the ear, known as the **middle ear**, by the **Eustachian** (u-stay-she-an) **tube**. Bacteria in the throat can pass through the Eustachian tube, causing a painful middle-ear infection.

## ③ Larynx

The larynx is the voice box and is a short passageway linking the pharynx to the trachea. It consists of cartilages, the largest of which forms the Adam's apple. During swallowing, the pharynx and larynx rise. A piece of flap-like cartilage called the **epiglottis** acts as a lid to cover the opening of the larynx.

## ④ Trachea (windpipe)

The trachea, or windpipe, is a tube that acts as a passageway for air. It is held open by up to 20 C-shaped rings of cartilage, which give the trachea some rigidity to ensure that there is no obstruction of airflow. The trachea extends into the thorax (chest cavity) and branches off to form the bronchi.

## ⑤ Bronchi

The bronchi are two tubes, each individually known as a **bronchus**, which carry air into the lungs. Like the trachea, they contain cartilage rings that keep the tubes fairly rigid to ensure adequate airflow.

The trachea and bronchi contain cilia and cells that produce mucus. The mucus and cilia trap dust and other harmful substances. The cilia waft to and fro, carrying the mucus and dust towards the throat, where it is swallowed and then dealt with by acid in the stomach.

## ⑥ Bronchioles

The bronchi divide into branches called bronchioles. The bronchioles become progressively smaller until they join on to the alveoli.

## ⑦ Alveoli

Alveoli are round, sac-like structures and their shape ensures a large surface area for the exchange of gases. The alveoli have very thin walls and each alveolus is surrounded by a network of capillaries. This ensures that an efficient exchange of oxygen and carbon dioxide can take place.

## ⑧ Lungs

The lungs are large organs situated on either side of the thoracic cavity and separated by the heart. They are each enclosed in a **pleural membrane** that consists of two layers: the **visceral** (vis-ser-raal) **pleura** and **parietal pleura**. Between these layers is a space called the **pleural cavity**, containing fluid. The fluid allows the membranes to slide over each other during breathing, preventing friction.

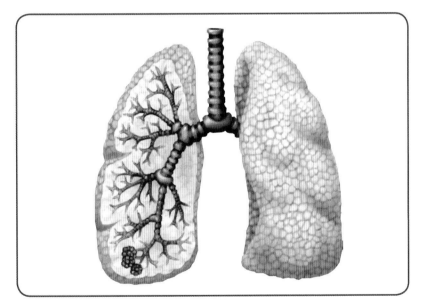

**Figure 7.2** Lungs

## ⑨ Diaphragm

The diaphragm is a large, dome-shaped muscle found directly under the lungs. It separates the thoracic cavity from the abdominal cavity. The diaphragm plays a major role in breathing and helps to ensure that the thoracic cavity is airtight.

**FAST FACT**

Each lung contains approximately 150 million alveoli.

**MEMORY JOGGER**

To help you memorise the sequence of organs involved with inhalation remember the following sentence: 'Nosey Phil Lied To Broncho Billy Again' (nose, pharynx, larynx, trachea, bronchi, bronchioles and alveoli).

If you make up your own sentence you will find it's more memorable.

## MEMORY JOGGER

Make up flashcards that contain a picture of the respiratory organs.

Keep the cards handy so you can regularly test yourself regarding the names and functions of the different structures.

Write the structures and functions of the respiratory system on the back of the card, so they are at hand if you need to refer to them.

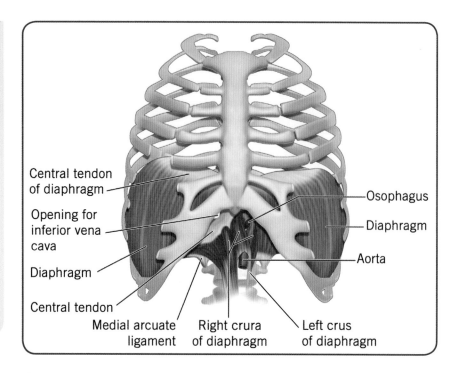

Central tendon of diaphragm

Opening for inferior vena cava

Diaphragm

Central tendon

Medial arcuate ligament

Right crura of diaphragm

Left crus of diaphragm

Osophagus

Diaphragm

Aorta

**Figure 7.3** Diaphragm

## ACTIVITY 7.2

Match the terms in the bubbles with the correct description in the list.

- The throat ............
- Round sac-like structures ............
- Prevents food from entering the trachea during swallowing ............
- The membrane surrounding a lung ............
- Two tubes that enter each lung ............
- Small tubes that branch out in the lungs ............
- Moistens and warms the air breathed in ............
- Contains the voice box ............
- The windpipe ............

1. Nose
2. Bronchioles
3. Alveoli
4. Larynx
5. Trachea
6. Bronchi
7. Pharynx
8. Pleural membrane
9. Epiglottis

## Gas exchange in the lungs

Air is breathed into the lungs, where oxygen diffuses through the walls of the alveoli and into the blood. It is picked up by the red blood cells and taken around the body to provide oxygen for the body's cells. The cells produce carbon dioxide, which has to be removed from the body. The carbon dioxide diffuses from the cells into the surrounding capillaries. When it reaches the capillaries surrounding the alveoli, it passes through the walls of the alveoli and is breathed out. The **deoxygenated blood** becomes oxygenated once again. This is a process that is continually happening and is essential for life (see Figure 7.4).

**FAST FACT**

Essential oils used in aromatherapy are also able to pass into the bloodstream through the respiratory system.

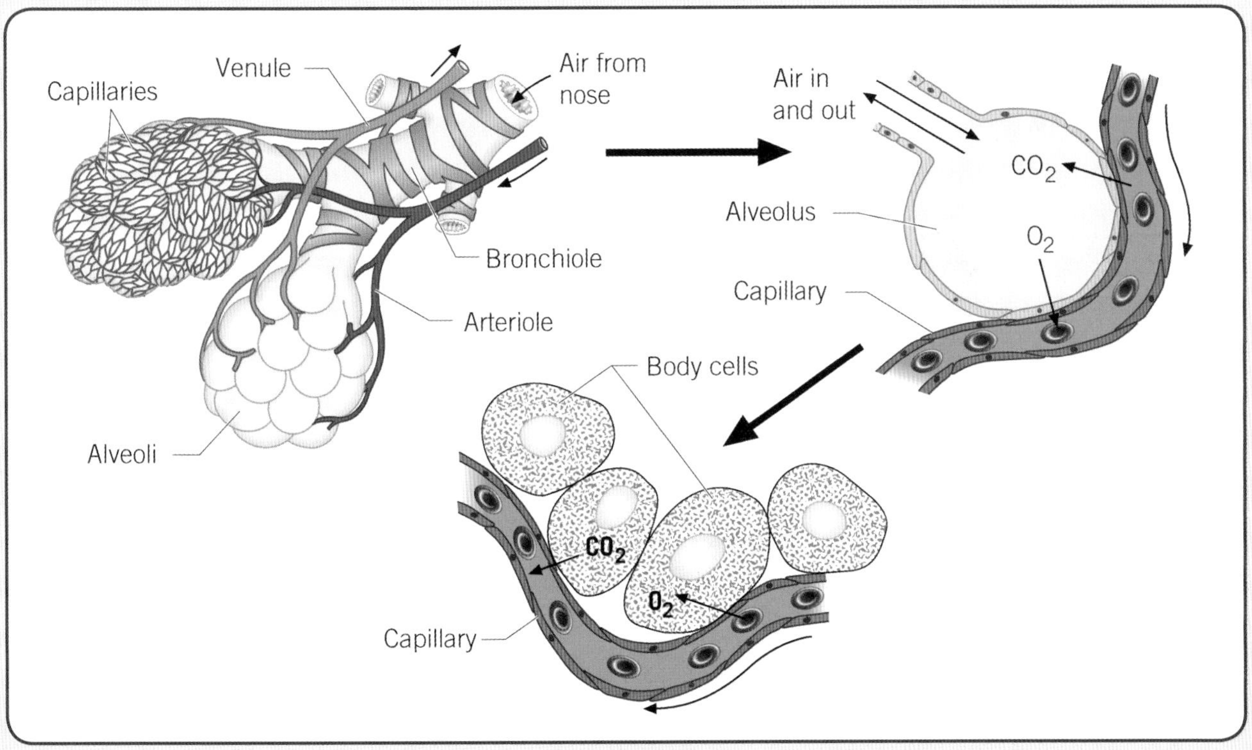


**Figure 7.4** Gas exchange in the lungs and in the cells of the body

## Composition of air

The air that we breathe is a mixture of gases. It is usually made up of:

- 78 per cent nitrogen
- 21 per cent oxygen

**don't forget**

**The pulmonary circulation carries the blood to and from the lungs. See Chapter 8 for more information.**

- Around 0.9 per cent inert gas, such as argon
- 0.04 per cent carbon dioxide
- a little moisture.

However, the air we breathe out contains less oxygen and more carbon dioxide and water. It is made up of:

- 78 per cent nitrogen
- 17 per cent oxygen
- 1 per cent inert gas, such as argon
- 4 per cent carbon dioxide
- lots of moisture.

**don't forget**

**External respiration is the exchange of oxygen and carbon dioxide between inhaled air and the blood. Internal respiration is the exchange of gases between the blood, tissue fluid and cells (see Chapter 1 for more information).**

## ACTIVITY 7.3

Air firstly travels through the nose and eventually the oxygen reaches the cells of the body. What is the pathway of oxygen through the body? Write the names of the organs from the bubbles on the correct line of the list below. You may need to refer to Chapter 8 to complete this activity.

Aorta | Pulmonary veins | Trachea | Bronchioles | Pharynx | Nose | Alveoli | Capillaries | Bronchi | Heart | Larynx | Cells of the body

| | | |
|---|---|---|
| 1 ........ | 5 ........ | 9 ........ |
| 2 ........ | 6 ........ | 10 ........ |
| 3 ........ | 7 ........ | 11 ........ |
| 4 ........ | 8 ........ | 12 ........ |

# The mechanism of inhalation and exhalation

During inspiration, the external intercostal muscles found between the ribs contract, moving the ribs up and out. The diaphragm muscle also contracts and so the dome shape is flattened. This increases the space in the lungs and causes air to be automatically drawn into them.

During expiration, the external intercostal muscles relax and the ribs return to their resting position. The diaphragm relaxes, returning to its original dome shape. This causes the space in the lungs to get smaller, forcing air out of them (Figure 7.5).

*don't forget*

This process can be likened to having your hands glued to a balloon (which represents the lung attached to the chest wall) and pulling it wider to increase the space inside.

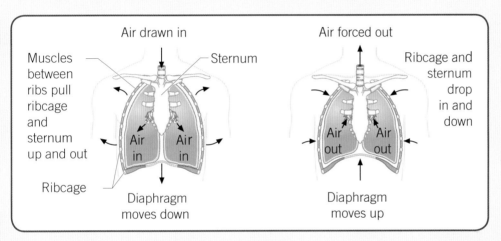

**Figure 7.5** The mechanism of breathing

# The role of the brain in respiration

Breathing is controlled by the **medulla oblongata** and **pons varolii** in the brain stem. Messages are sent from the brain, through phrenic nerves to the diaphragm, and by the intercostal nerves to the external intercostal muscles, causing these muscles to contract. This causes us to breathe in. When the messages stop, relaxation of the muscles occurs, and so expiration takes place.

## Chemical control

When exercising, the body requires more oxygen. Therefore, the body produces more carbon dioxide as a by-product. The body needs to get rid of this carbon dioxide, and does so by increasing the breathing rate. **Chemoreceptors** are found in the medulla

**Q.** What effects does smoking have on the respiratory system?

**A.** Cigarette smoking is well known for being bad for a person's health and for having the following effects on the respiratory system.

- It coats the inside of the lungs with tar so they become inefficient – a heavy smoker will often sound wheezy.
- It covers the cilia in tar, preventing them from getting rid of bacteria from the lungs. Smokers will often develop a 'smoker's cough', which is the body's way of trying to get rid of the unwanted substances in the lungs.
- It can lead to diseases such as emphysema and bronchitis.
- It can cause lung cancer. Most patients with lung cancer have been smokers.

oblongata and in the walls of the **aorta** and **carotid arteries**. They are sensitive to carbon dioxide levels in the blood. When stimulated, they send messages to the respiratory centres in the brain, which leads to an increase in the breathing rate.

## Relationship with other body systems

### Circulatory system

Air is breathed into the lungs and oxygen is carried around in the blood and delivered to the cells. Carbon dioxide is picked up from body cells and carried in the blood; it is then exhaled.

### Nervous system

Nerves connect from the brain to the diaphragm and intercostal muscles to help control breathing.

### Muscular system

The diaphragm and intercostals are muscles that aid with breathing.

# The olfactory system

The olfactory system provides us with the sense of smell, also known as **olfaction**. The brain is able to distinguish about 20 000 different scents with the help of the nervous system. Millions of olfactory receptors in the nose transmit messages in the form of nerve impulses to the brain.

## How is smell perceived?

Substances, such as essential oils (oils used in aromatherapy), give off (1) **smelly gas particles**. These particles are drawn into the nose as we inhale, and dissolve into the upper part of the moist mucous membrane of the nasal cavity.

The ②  **mucus** surrounds small hairs called ③  **cilia** that stick out from the bottom of ④  **olfactory cells**. The gas particles reach the cilia and stimulate nerve impulses to travel along the ⑤  **axon of the nerve cell**, through bones in the skull and to the ⑥  **olfactory bulb**, of which there are two.

## ACTIVITY 7.4

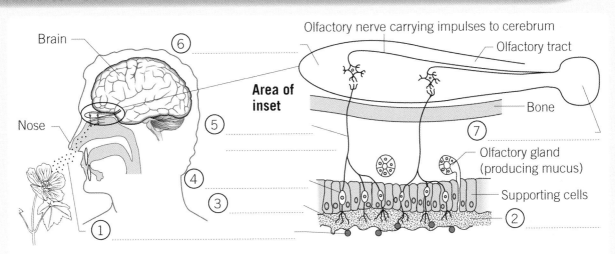

**Figure 7.6** The olfactory system

Label the diagram in Figure 7.6, matching the numbers to the numbered terms in the text on pages 204–205. Use this key to colour the diagram.

Unshaded – gas particles
Green – mucus
Blue – olfactory cell, cilia and axon

Yellow – olfactory bulb
Red – the limbic system

## don't forget

The olfactory receptor consists of the olfactory cell, cilia and axon. Nerves from the olfactory bulb then carry nerve impulses to the brain, many of which are part of the ⑦ **limbic system**. The limbic system is involved with emotions, such as pain, anger, pleasure, affection and memory. This is why smells can evoke different emotional responses and can bring back a flood of memories.

## Adaption

We can become adapted to a smell. If we spray perfume, we will soon stop noticing its smell because the olfactory receptors, of which there are millions, will stop being stimulated until a new smell comes along.

### ACTIVITY 7.5

Decide the order of sequence of the events described below and place the correct letter in each box.

**A** Smell is perceived in the olfactory area of the brain.

**B** Particles of a substance are in the air.

**C** Olfactory cells connect directly with the brain.

**D** Particles stimulate olfactory cells.

**E** Particles dissolve in the mucous layer in nasal cavities.

| 1 | 2 | 3 | 4 | 5 |
|---|---|---|---|---|
|   |   |   |   |   |

# Conditions associated with the respiratory system

## Asthma

Asthma is a chronic (long-term) condition that causes symptoms such as coughing, wheezing, breathlessness and a tight chest. It involves inflammation and contraction of the bronchi muscles, and also an increased production of mucus. These factors cause narrowing of the airways and so make it difficult for a person to breathe. There is no single cause but triggers include an allergy, infection, exercise or stress. Certain factors may increase the likelihood of developing it for example genetic factors and the environment. Asthma can be controlled well in most sufferers.

# Bronchitis

Bronchitis is inflammation of the bronchi. Symptoms include a cough, shortness of breath and wheezing. Cigarette smoke is the main cause of chronic bronchitis.

# Common cold

There are around 200 viruses that can cause the common cold. Symptoms include a blocked nose, cough, sore throat and generally feeling unwell. A **cough** occurs to clear the airways of mucus and other irritating substances. A cold is caused either by breathing in tiny droplets of infected liquid, such as those released when a person sneezes, or by touching a contaminated item, such as a door handle.

# Emphysema

This is a disorder in which the walls of the alveoli are destroyed, thus producing abnormally large air spaces. These remain filled with air during breathing out, so breathing becomes very difficult. Common causes include cigarette smoking and air pollution.

# Hay fever

Caused by an allergy to certain pollens, the hay fever season begins in early spring and lasts until late autumn. Symptoms include a runny nose, sneezing and itchy eyes.

# Influenza

Flu is different to the common cold as the symptoms are generally more severe. Symptoms include fever, cough, sore throat, tiredness, aching muscles and a blocked or runny nose. The flu virus is spread by coughs and sneezes. A person may either breathe in the virus or touch a contaminated item, such as a telephone handset, then touch their nose or mouth. The virus can live on a surface for up to 24 hours. Using tissues to blow the nose and promptly throwing them away, and regularly washing the hands can help to prevent the spread of flu.

## Laryngitis

This is inflammation of the larynx (voice box) and can be the result of factors such as a cold or tonsillitis; it may also be caused by straining the voice, for instance, while singing. Chronic laryngitis can be caused by cigarette smoking and excess alcohol consumption. Symptoms include hoarseness, loss of voice and sore throat.

## Pharyngitis

This is a sore throat and is commonly caused by a viral or bacterial infection, such as a cold. Symptoms include swollen tonsils, enlarged glands in the neck and discomfort when swallowing.

## Pleurisy

Pleurisy is the inflammation of the pleura and is usually caused by a viral or bacterial infection, and can be the result of pneumonia. It commonly causes a sharp pain in the chest.

## Pneumonia

This is inflammation of the lungs. It can be caused by a viral or bacterial infection. Symptoms include a cough, fever and difficulty with breathing.

## Rhinitis

Rhinitis is an inflammation of, and discharge from, the mucous membranes in the nose. The swelling of the membrane blocks the free flow of air though the nose. Rhinitis is a symptom of the common cold, hay fever and sinus problems.

## Sinusitis

This is a viral or bacterial infection (usually associated with a cold or flu), which causes inflammation of the membrane lining of the sinuses. The symptoms include a high temperature, blocked or runny nose, and a painful throbbing feeling in the cheeks and behind the nose and eyes. There may also be a reduction or loss of the sense of smell.

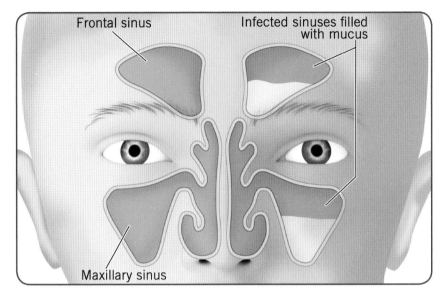

**Figure 7.7** Sinusitis

## Tonsillitis

The tonsils are two glands found at the back of the throat. If they become infected with a virus or bacteria (usually a virus), tonsillitis may result. Symptoms include a sore throat, a reddened throat with white pus-filled spots, swollen lymph nodes in the throat area, and fever.

## Tuberculosis

Tuberculosis (TB) is a bacterial infection that can affect the lungs or other parts of the body, such as the bones, skin and heart. Symptoms include fever, persistent cough, chest pain and tiredness.

## Whooping cough

This is a bacterial infection of the lining of the trachea and bronchi, and is highly infectious. The main symptom is a hacking cough, which is commonly followed by a 'whoop' noise as a person gasps for breath. The condition mostly occurs in children, but is now very uncommon owing to vaccination.

# What you should know

## Functions of the respiratory system

☐ Oxygen supply to body tissues and carbon dioxide removal from body tissues

## Location, structure and function

☐ Respiratory system – mouth, nose, nasal cavity, larynx, pharynx, epiglottis, trachea, primary bronchi, bronchioles, alveoli, lungs, pulmonary capillary network, pleural membranes, diaphragm, intercostal muscles

☐ Mechanism of inhalation and exhalation, gaseous exchange, composition of inspired and expired air, process of internal and external respiration, control of respiration (chemical, nervous), process of pulmonary circulation (see Chapter 8)

☐ Relationship of respiratory system with other body systems (circulatory, nervous, muscular), growth and repair (see Chapter 1)

## Pathologies

☐ Conditions associated with the respiratory system, including their causes, signs and symptoms – obstructive conditions such as emphysema, bronchitis and asthma, pneumonia, tuberculosis, hay fever, rhinitis, whooping cough, sinusitis, laryngitis, pharyngitis, cancer, common cold, flu, tonsillitis, pleurisy

# Cardiovascular system and common pathologies

# 8

The cardiovascular system consists of the heart, blood and blood vessels. The function of the heart is to act as a pump to move the blood around the body. The blood carries oxygen and nutrients and is transported in the body by blood vessels.

# Blood and its functions

## Blood plasma

Plasma is the liquid part of the blood and mainly consists of water. It makes up about 55 per cent of what's inside blood vessels. Many substances can travel in the blood plasma, including blood cells, hormones, nutrients and the waste products produced by cells. Plasma proteins are also found in the blood.

Plasma proteins include albumin, globulin and fibrinogen, which are all made in the liver. Clotting factors are also plasma proteins and, along with fibrinogen, help to clot the blood to prevent bleeding.

## Functions of the cardiovascular system

The blood has several functions.

✻ It **transports** oxygen, nutrients, **antibodies** and hormones to the cells of the body.

✻ Heat is transported around the body from the muscles and liver, which helps regulate the body temperature.

- It **removes** carbon dioxide and waste from the cells.
- It **helps with immunity against disease** as it carries white blood cells, which attack harmful organisms such as bacteria. This helps to protect the body against disease and infection.
- It **clots** to prevent excessive loss of blood if an injury occurs to the body.

## Blood cells

### Red blood cells

Red blood cells (**erythrocytes**) are button-shaped cells that are made in the bone marrow and live for about three months.

FAST FACT

There are approximately 5 million red blood cells in a drop of blood and around 30 trillion of them in the body.

There are approximately 5 million of these cells in a drop of blood. Red blood cells contain the pigment **haemoglobin**. The oxygen picked up from the lungs combines with the haemoglobin.

The function of red blood cells is to carry oxygen around the body and deliver it to the cells. The body cells use the oxygen and nutrients (internal respiration) and produce carbon dioxide. Carbon dioxide can be carried away by the red blood cells and taken back to the lungs to be breathed out.

FAST FACT

Lack of iron leads to a condition called anaemia.

Haemoglobin is rich in iron and needs a constant supply of it. Iron comes from the food we eat and also from old or damaged red blood cells that have been destroyed by the liver. Lack of iron leads to a condition called **anaemia**; symptoms include tiredness, dizziness and shortness of breath.

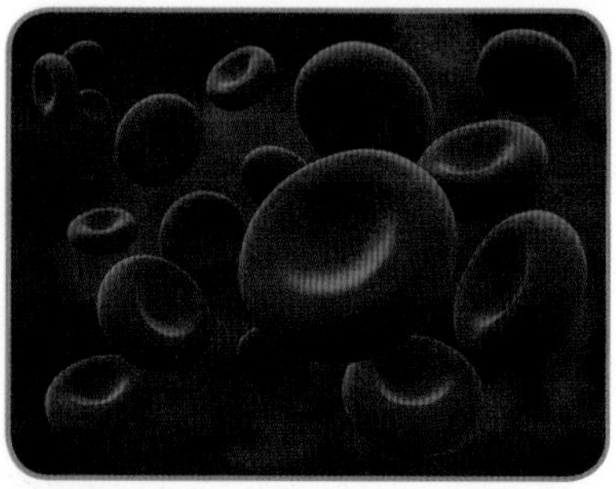

**Figure 8.1** Red blood cells

### White blood cells

White blood cells (**leucocytes**) contain a nucleus and are larger than red blood cells. They are made in the bone marrow and lymphatic system. There are up to 10 000 in a drop of blood and around 60 billion in the body. They help to fight harmful germs and so protect us from disease. Most types of white blood cell can change their shape so they are able to squeeze through small spaces. White blood cells are able to reach almost anywhere in the body.

FAST FACT

Leukaemia is a cancer of the blood caused by the overproduction of white blood cells.

Leucocytes are made up of granulocytes and agranulocytes.

- About 75 per cent of white blood cells are made in the bone marrow. These cells are called **granulocytes** because they have tiny granules in their cytoplasm. Most granulocytes are **phagocytes** – this means that they are able to engulf and digest (eat) bacteria and any other harmful matter.
- **Agranulocytes** do not have granules in their cytoplasm. These white cells make up the remaining 25 per cent of white blood cells and are mostly produced in the lymphatic system. Lymphocytes and monocytes are types of agranulocyte.

### Platelets

Platelets (**thrombocytes**) are tiny fragments of cells, which are smaller than white and red blood cells. They are produced in the bone marrow and live for up to two weeks. There are about 200 000 in a drop of blood. Platelets are involved in the clotting process of the blood following an injury to the body. Their function is to help to prevent loss of blood from damaged blood vessels by forming a plug.

## Process of blood clotting

A blood clot is formed at the site of an injury to the body and prevents the further loss of blood. If this process did not occur we would bleed to death. In haemophiliacs the blood clots very slowly, so a great deal of blood may be lost from even small cuts. Clotting factors can be injected so that haemophiliacs can lead normal lives.

### Stages of blood clotting

1. A wound to the skin stimulates the platelets to release an enzyme called thromboplastin (Figure 8.4 A). An enzyme is a protein that speeds up a chemical reaction.
2. Thromboplastin changes a protein found in the blood plasma called prothombin into another enzyme known as

### don't forget

**An autoimmune disease is one in which antibodies produced by the immune system attack the body's own tissues. Examples include arthritis, psoriasis and multiple sclerosis.**
**The job of lymphocytes is to produce antibodies. Antibodies are chemicals made by the body in response to bacteria and any other harmful matter. They have the function of destroying the harmful matter so that it is no longer a threat to the body. Monocytes also destroy harmful matter, for example bacteria, by engulfing and digesting it, like most of the granulocytes. These cells gather around wounds and kill invading bacteria to prevent them from entering the body.**

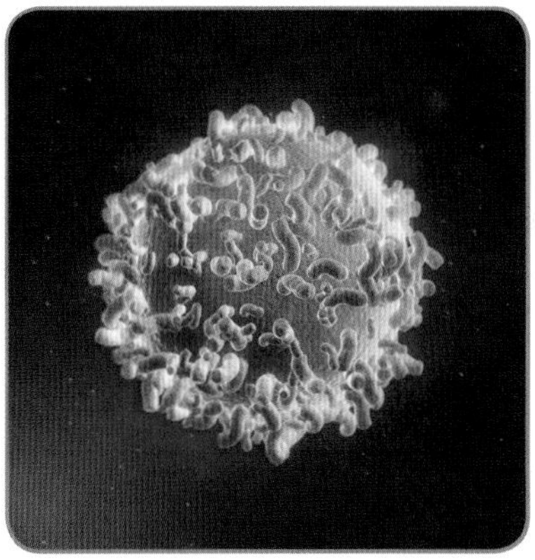

**Figure 8.2** White blood cell

**Figure 8.3** Platelet

thrombin. Vitamin K and calcium are also needed for this process (Figure 8.4 B).

3. Thrombin will act on a soluble protein, also found in the blood plasma, called fibrinogen. Thrombin converts fibrinogen into an insoluble substance called fibrin. Fibrin consists of fibrous strands, which form a net (Figure 8.4 C). The blood cells become trapped in the net and so a blood clot is formed.

4. The clot dries out to form a scab, which is a natural plaster to protect the skin underneath (Figure 8.4 D).

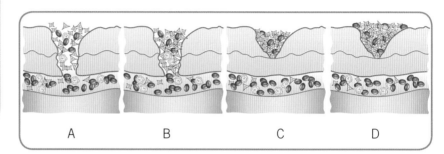

**Figure 8.4** Stages of blood clotting

# The heart

The heart is situated between the lungs in the thoracic cavity (chest region), lying slightly to the left of the body. It is roughly the size of its owner's closed fist and is an organ made up mainly of cardiac muscle.

The heart consists of four chambers: the ① **right atrium**, ② **left atrium**, ③ **right ventricle** and ④ **left ventricle**. The upper chambers are together called the atria and the lower chambers of the heart are called the **ventricles**.

The heart also contains **valves**, including the ⑤ **bicuspid**, ⑥ **tricuspid** and ⑦ **pulmonary valves**, and ⑧ **aortic valve** to prevent the blood from flowing backwards. The right side of the heart is separated from the left side by a muscular wall called the ⑨ **septum** (Figure 8.5).

## ACTIVITY 8.1

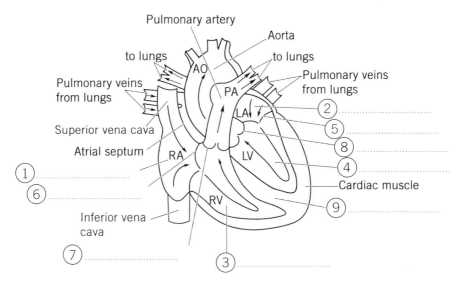

**Figure 8.5** A simplified cross-section showing the structure of the heart and how blood passes through it (see also Figure 1.3)

Label and colour the diagram in Figure 8.5 using the following information.

Use a red colour to lightly shade the following.

- Aorta
- Pulmonary veins
- Left atrium
- Left ventricle
- Cardiac muscle
- Septum

Use a blue colour to lightly shade the following.

- Pulmonary artery
- Superior vena cava
- Right atrium
- Inferior vena cava
- Right ventricle

The areas shaded red show the flow of oxygenated blood through the heart. The blue shading shows the flow of deoxygenated blood through the heart.

## Blood

The blood that passes through the right side of the heart is known as **deoxygenated blood** because it carries very little oxygen. The blood that passes through the left side of the heart is rich in oxygen so is called **oxygenated blood**. Blood vessels that transport blood away from the heart are called **arteries**, while blood is brought to the heart in **veins**.

The **heart wall** consists of three layers.

✖ The **endocardium** is the inner layer of the heart wall.

✖ The **myocardium** is the middle layer of the heart and contains the cardiac muscle that contracts to pump the blood.

✖ The **pericardium** is the outer layer of the heart.

# Pulmonary circulation

The pulmonary circulation is the circulation of blood between the heart and the lungs.

✖ Deoxygenated blood travels through veins called the **inferior vena cava** and **superior vena cava** into the right atrium.

✖ Blood flows from the right atrium through a valve and into the right ventricle.

✖ From the right ventricle the blood passes through another valve and travels into the **pulmonary arteries**.

✖ From the pulmonary arteries the blood is carried to the lungs. An exchange of gases occurs in the lungs. The blood gets rid of the carbon dioxide, which is breathed out, and a fresh supply of oxygen is picked up from the lungs. The blood now becomes oxygenated.

✖ The oxygenated blood is then returned to the left atrium of the heart by the **pulmonary veins**.

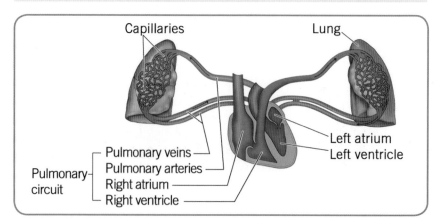

**Figure 8.6** Pulmonary circulation

# General (systemic) circulation

The general circulation is the circulation of blood from the left side of the heart to the rest of the body's tissues.

✖ The oxygenated blood passes from the left atrium through a valve and into the left ventricle.

✖ The blood leaves the left ventricle of the heart and passes into a large blood vessel (artery) called the **aorta** which includes the **aortic arch**. The blood, which also transports nutrients, is then carried around the body to supply oxygen and nutrients to all the cells. Carbon dioxide is picked up from the tissues and the blood now contains little oxygen, so it becomes deoxygenated again.

✖ The deoxygenated blood is eventually returned to the right atrium of the heart by the superior vena cava and inferior vena cava.

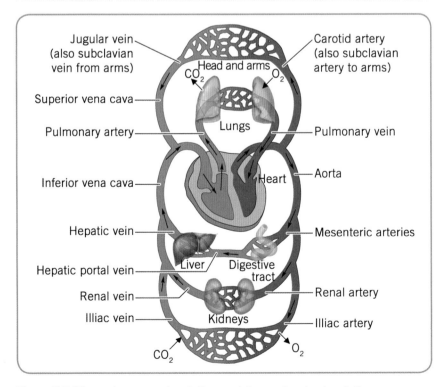

**Figure 8.7** The pulmonary circulation and the systemic circulation

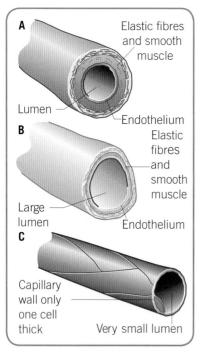

**A**
Elastic fibres and smooth muscle

Lumen

Endothelium

**B**
Elastic fibres and smooth muscle

Large lumen

Endothelium

**C**

Capillary wall only one cell thick

Very small lumen

**Figure 8.8** Blood vessels: **A** artery, **B** vein, **C** capillary

### Portal circulation

The portal circulation is the circulation of the blood from the small intestine to the liver, which is delivered by the portal vein.

### Coronary circulation

This is the circulation of blood in the blood vessels of the heart muscle. The right and left coronary arteries branch off the aorta to deliver oxygen-rich blood to the myocardium of the heart. Coronary veins return deoxygenated blood to the right atrium of the heart. These blood vessels are commonly affected by **atherosclerosis** (narrowing of the arteries), which is known as coronary heart disease. If these vessels become blocked it may result in angina or a heart attack.

Blood is transported around the body in a series of pipes called blood vessels (Figure 8.8). These blood vessels are called arteries, arterioles, capillaries, venules and veins, and form an intricate network within the body.

## Arteries

Arteries have thick, elastic, muscular walls because the blood within them is carried under high pressure owing to the pumping action of the heart. Arteries carry blood **away** from the heart. All arteries carry **oxygenated** blood, with the exception of the pulmonary arteries which carry deoxygenated blood from the heart to the lungs. Arteries are generally deep-seated, except where they cross a pulse spot, such as the radial artery in the wrist and carotid artery in the neck, where a pulse can be felt. As arteries get further from the heart they branch off and become smaller. The oxygenated blood eventually reaches very small arteries called **arterioles**.

## Capillaries

Arterioles are connected to the capillaries. Capillaries are the smallest vessels, about a hundredth of a millimetre thick. Unlike arteries and veins, the walls of the capillaries are thin enough to allow certain substances to pass through them – this is known as **capillary exchange**. Oxygen and nutrients are delivered to the cells of the body, and carbon dioxide and waste products are removed.

The capillaries connect with larger vessels called **venules**. Now that oxygen has been removed from the blood, and carbon dioxide has been picked up, the blood that reaches the venules has become deoxygenated (Figure 8.10).

## Veins

Blood flows through the venules until it reaches larger vessels called veins. The veins carry blood, called venous blood, towards the heart. Their walls are thinner and less elastic than arteries. Veins carry deoxygenated blood, with the exception of the pulmonary veins that carry oxygenated blood from the lungs to the heart. Veins are nearer the surface of the body than the arteries. Unlike the other blood vessels, veins contain valves that prevent the blood from flowing backwards.

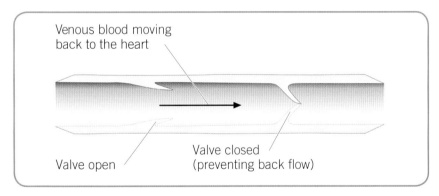

**Figure 8.9** Valves in the veins

Unlike arteries, the veins carry blood at low pressure because they are not helped by the pumping action of the heart. Blood in the veins is moved through the body by the squeezing action of the voluntary muscles, such as during walking, and the involuntary muscles, such as the movement of breathing. Therefore, exercise and massage are particularly useful to help the venous flow.

## ACTIVITY 8.2

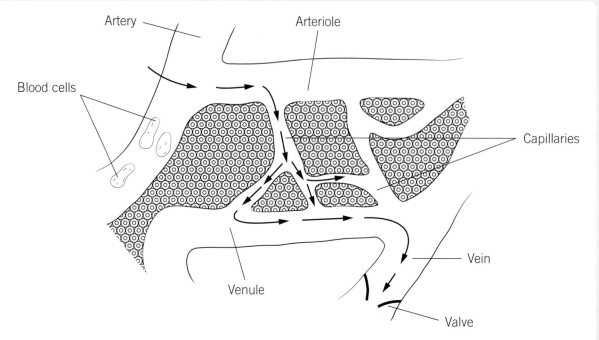

**Figure 8.10** How blood passes from arteries through capillaries to veins

In the diagram in Figure 8.10, colour the artery and arteriole red, the veins and venule blue, and the capillaries yellow.

## ACTIVITY 8.3

Fill in the table showing the differences between arteries and veins.

|  | Arteries | Veins |
|---|---|---|
| Thickness of walls |  |  |
| Pressure of blood |  |  |
| Do they have valves? |  |  |
| Blood carried oxygenated/deoxygenated? |  |  |
| Blood to heart/away from heart? |  |  |
| How blood is moved along vessels |  |  |
| Deep-seated or near surface of body? |  |  |

## Arteries of the head and neck

The blood to the head arrives via the **carotid arteries**. There are two main carotid arteries, one either side of the neck:

(1) the **internal carotid artery**, which supplies oxygenated blood to the brain

(2) the **external carotid artery**, which carries blood to the more superficial structures of the head: muscle, skin and bone.

Important arteries of the head and neck include the (3) **common carotid**, the (4) **occipital**, the (5) **superficial temporal**, the (6) **maxillary**, the (7) **facial**, the (8) **lingual** and the (9) **thyroid** arteries.

### ACTIVITY 8.4

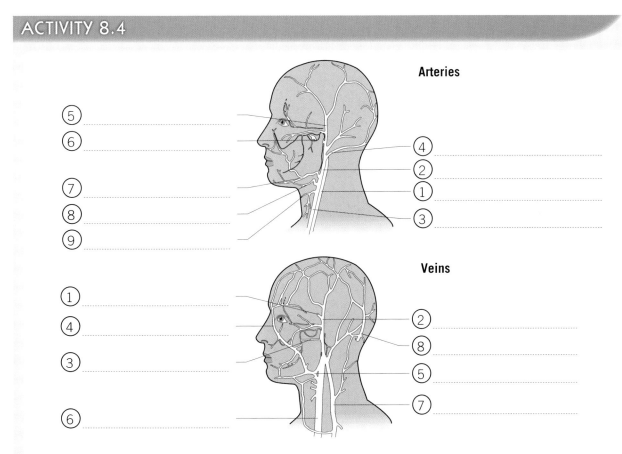

**Figure 8.11** Blood vessels of the head and neck

Label the diagrams in Figure 8.11 using the information on pages 221–222. Colour the arteries in red and the veins in blue.

## Veins of the head and neck

Important veins of the head and neck include the ① **middle temporal**, the ② **superficial temporal**, the ③ **maxillary**, the ④ **anterior facial**, the ⑤ **common facial**, the ⑥ **internal jugular**, the ⑦ **external jugular** and the ⑧ **occipital** veins.

## Arteries of the body

The ① **aorta** is the largest artery of the body. Its diameter is about the size of a ten pence piece. This artery subdivides to become smaller arteries and supplies blood to the whole body. Other arteries of the body include: ② coronary, ③ subclavian, ④ common carotid, ⑤ intercostal, ⑥ common hepatic, ⑦ splenic, ⑧ renal, ⑨ superior mesenteric, ⑩ common iliac, ⑪ vertebral, ⑫ axillary, ⑬ brachial, ⑭ ulnar, ⑮ radial, ⑯ deep palmar arch, ⑰ external iliac, ⑱ femoral, ⑲ popliteal, ⑳ anterior tibial, ㉑ plantar arch, ㉒ digital arteries, ㉓ posterior tibial.

## Veins of the body

The **jugular veins** bring deoxygenated blood from the head back to the heart via the superior vena cava. The ① inferior vena cava is the largest vein in the body, about 3.5 cm in size. The ② superior vena cava has a diameter about the size of a ten pence piece.

Other important blood vessels include: ③ subclavian, ④ axillary, ⑤ cephalic, ⑥ brachial, ⑦ intercostal, ⑧ basilic, ⑨ ulnar, ⑩ palmar arch, ⑪ hepatic, ⑫ splenic, ⑬ renal, ⑭ common iliac, ⑮ long saphenous, ⑯ femoral, ⑰ popliteal, ⑱ tibial, ⑲ deep plantar, ⑳ short saphenous, ㉑ dorsal venous arch veins.

## ACTIVITY 8.5

Label the diagram in Figure 8.12 using the information on page 222. Colour the arteries in red.

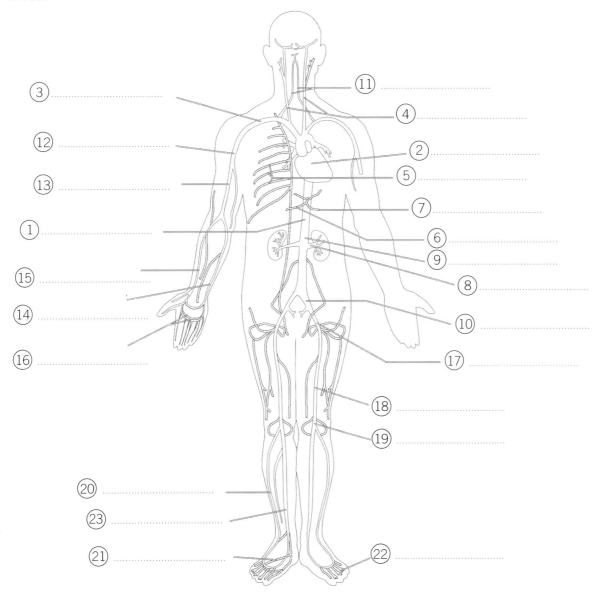

**Figure 8.12** Arteries of the body

## ACTIVITY 8.6

Label the diagram in Figure 8.13 using the information on page 222. Colour the veins in blue.

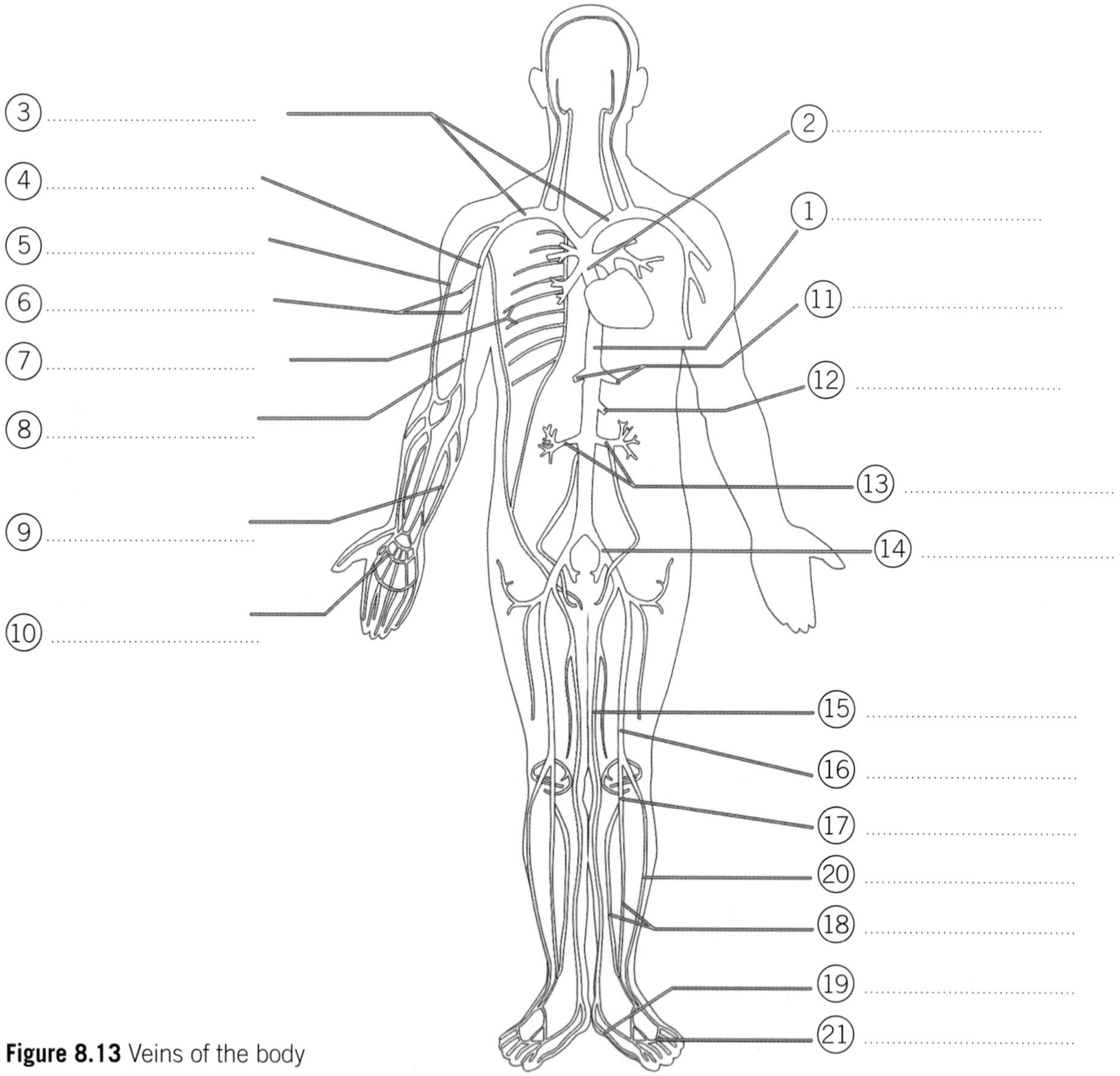

**Figure 8.13** Veins of the body

# How the circulation works

## The cardiac cycle

The technical name for the contraction of the heart is **systole**. **Atrial systole** begins as a wave of muscle contraction running down and across the atria from left to right, forcing blood into each of the ventricles. A fraction of a second later, the wave reaches the ventricles and they too contract (**ventricular systole**), forcing blood into the aorta and pulmonary arteries.

After the heart has contracted, the atria and ventricles relax, known as **diastole**. The atria again fill with blood and the **cardiac cycle** starts again. One systole and one diastole form a cardiac cycle. It is one complete heartbeat and lasts for 0.8 seconds.

MEMORY JOGGER

To help you remember diastole, think of DR (doctor) – D is for diastole and R for relaxation, as the atria and ventricles relax during diastole.

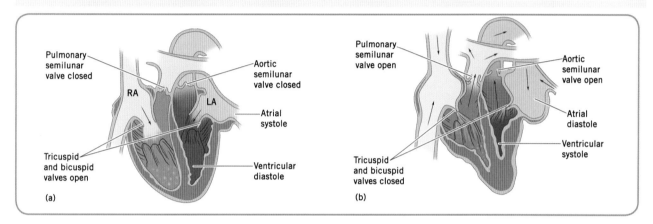

**Figure 8.14** Contraction of the heart

## Electrical conduction in the heart

In the upper part of the right atrium of the heart there is a tiny group of nerve cells known as the sinoatrial node (SA node), which acts as the heart's natural pacemaker. The SA nodes send out electrical impulses across the heart, which cause it to beat at around 60–70 beats per minute for a resting heart. The atrioventricular node (AV node) lies near the bottom of the right atrium. It conducts the impulses received from the sinoatrial node but delays the signal across the heart to allow time for the atrium to contract. When there is a problem with this process, a person may require a pacemaker – a small device that is put into the chest and helps the heart to beat regularly.

## Blood pressure

When blood reaches the capillaries, it is vital that oxygen and nutrients pass out of the blood and into the cells. It is the pressure of blood that forces fluid out through the capillary walls. The fluid contains oxygen and nutrients that pass into the cell by diffusion. Therefore, it is important for the body to maintain the correct level of blood pressure.

With each heartbeat, the atria and ventricles contract (systole). As a chamber of the heart contracts, the blood pressure inside it will increase. Blood pressure measures the force with which the heart pumps blood around the body. It is the force of pressure the blood exerts against the walls of the arteries. Blood pressure can be likened to the pressure in a hosepipe, which increases and decreases as the tap is turned on and off. The blood pressure varies during a complete heartbeat.

The greater the blood volume (amount of blood) in the body, the higher the blood pressure will be. A high blood volume means there is more blood flowing through the blood vessels, which means a greater pressure is exerted on the blood vessels' walls. This increases blood pressure. Diuretics may be used to treat high blood pressure; they work by decreasing the amount of sodium (salt) and water that are reabsorbed into the bloodstream by the kidneys. Therefore, the body produces more urine and so results in a reduction of the amount of fluid left in the bloodstream. As the blood volume is reduced in the body, the heart does not need to work so hard to pump the blood; this helps to lower the blood pressure.

**FAST FACT**

People who exercise regularly often have slightly lower-than-normal blood pressure.

A doctor uses a sphygmomanometer to measure blood pressure. Two phases of blood pressure are measured.

- **Systolic pressure** – the force exerted by blood on the walls of the arteries during the contraction of the ventricles. This shows the highest pressure the heart can produce. It is the first number in a blood pressure reading and also the first sound heard as the large heart valves close.
- **Diastolic pressure** – the measure of the pressure on the walls of the arteries during relaxation of the ventricles. It is the second number in a blood pressure reading and is the lowest blood pressure measured in the large arteries. At this time, the smaller heart valves close, producing the second, quieter heartbeat.

**don't forget**

**Complementary therapies promote relaxation and so can help to lower a person's blood pressure.**

A normal blood pressure will measure around 120 mmHg systolic and 80 mmHg diastolic, or 120/80. At this level, there is a much lower risk of heart disease or stroke. A person is considered to be hypertensive when their blood pressure readings are consistently over 140/90, or higher. This higher pressure places additional strain on the heart and blood vessels, which increases the risk of suffering with a heart attack or stroke. High blood pressure can also cause heart and kidney disease. Lifestyle changes should be made and the sufferer may be given medication to help lower it.

Lifestyle changes to lower blood pressure include the following.

- Try to maintain a healthy weight. Being overweight increases the chances of suffering with high blood pressure.
- Eat less salt as too much can raise blood pressure. A high intake of salt in the diet causes water to be retained in the body. This may result in an increased amount of blood in the body, leading to raised blood pressure, as the heart has to work harder to pump the extra blood around the body.
- Eat more fruit and vegetables (around five portions each day). Fruit and vegetables are rich in potassium, and there is evidence that suggests a diet rich in potassium and low in salt can help to lower blood pressure levels.
- Limit alcohol intake as, over a period of time, increased levels can raise blood pressure.
- Regular exercise, particularly aerobic, will help to lower blood pressure.
- Regularly carry out relaxing activities, such as yoga, to help lower stress levels.

A person is considered to have low blood pressure if they have a reading of 90/60 or less, and it is usually not a cause for concern. If a person has a blood pressure lower than normal, it means a lower risk of stroke or heart disease.

Blood pressure is used as an indicator of the health of the blood vessels and heart. Damaged blood vessels that are less elastic or have a partial blockage will show a raised blood pressure. A

**FAST FACT**

Sufferers may be prescribed medication to lower their blood pressure. There are four main types that are commonly used.

- ACE inhibitors
- Angiotensin receptor blockers
- Calcium channel blockers
- Thiazide diuretics

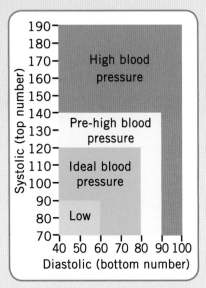

**Figure 8.15** Blood pressure chart

weak heart will show low blood pressure. People who exercise regularly often have slightly lower-than-normal blood pressure. Exercise helps to strengthen the heart, so it has to do less work to pump the same amount of blood.

## Viscosity of the blood

**Viscosity** (thickness) of blood can affect blood pressure. A decrease in viscosity, or thinning of blood, can lower blood pressure. However, increasing viscosity, or thickening of the blood, raises blood pressure. Poorly controlled diabetes, elevated cholesterol in the body, genetic factors, and smoking cigarettes, can all thicken the blood.

## Blood flow resistance in the arteries

The pressure of blood flow through an artery is determined by the force of the blood against the blood vessel walls and the resistance of the blood vessel to the blood flow. Hardening, narrowing and loss of elasticity of the arteries (arteriosclerosis) means the heart has to work harder to move blood around the body. This increases the force of blood against the artery wall and so there is an increase in blood pressure.

## Control of blood pressure by nerves

Nerves can control the diameter of the blood vessels. If the blood pressure is too low, the sympathetic nerves of the autonomic nervous system cause the blood vessels to contract. Contraction of these vessels leads to a decrease in the diameter of the vessels. This causes the pressure of blood inside the vessels to increase so that the blood pressure can return to normal. If the blood pressure is too high, the muscles in the walls of the blood vessels will relax so that the diameter of the vessels increases. This will cause the blood pressure to be lowered and so return to normal.

## Heart rate/pulse rate

The heart rate, or pulse rate, can be felt in arteries that lie close to the surface of the body, such as the radial artery in the wrist and the carotid artery in the neck. The number of pulse beats per minute represents the **heart rate**. The pumping action of the left ventricle in the heart is strong so it can be felt as a pulse in the arteries. The average pulse of an adult at rest is 60–80 beats per minute.

### Factors affecting the pulse rate

✖ **Exercise**. Any form of exercise will cause the pulse rate to increase. During strenuous exercise, the pulse rate can double.

✖ **Emotion**. The pulse rate can increase at times of stress, excitement, fear, anger and any other strong emotional states.

✖ **Age**. Children have a higher pulse rate than adults.

✖ **Gender**. The pulse rate in females is higher than in males.

✖ **Drugs**. Certain drugs can influence the pulse rate.

## Effects of adrenalin on the heart

The hormone adrenalin is released from the adrenal glands, which sit on top of each kidney. Adrenalin is released in response to stress, fear, exercise and excitement. It causes the heart rate to speed up and the coronary blood vessels to dilate, increasing the blood supply to the heart muscle. The increase in blood pressure means that a greater volume of blood is pumped with each beat, allowing more blood to reach vital organs and muscles.

## Control of heart rate by nerves

The cardiac muscle of the heart has the ability to contract without the need of a nerve supply from the brain. If removed from the body, it can still continue to contract as long as it is provided with

### don't forget

The heart rate is the number of heartbeats per unit of time, which is typically expressed as beats per minute. A female's heart rate tends to be higher than a male's as they have smaller hearts. Regular exercise can help to lower resting heart rate, which increases the heart's health.

oxygen. The heart has a built-in pacemaker, so it will naturally beat at 60–100 beats per minute. However, nerves are able to control the rate at which the heart beats. **Sympathetic nerves** can cause the heart rate to speed up and **parasympathetic nerves** can cause the heart rate to slow down.

Whether at rest or undertaking exercise, the sympathetic and parasympathetic nerves ensure that the heart rate can be adjusted to meet demands. When at rest, the parasympathetic nerves will cause the heart to beat at about 75 beats per minute, which is the average heart rate for a person.

## Blood groups

A person's blood can be classified as belonging to a particular blood group. During a blood transfusion, if the blood groups of the donor and patient (recipient) are not compatible, the red blood cells clump together, which is known as **agglutination**. This results in a blockage of the blood vessels, and can be fatal.

People can have blood types that belong to one of four groups: A, B, AB and O (Table 8.1).

**Table 8.1** The compatibility of blood groups

| Type | May give to | May receive from |
|---|---|---|
| O | Any blood group | O |
| A | A and AB | O and A |
| B | B and AB | O and B |
| AB | AB | Any blood group |

- In the UK, O is the most common blood group.
- Type O is the **universal donor** because it can be given to a patient with either type A, B or AB blood. If a patient has blood group type O they can only receive type O.
- Type AB is called the **universal recipient** because a patient with this type can receive blood from all blood groups. A donor with type AB blood can only give to people with type AB blood.

# Effects of massage on the circulatory system

Massage causes the blood vessels to be compressed, forcing blood forward. As pressure is released, the blood vessels return to their normal size and blood rushes in to fill the space created. Reddening of the skin, called erythema, results. Fresh, oxygenated blood and nutrients are brought to the area and so will nourish the tissues and help with tissue repair. Waste products (metabolic waste) are removed and carried away by the veins. A build-up of waste products can cause pain and stiffness, so massage can help to relieve these symptoms.

Massage movements such as effleurage (stroking) will help to return the blood in the veins back to the heart (venous return). This is why strokes are performed in the direction of the venous flow.

# Conditions associated with the cardiovascular system

## Anaemia

There are various types of anaemia, but the most common is anaemia caused by iron deficiency. The body requires iron to make the haemoglobin part of red blood cells (haemoglobin stores and carries oxygen). Iron-deficiency anaemia is caused by a decreased amount of red blood cells as the body has insuffient iron to make them. The main symptoms include tiredness and lack of energy. Iron supplements are often recommended to sufferers.

## Aneurysm

A weakness in the wall of a blood vessel can cause an aneurysm to form: this is a bulge in a blood

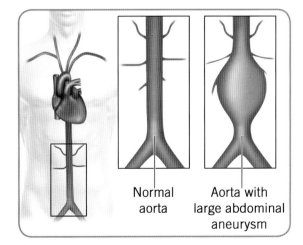

Normal aorta

Aorta with large abdominal aneurysm

**Figure 8.16** Aneurysm

vessel. If the bulge grows too big it can split, which can cause internal bleeding, and may result in death. Risk factors include smoking, high blood pressure and atherosclerosis.

## Angina

Angina occurs when there is a restriction of blood to the heart muscle. It commonly happens when the coronary arteries become narrowed and hardened. When a person suffers an angina attack, they will commonly experience a heavy or tight pain in the chest, which may also be felt in the left arm, neck, jaw and back. It can be brought on by physical activity or stress.

## Arteriosclerosis and atherosclerosis

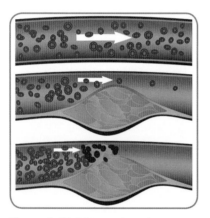

**Figure 8.17** Atherosclerosis

Arteriosclerosis is a group of diseases that feature a thickening and a loss of elasticity of the artery walls (including small arteries and arterioles).

Atherosclerosis (furring of the arteries) is the most common type of arteriosclerosis and happens when fatty, yellowish plaques form on the artery walls. This causes narrowing of the artery, which restricts the blood flow through it. A diet high in saturated fats, such as animal fats, often causes this condition. Other causes include smoking, high blood pressure, hereditary factors and poorly controlled diabetes.

## Coronary thrombosis

This is a thrombosis that occurs in a coronary artery and causes it to narrow. This increases the chance of a heart attack as the blood supply becomes disrupted.

## Embolism

This is a blockage of an artery with a clot of material that is contained within the bloodstream. A piece broken away from a thrombosis can be the cause. It circulates in the bloodstream until it becomes wedged somewhere in a blood vessel and blocks the flow of blood. Such a blockage may be extremely harmful. Do not treat clients with thrombosis or embolism, and if they have a history of these conditions it may be wise to check with their doctor before treatment.

## Haematoma

This is a swelling that contains clotting blood and is found outside the blood vessels. It may be caused by injury or disease.

## Haemophilia

Haemophilia is an inherited disorder and nearly always affects males. It involves a problem with clotting factors in the blood, which affects the blood's ability to clot; it can cause bleeding for longer than normal, or even severe bleeding, both internally and externally. It can usually be well managed with medication.

## Hepatitis A, B, C

Hepatitis is inflammation of the liver. This is mainly caused by a viral infection but can also be the result of excess alcohol consumption and drugs. There are many types of virus responsible for hepatitis.

- **Hepatitis A** virus is a common infection in many parts of the world. It can be caught through eating or drinking contaminated food or water.
- **Hepatitis B** is very infectious and the virus can be spread through unprotected sex, sharing contaminated needles and using non-sterilised equipment for tattooing and body piercing.
- **Hepatitis C** can be caught through contaminated needles, non-sterilised equipment for tattooing and body piercing, and unprotected sex.

If a person continues to be infected over a number of years, they could develop chronic hepatitis, liver cirrhosis or liver cancer.

The symptoms of hepatitis A, B and C are similar and include flu-like illness, nausea, vomiting, diarrhoea and jaundice (yellow skin and whites of eyes).

# High cholesterol

Cholesterol is a fatty substance that the liver makes from fatty foods that have been eaten. If cholesterol accumulates in the blood it can increase a person's risk of suffering with a heart attack or stroke, as it can build up on an artery wall. Eating a healthy diet that is low in **saturated fats** (animal fats) can help to prevent high cholesterol levels.

# High/low blood pressure

High blood pressure (**hypertension**) is when the blood pressure is consistently above normal. It can lead to strokes and heart attacks as the heart has to work harder to force blood through the system. High blood pressure can be caused by smoking, obesity, lack of exercise, eating too much salt, stress, too much alcohol, the contraceptive pill, pregnancy and hereditary factors.

Low blood pressure (hypotension) is when the blood pressure is below normal for a substantial time. Blood pressure must be sufficient to pump blood to the brain when the body is in the upright position. If it is not, then the person will feel faint. Some people with low blood pressure may feel faint when sitting up suddenly from the lying position. The causes of low blood pressure include Addison's disease, loss of blood and heart conditions.

**Tachycardia** means a fast resting heart or pulse rate of over 100 beats per minute. If a person has tachycardia while at rest, too much coffee or tea, certain drugs, anxiety or fever may be the cause. Sometimes it can be a symptom of coronary heart disease.

**Bradycardia** means a slow resting heart or pulse rate of less than 60 beats per minute. Athletes who compete in endurance sports normally have bradycardia.

## HIV/AIDS

HIV (human immunodeficiency virus) is the cause of AIDS. HIV destroys or damages many helper T-lymphocytes, which play an important part in the defence against other viruses, bacteria and fungi. In fully developed AIDS, immunity is lost, so the body becomes susceptible to illness.

## Palpitations

A palpitation is a sensation in the heart area, such as a sudden pounding, fluttering or irregular beating, which lasts for a short period of time. A release of adrenalin can cause palpitations, perhaps owing to feeling nervous, anxious or emotional. Smoking, excessive caffeine or alcohol intake, or using recreational drugs can trigger them. They are usually harmless. However, in a few cases they could indicate heart problems.

## Phlebitis

This is an inflammation of the walls of veins caused by tiny blood clots. There is redness, tenderness and swelling along the affected veins. No treatment should be given to anyone suffering with this condition.

## Septicaemia

This is blood poisoning and is caused by a bacterial infection. It can be a life-threatening condition; symptoms begin with fever, a rapid breathing rate and increased heart rate. If uncontrolled, it can lead to septic shock in which blood pressure becomes low.

## Varicose veins

Varicose veins is a condition that occurs if valves in the veins stop functioning properly. The veins become permanently dilated (widened) as the valves can no longer prevent blood from flowing backwards down them. The blood pools in the veins and causes them to swell and bulge. Varicose veins commonly occur in the veins near the surface of the leg. They can also occur in the anus, where they are called haemorrhoids or piles. The causes of varicose veins include hereditary factors, ageing, obesity, pregnancy and jobs that involve long periods of standing. The affected veins must not be touched during treatment.

## Thrombosis

A thrombosis is a blood clot within a blood vessel. It is dangerous as it may constrict or cut off the flow of blood. There are often no symptoms. However, if someone has a blood clot in the vein (venous thromboembolism, or VTE), they may experience pain, swelling and redness, as well as other symptoms. The main causes of a VTE are slow blood flow, damage to a blood vessel and blood clotting too readily. Deep vein thrombosis (DVT) is a blood clot in a deep vein, which affects a leg.

An arterial thrombosis is a blood clot in an artery and can lead to heart disease, angina and stroke. It is caused by many factors including smoking, high blood pressure, and obesity.

If massage is carried out, there is a risk that the clot may be moved or broken up and taken to the heart, lungs or brain, which could prove fatal.

### ACTIVITY 8.7

Which condition am I?

1. A group of diseases that include thickening and a loss of elasticity of artery walls.

   ....................................................................................................

2. Blood clot in a blood vessel.

   ....................................................................................................

3. Inflammation of the liver.

   ....................................................................................................

4. Blood pressure that is consistently above normal.

   ....................................................................................................

5. This may occur if the valves in veins do not work properly.

   ....................................................................................................

# What you should know

## Functions of the cardiovascular system

☐ Transportation – nutrients, gases, hormones, antibodies, waste products

☐ Heat regulation, protection and immunity, blood flow distribution, clotting

## Location of blood vessels

☐ Arteries of the head and neck – innominate, common carotid, internal carotid, external carotid, facial, occipital, superficial, temporal

☐ Veins of the head and neck – posterior external jugular, occipital, superficial, temporal, maxillary, anterior facial, common facial, internal jugular, external jugular

☐ Arteries of the body – coronary artery, ascending and descending aorta, left and right common carotid, left and right subclavian, intercostal, pulmonary, right hepatic, splenic, renal, superior mesenteric, right iliac, inferior mesenteric, left iliac, vertebral, axillary, brachial, left and right ulnar, left and right radial, left and right deep palmar arch, left and right superficial palmar arch, external iliac, left and right femoral, left and right popliteal, left and right anterior tibial, left and right posterior tibial, plantar arch, digital arteries

☐ Veins of the body – inferior vena cava, pulmonary, right hepatic, hepatic portal, splenic, right renal, left and right iliac, left and right axillary, left and right brachial, left and right basilica, left and right cephalic, left and right subclavian, long saphenous, left and right short saphenous, dorsal venous arch, left and right femoral, left and right popliteal, left and right posterior tibial, left and right anterior tibial

## Location, structure and function

☐ Blood – plasma, erythrocytes, leucocytes, thrombocytes

☐ Blood vessels – arteries, arterioles, veins, venules, capillaries

☐ Heart – superior vena cava, inferior vena cava, right atrium, tricuspid valve, right ventricle, pulmonary valve, pulmonary artery, septum, pulmonary veins, left atrium, bicuspid valve, left ventricle, aorta, aortic arch, endocardium, myocardium, pericardium), coronary circulation

☐ Cardiac cycle – diastole, atrial systole, ventricular systole

☐ Electrical conduction in the heart – sinoatrial node, atrioventricular node, type of circulation

☐ Definition of heart rate. Heart rate values

☐ Heart rate control – nervous system, hormonal

☐ Definition of blood pressure – systolic, diastolic

☐ Blood pressure measurements and classifications, blood pressure regulation

☐ Factors affecting blood pressure

## Growth and repair

☐ Process of blood clotting – thrombocytes, thromboplastin, prothrombin, calcium, thrombin, fibrinogen, fibrin

## Pathologies

☐ Conditions associated with the cardiovascular system, including their causes, signs and symptoms – anaemia, angina, haematoma, haemophilia, septicaemia, aneurysm, arteriosclerosis, atherosclerosis, coronary, deep vein thrombosis, hypertension, hypotension, varicose veins, palpitations, high cholesterol, high/low blood pressure

# 9

# Lymphatic system and common pathologies

## The lymphatic system

Have you noticed that certain glands swell up when you are ill? For example, the glands in the neck inflame during a throat infection. The glands you can feel are lymph nodes. Lymph nodes, lymph, lymph vessels and lymphatic ducts all make up the lymphatic system, which is closely related to blood circulation.

### How is lymph produced?

Blood does not flow into the tissues but remains inside the blood vessels. However, plasma from the blood is able to seep

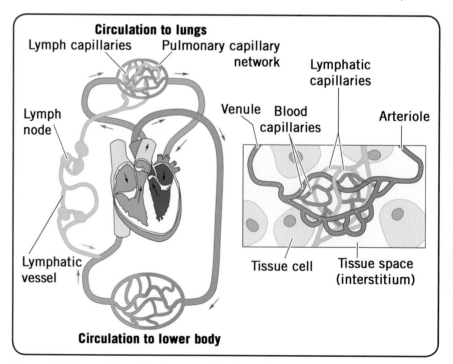

**Figure 9.1** The relationship between blood and lymph

through the capillary walls and enter the spaces between the tissues. This fluid provides the cells with nutrients and oxygen. It has now become tissue fluid, also known as interstitial fluid. More fluid passes out of the blood capillaries than is returned to the blood. The excess tissue fluid passes into the **lymphatic capillaries** and now becomes **lymph**. Lymph is similar to blood plasma but contains more white blood cells.

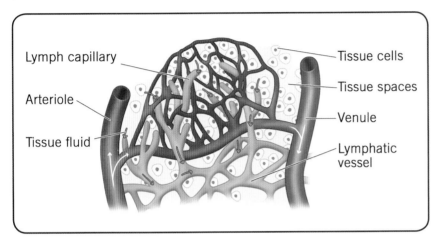

**Figure 9.2** Lymph capillaries in tissue spaces

## The functions of the lymphatic system

✖ **Helps to fight infection**. The lymphatic system is an important part of the body's immune system and helps protect us against disease. It produces specialised white blood cells (**leucocytes**) called **lymphocytes**, which recognise harmful substances and destroy them. Lymph nodes and other lymphatic organs filter the lymph to remove microorganisms and other foreign particles, and also help to get rid of waste and toxins.

✖ **Distributes fluid in the body**. Lymphatic vessels drain approximately 3 litres of excess tissue fluid daily from tissue spaces.

✖ **Transport of fats**. Carbohydrates and protein are passed from the small intestine directly into the bloodstream. However, fats are passed from the small intestine into lymphatic vessels called **lacteals** before eventually passing into the bloodstream.

## ACTIVITY 9.1

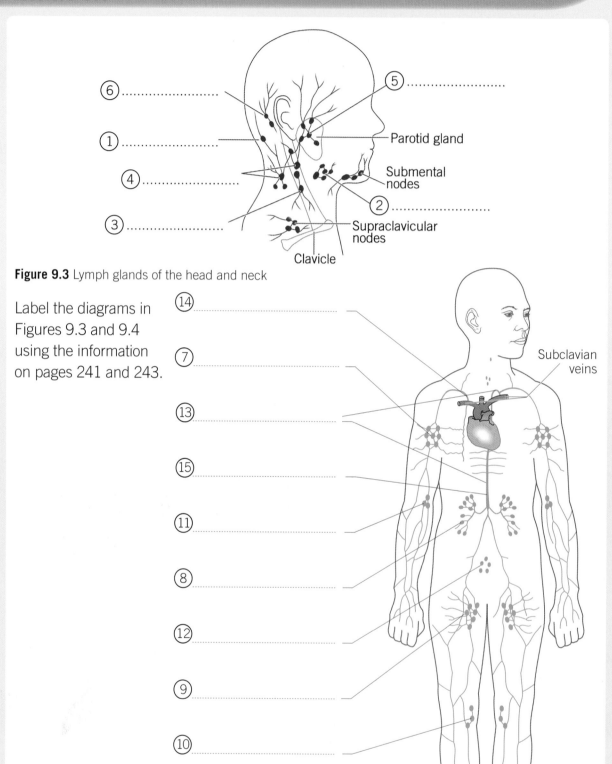

**Figure 9.3** Lymph glands of the head and neck

Label the diagrams in Figures 9.3 and 9.4 using the information on pages 241 and 243.

**Figure 9.4** Lymph glands of the body

# Lymph nodes

There are approximately 600 bean-shaped lymph nodes scattered throughout the body. They lie mainly in groups around the groin, breast, armpits and round the major blood vessels of the abdomen and chest.

Lymph is a watery, colourless fluid that passes through the lymph nodes. Lymph nodes filter out harmful substances from the lymph, such as bacteria, which could cause an infection in the body. They contain specialised white blood cells called monocytes and lymphocytes.

✼ **Monocytes** destroy harmful substances by ingesting (eating) them.

✼ **Lymphocytes** produce **antibodies** that stop the growth of bacteria and prevent their harmful action. During an infection there are more bacteria and so the lymph nodes produce more lymphocytes to destroy them. This causes the lymph nodes to enlarge and is a sign that the glands are working to fight the infection.

Important groups of lymph nodes in the head are: the (1) **occipital**, (2) **submandibular**, (3) **deep cervical** and (4) **superficial cervical**, (5) **anterior auricular** and (6) **posterior auricular** nodes.

Important groups of lymph nodes in the rest of the body include the (7) **axillary**, (8) **abdominal**, (9) **inguinal**, (10) **popliteal**, (11) **supratrochlear** and (12) **iliac** nodes.

| FAST FACT ❯ |
| --- |
| A lymph node within the breast is called an intramammary lymph node. |

# Structure of lymph nodes

Lymph nodes have a fibrous outer capsule containing **lymphoid tissue**. Lymph enters the node through the **afferent lymphatic vessels** and leaves the node via the **efferent lymphatic vessels**.

As many as five afferent lymph vessels may enter a node while only one or two efferent vessels carry lymph away from it. **Trabeculae** divide the node into sections, provide support and enable blood vessels to enter into the node.

## Lymph vessels

Lymph travels around the body in one direction only, towards the heart. It is carried in vessels that begin as **lymphatic capillaries**. Lymph capillaries are blind-ended tubes, situated between cells, and are found throughout the body. The walls of lymphatic capillaries are structured in such a way that tissue fluid can pass into them but not out of them (Figure 9.5).

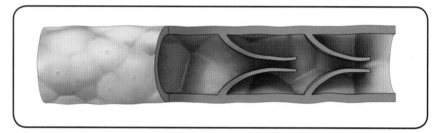

**Figure 9.5** Lymph vessel

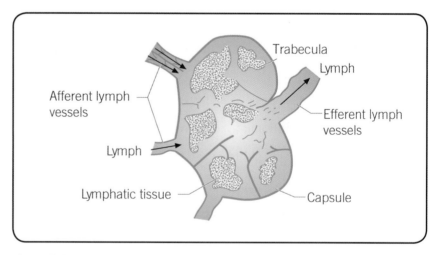

**Figure 9.6** Structure of a lymph gland

Lymphatic capillaries join up and become wider tubes, known as **lymphatic vessels**. The lymph vessels generally run parallel to the veins. These vessels are similar to veins as they contain valves, although they generally have thinner walls. The lymph flows around the body through these lymph vessels and passes through a number of lymph nodes to be filtered. Eventually, the lymph will be passed into **lymphatic ducts**.

## Lymphatic ducts

The lymphatic ducts are known as the ⑬ **thoracic duct** and ⑭ **right lymphatic duct**. The thoracic duct is approximately 40 cm long. Lymph vessels from the lower body join up to form a large lymph vessel called the ⑮ **cisterna chyli**, which leads to the thoracic duct. The cisterna chyli is situated in front of the first two lumbar vertebrae. The thoracic duct is the main collecting duct of the lymphatic system. It receives lymph from the left side of the head, neck and chest, the upper limbs and the whole body beneath the ribs. The thoracic duct drains the lymph directly into the left subclavian vein, so that it is returned back to the blood circulation (Figure 9.7).

The right lymphatic duct is about 1.25 cm long and drains lymph from the upper right hand side of the body. The lymph passes into the right subclavian vein, where it joins the venous blood to become part of the blood circulation once again.

The lymphatic system does not have a pump like the heart but, like veins, relies on the movement of the body and the contraction of the skeletal muscles. The squeezing action of the muscles forces the lymph along its vessels. Involuntary actions, such as breathing and the heartbeat, also help the movement of lymph through the vessels.

Tonsils, adenoids, the appendix and Peyer's patches contain lymphatic tissue. **Tonsils** are found in the throat and **adenoids** are found at the back of the nose. The appendix is found in the lower right-hand abdomen (see Chapter 10). They help to destroy bacteria and other harmful matter as air is taken into the body. **Peyer's patches** are found in the small intestine and also help to destroy harmful substances to prevent infection.

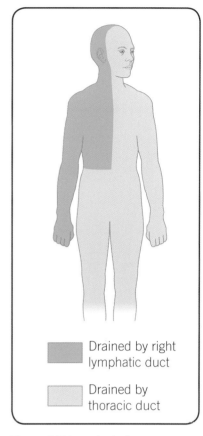

Drained by right lymphatic duct

Drained by thoracic duct

**Figure 9.7** Lymph drainage

## ACTIVITY 9.2

Decide the order of sequence of the events described below and place the correct letter in each box.

**A** Tissue fluid passes into lymphatic capillaries.

**B** Plasma now becomes tissue fluid.

**C** Tissue fluid now becomes lymph.

**D** Tissue fluid provides the cells with nutrients and oxygen.

**E** Plasma in the blood seeps through the capillary walls.

| 1 | 2 | 3 | 4 | 5 |
|---|---|---|---|---|
|   |   |   |   |   |

## The spleen

The spleen consists of lymphatic tissue and is part of the lymphatic system. It is oval in shape and weighs approximately 200g. The spleen is situated in the left side of the abdomen, beneath the diaphragm and behind the stomach. The normal adult spleen is about the size of a large apple.

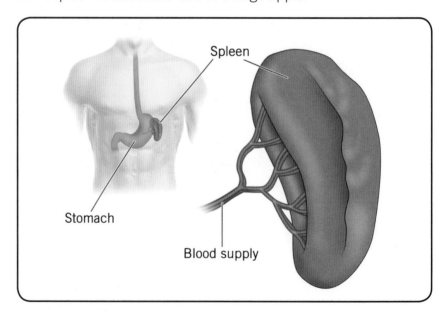

**Figure 9.8** Spleen

**Functions of the spleen**

✖ The spleen acts as a reservoir for blood. If blood is needed elsewhere in the body, perhaps because of a haemorrhage, it can be diverted.

✖ Lymphocytes are produced here, so the spleen is an important part of the immune system. If the spleen has to be removed, resistance to disease may be slightly lowered.

✖ The spleen has a good blood supply. Old, worn-out red blood cells are filtered from the blood and destroyed after their 120-day life.

The spleen can be easily damaged by trauma. If this happens, a haemorrhage can occur so the damaged spleen has to be removed quickly. The body can still survive without it.

## Thymus

The thymus is a small gland made from lymphoid tissue and is found behind the breast bone (sternum). It produces white blood cells and is most active during teenage years, but it shrinks in adulthood (see Chapter 6).

## Immunity

The body's immune system defends us against harmful germs and microorganisms and so helps to prevent infections.

### Natural immunity

Everyone is born with natural immunity. It includes the skin and mucous membranes, which help prevent germs from entering the body. Babies have some natural immunity passed to them by their mother, but this is for a limited time.

### Acquired immunity

This is immunity, also known as active immunity, that develops throughout a person's life and involves the lymphocytes. It develops as people are exposed to diseases,

**ASK FRAN...**

**A.** What causes the symptoms of an allergy?
**Q.** The symptoms are caused by the release of histamine and other allergy mediators into the tissues and blood. It causes widening of surface blood vessels and causes spaces between cells to fill with fluid. A mild case of an allergic reaction may only cause itching and inflammation. Extreme allergic reactions may include difficulty breathing and anaphylactic shock. Anaphylactic shock causes the throat to swell and can be potentially fatal. Treatment involves an injection of adrenalin, which opens the airways and constricts the blood vessels.

such as infections, or vaccinated against diseases. The acquired immune system is responsible for the destruction of foreign particles, also known as **antigens**, once they have entered the body. The first time the antigens invade the body (for example a bacterium or virus), the acquired immune system must learn how to attack and destroy it. The immune system will produce a response to deal with it and will produce memory cells to 'remember' it (the infectious germ), so it will be able to fight it more effectively next time. This is also how vaccines work. They may contain a dead or weakened form of a harmful bacteria or virus. The germ in the vaccine won't cause illness but the body treats it like a real germ. If it comes into contact with it in the future, the immune system will recognise it and effectively fight it so that the person does not become ill.

### Allergy triggers and the body's response

An allergy is an abnormal response by the body's immune system to a foreign substance (allergen). Some people can react to ordinary substances that are normally harmless to people. Allergens include pollen, mould, dust mites, metals, insect stings and food. The parts of the body that are prone to react to allergies include the eyes, nose, lungs, skin and stomach. Symptoms include itching, sneezing, wheezing, hives and nausea.

## Relationship with other body systems

### Circulatory system

Lymph originates from blood, is filtered by the lymphatic system then returned to the blood. The lymphatic system helps to purify the blood.

### Muscular system

The contraction of muscles helps to move lymph along lymph vessels.

### Digestive system

Peyer's patches are found in the small intestine and help to destroy harmful substances to prevent infection. Fats are passed from the small intestine into lymphatic vessels before eventually passing into the bloodstream.

### Immune system

The lymphatic system is an important part of the body's immune system and helps protect us against disease.

## Conditions associated with the lymphatic system

### Cancer

Lymphoma is a cancer of the lymphatic system. The most common type of lymphoma is non-Hodgkin's lymphoma; the other is Hodgkin's lymphoma. Non-Hodgkin's lymphoma is associated with ageing. Hodgkin's lymphoma is one of the most common cancers among younger people. Most young people will be cured of this cancer, although, the cure rate for people over 50 is around 80%.

Both these types of lymphoma cause symptoms such as swellings in lymph nodes, commonly the ones in the neck, armpits or groin, which causes aching. If the cancer is advanced it can cause symptoms such as weight loss, fatigue, night sweats and fever. The exact cause is unknown.

### Cellulitis

Cellulitis is mostly caused by a bacterial skin infection that affects the tissues under the skin. Injury to the skin, such as a cut, graze or burn, can allow bacteria to enter and attack the tissues underneath the skin. Cellulitis commonly affects one of the legs, although symptoms can occur anywhere on the body. It affects the skin and features red, swollen, hot, painful and tender areas. Blisters may also develop on the skin. Other symptoms include shivering, chills and generally feeling unwell.

### Fever

Fever is an increase in the body's temperature in response to a disease or illness. Normal body temperature can vary throughout the day but is highest in the evening. An adult body is feverish when it exceeds temperatures of 38 degrees Celsius (100.4 degrees Fahrenheit). Most bacteria and viruses prefer an environment of 37 degrees Celsius (98.6 degrees Fahrenheit), so the body raises its temperature to help prevent them thriving and causing illness. A fever shows that the body is fighting against the infection or disease. Symptoms of fever include sweating, shivering and general weakness.

### Glandular fever

This is caused by a viral infection (Epstein-Barr virus) and mostly affects young adults. It is spread through saliva and in droplets released while sneezing or coughing. Symptoms include a very painful sore throat, swollen lymph glands and fever.

### Lymphoedema

If the lymphatic system is unable to drain excess fluid from tissues, which can be caused by factors such as infection, injury and cancer, the fluid can build up in the tissues, making them swell. Lymphoedema is a chronic (long-term) condition that usually affects the arms or legs, although other parts of the body, such as the head, chest and genitals, may also be affected. It can cause pain and mobility problems.

### Oedema (fluid retention)

Fluid retention is a common problem in which there is an accumulation of excess fluid in the body tissues. Depending on the cause, it can either be localised (affecting only a certain part of the body) or generalised (affecting the whole body). Fluid retention causes swelling, which is commonly seen around the ankles. It can be differentiated from other types of swelling by the fact that slight pressure will leave a dent in the skin that takes a few seconds to return to normal. It often occurs in women just before a period and also in the last three months of pregnancy. It can also be a symptom of high blood pressure or injury, and a side effect of certain drugs.

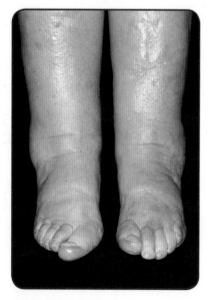

**Figure 9.9** Oedema

# What you should know

## Functions of the lymphatic system

- ☐ Transportation – excess fluid, foreign particles, fats
- ☐ Purification – waste and toxins
- ☐ Protection – antibodies for defence

## Location, structure and function

- ☐ Lymph – leucocytes, lymphocytes, waste products, lymphatic capillaries, lymphatic vessels, lymphatic nodes (superficial and deep cervical, submandibular, axillary, supratrochlear, iliac, inguinal, popliteal)
- ☐ Lymphatic ducts – general, thoracic duct, right lymphatic duct, cisterna chyili

- ☐ Lymphoid tissue – spleen, thymus, tonsils, appendix, Peyer's patches
- ☐ Immunity – antigens, antibodies, acquired immunity, natural immunity, allergy triggers and the body's response.
- ☐ Relationship with other body systems – muscular, digestive, immune
- ☐ Growth and repair (see Chapter 1)

## Pathologies

- ☐ Conditions associated with the lymphatic system, including their causes, signs and symptoms – cancer, fever, cellulitis, rheumatoid arthritis (see Chapter 3), oedema, Hodgkin's lymphoma, non-Hodgkins lymphoma, lymphoedema, glandular fever, lymphadenitis.

# 10 Digestive system and common pathologies

**FAST FACT**

Food takes on average 24 hours to pass through the digestive tract.

The digestive system changes the food we eat into small, simple molecules that can be absorbed into the bloodstream. The body uses these to produce energy or as building materials for repairing itself or growing.

## Digestion

### ACTIVITY 10.1

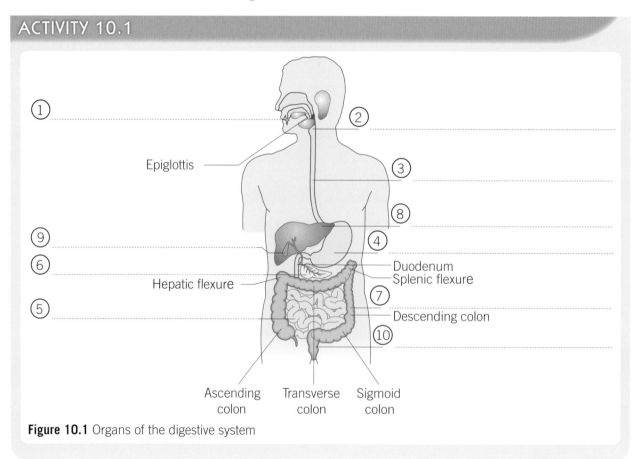

**Figure 10.1** Organs of the digestive system

Epiglottis

Hepatic flexure

Duodenum
Splenic flexure

Descending colon

Ascending colon

Transverse colon

Sigmoid colon

Label the diagram in Figure 10.1, matching the numbers to the numbered terms in the following text. Use this key to colour the organs of the digestive system.

Pink – mouth, oesophagus, stomach, small intestine, large intestine and rectum
Brown – liver
Green – gall bladder
Yellow – pancreas

The digestive tract, also known as the gastrointestinal tract (GIT) or the alimentary canal, is more than 10 metres long; it begins at the mouth and ends at the anus.

## ① Mouth (buccal cavity)

Food and liquids pass through the **lips** into the mouth (**ingestion**). The action of the teeth helps to break down the food during chewing, also called **mastication**. The tongue allows us to taste and sense the texture and temperature of food. It aids with chewing and shapes the foods to allow swallowing.

> **don't forget**
>
> **The adult set of teeth consists of 32 teeth.**

There are three main pairs of **salivary glands** which produce saliva.

✖ The **parotid glands** are located in front of, and below, the ears, between the skin and the masseter muscle.

✖ The **submandibular glands** and **sublingual glands** are found below the tongue.

The saliva lubricates the food and, in most people, contains an enzyme called **salivary amylase**. An enzyme is a protein that speeds up chemical reactions. This enzyme begins the chemical breakdown of starch in cooked foods. Starch is found in foods like bread, potatoes and grains. It breaks it down to a sugar called maltose.

## ② Pharynx

The muscles of the pharynx (throat) push the food down into the **oesophagus** (foodpipe). A flap of cartilage, known as the

**epiglottis**, prevents the food being swallowed and entering the lungs.

## ③ Oesophagus

This is the foodpipe, which is a muscular tube leading to the stomach. The passage of food is aided by the release of mucus from the wall of the oesophagus. The food is propelled downwards towards the stomach by the process of **peristalsis**. Peristalsis is a wave of contractions occurring in the muscles of the oesophagus wall. The walls squeeze and relax to push food along the digestive tract.

## ④ Stomach

This is a muscular, J-shaped, bag-like organ and is made of three layers: the inner oblique, the middle circular, and the outer longitudinal layers, which help to mix and churn the food. It is situated on the left side of the abdominal cavity, beneath the diaphragm. At either end of the stomach is a sphincter muscle, which contracts and relaxes to control the movement of food in and out of the stomach. The cardiac spincter is located at the top of the stomach and prevents food from going back up into the oesphagus. The pyloric sphincter closes the bottom end of the stomach and allows food to pass from the stomach into the duodenum.

**don't forget**

Rennin is an enzyme that curdles milk; it is only found in the stomachs of infants.

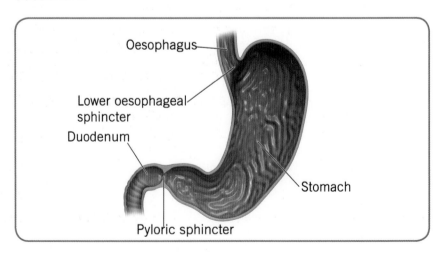

**Figure 10.2** Stomach

The stomach is lined with millions of gastric glands, which release gastric juices to help break down the food. The gastric juices contain hydrochloric acid and enzymes, such as pepsin.

- **Hydrochloric acid** kills any harmful bacteria and helps to dissolve the food.
- **Pepsin** is an enzyme that begins the digestion of protein by breaking it down and turning it into **polypeptides** and **peptones**.

Substances including water, alcohol, aspirin and glucose are absorbed directly into the bloodstream from the stomach. Food stays within the stomach for about five hours and leaves in a liquid form called **chyme**.

## (5) The small intestine

The small intestine is over 6 metres long and is the place where most of the nutrients are absorbed. There are three parts to the small intestine: the first part is called the **duodenum**, followed by the **jejunum** and then the **ileum**. Food in the process of digestion is pushed through the small intestine by peristalsis. In the duodenum, the enzyme **maltase** breaks down each maltose molecule to two molecules of glucose. **Sucrose**, the sugar used as a sweetener, is broken down by the enzyme **sucrase** into glucose and fructose, and **lactose** (milk sugar) is broken down by the enzyme **lactase** into glucose and galactose.

**don't forget**

**A protease is the name for a group of enzymes that can break down a protein. It can break down protein into small molecules, such as peptone, peptide and amino acids. Pepsin and trypsin are examples of proteases.**

The inside of the small intestine is covered with millions of tiny finger-like projections called **villi** (singular: villus). Villi have a rich blood supply and their shape ensures a large surface area so that digested food can be absorbed quickly (see Figure 10.3). Intestinal glands (known as crypts of Lieberkuhn) are attached to the villi and produce digestive enzymes, including maltase and sucrase.

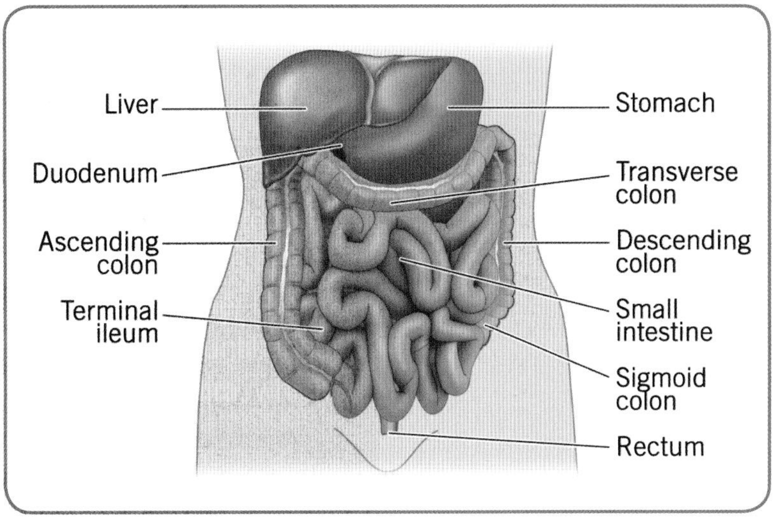
Liver
Duodenum
Ascending colon
Terminal ileum
Stomach
Transverse colon
Descending colon
Small intestine
Sigmoid colon
Rectum

**Figure 10.3** Intestines

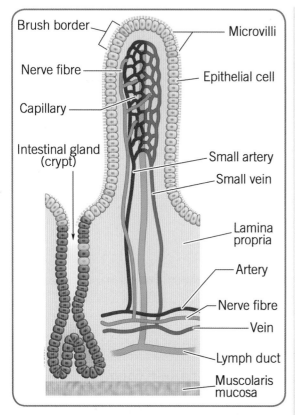

Brush border
Microvilli
Nerve fibre
Epithelial cell
Capillary
Intestinal gland (crypt)
Small artery
Small vein
Lamina propria
Artery
Nerve fibre
Vein
Lymph duct
Muscolaris mucosa

**Figure 10.4** Villus

Proteins are made up of smaller molecules called **amino acids**.

Protein digestion begins in the stomach with the enzyme **pepsin**, which breaks down most proteins into smaller units called **polypeptides**.

In the duodenum, the enzyme **trypsin** (which is converted from **trypsinogen**), found in the pancreatic juice, breaks down proteins and polypeptides into smaller substances called **peptides**. Peptides are broken down by enzymes to become **amino acids**:

Pepsin                          Trypsin

Protein → Polypeptides → Peptides → Amino acids

The nutrients are passed into the bloodstream, with the exception of fat. Fat is absorbed directly into lymphatic capillaries, called **lacteals**, which gives lymph a milky colour. The fat joins the lymphatic system before finally reaching the blood circulation (see Chapter 9).

Organs such as the pancreas and liver also play a part in the digestion of food. The pancreas releases pancreatic juices into the duodenum and is responsible for breaking down protein, carbohydrates and fats. The liver produces **bile**, which also helps to break down fats.

## ⑥ Pancreas

The pancreas is a gland situated behind the stomach and is about 15cm long. As well as releasing hormones, it also produces the following enzymes.

✽ **Trypsin**, which breaks proteins down into amino acids.

✽ **Amylase**, which breaks down carbohydrates (starches) into sugars so they can be more easily absorbed.

✽ **Lipase**, which breaks down fats into **fatty acids** and **glycerol**. Lipase works with bile from the liver to break down fat molecules so they can be absorbed and used by the body.

The pancreas also keeps a check on the amount of glucose in the blood. If the level is too high or too low it produces hormones that stimulate the liver to adjust the balance (see Chapter 6).

## ⑦ Large intestine

The **appendix** is a narrow, worm-like tube closed at one end that leads off from the large intestine and has no known function.

The large intestine is also known as the **colon**; it is called 'large' because of its diameter, not its length. It is about 1.5 metres long and is divided into the **ascending**, **transverse** and **descending colon**. The **caecum** is the first portion of the large intestine and is located in the lower right-hand side of the abdomen. Faecal matter passes from the ileum into it. The appendix is attached to the caecum.

The **hepatic flexure** is found between the ascending and transverse colon, and the **splenic flexure** is found between the transverse and descending colon. The **sigmoid colon** is S-shaped and ends at the sacral vertebrae.

Any remaining undigested food and fibre (non-starch polysaccharides) is now waste matter and passes from the small intestine into the large intestine in liquid form. Any remaining nutrients and water are removed from this waste matter and reabsorbed into the body. This results in solid faeces being formed.

*don't forget*

The ileo-caecal (il-ee-o see-kal) valve lies between the small and large intestine and prevents faeces going in a backwards direction.

*don't forget*

The sigmoid colon is the last intestinal turn before waste is emptied into the rectum. It is an area that is worked on during a reflexology treatment.

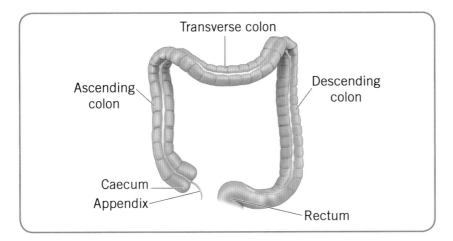

Transverse colon

Ascending colon

Descending colon

Caecum

Appendix

Rectum

**Figure 10.5** Large intestine

The large intestine contains millions of bacteria. These are useful as they produce vitamins B and K, which are absorbed and used by the body. These bacteria also have the ability to ferment some forms of carbohydrate found in foods, such as onions and beans, which are not digested by the enzymes of the small intestine. This fermentation produces large quantities of a gas, termed **flatulence** when it is excessive.

### ACTIVITY 10.2

State the order of sequence for the structure of the large intestine. Place the letters into the correct box.

**A** Hepatic flexure
**B** Sigmoid colon
**C** Ascending colon
**D** Transverse colon
**E** Splenic flexure
**F** Descending colon

| 1 | 2 | 3 | 4 | 5 | 6 |
|---|---|---|---|---|---|
|   |   |   |   |   |   |

### ⑧ Liver

The liver is a large organ found in the upper right corner of the abdomen, extending across to the left side. It lies below the diaphragm and is mostly protected by the ribs.

Most of the blood entering the liver passes through the **hepatic portal vein**, which carries blood from the stomach, intestines, spleen, pancreas and ⑨ **gall bladder**. The blood in the hepatic portal vein carries nutrients such as glucose, amino acids (protein), vitamins and minerals.

### ⑩ Rectum

The rectum is about 13 cm long and has two **sphincter** muscles at the end, which form the **anus**. Waste matter is expelled through the anus. This is called **defecation**.

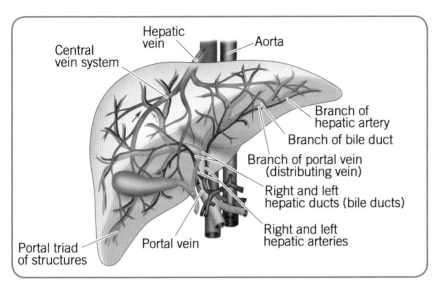

Central
vein system
Hepatic
vein
Aorta
Branch of
hepatic artery
Branch of bile duct
Branch of portal vein
(distributing vein)
Right and left
hepatic ducts (bile ducts)
Right and left
hepatic arteries
Portal vein
Portal triad
of structures

**Figure 10.6** Liver

## ACTIVITY 10.3

Fill in the gaps in the table below.

| Organ | Enzyme or acid | Action |
|---|---|---|
| Mouth | Salivary amylase | |
| Stomach | | Kills bacteria |
| Stomach | Pepsin | |
| Liver | Bile | |
| Pancreas | | Breaks down protein |
| Pancreas | Amylase | |
| Pancreas | | Breaks down fats |

The pear-shaped gall bladder stores **bile**, a greenish fluid produced by the liver. After food has been eaten, bile is released and travels down the **bile duct** to the duodenum. Here, it begins to break down fats into small droplets that are easier for lipase to digest.

## MEMORY JOGGER

Make up flashcards that contain a picture of the structures of the digestive system.

You can keep the cards at hand to regularly test yourself regarding the names and functions of the different structures.

Write the structures and functions of the digestive system on the back of each card so you can refer to it if needed.

### don't forget

Accessory organs are organs that do not make up part of the digestive tract but are helpful for digestion of food. They include the liver, pancreas and salivary glands.

### Functions of the liver

The functions include:

* storing and filtering the blood

* destroying bacteria and worn out red blood cells

* breaking down excess proteins into urea, which is excreted in the urine

* secreting bile to help break down fat

* detoxification of harmful substances, such as alcohol, paracetamol and other chemicals, into safer forms

* storage of vitamins A, D, E and K, and iron

* storage of glycogen, which can be broken down into glucose and used for energy by the body when required

* converting certain nutrients into others – amino acids (protein) can be turned into lipids (fats) or glucose (sugar), if required.

# Nutrition

Food contains substances called **nutrients** found within five basic food groups: protein, carbohydrates, fats, vitamins and minerals. Although fibre (known as non-starch polysaccharide (NSP)) is not nutritionally valuable, it is important for a healthy diet. All foods contain some nutrients, but hardly any food contains all of them.

For the body to remain healthy, a variety of foods need to be eaten (see Table 10.1).

## Sugars

There are two types of carbohydrate: simple and complex. Simple carbohydrates need little digestion and are a quick source of energy, such as fruit and confectionery. Complex carbohydrates take longer to digest and include vegetables, legumes and some grains.

**Table 10.1** Food groups, their effect on the body, and good sources

| Food group | Function | Good sources |
| --- | --- | --- |
| Protein | Vital for growth and repair of cells. | Meat, fish, eggs, milk, cheese |
| Carbohydrates | Provide energy for the body. | Potatoes, bread, sugar, cereals, pasta |
| Fats | Provide energy for the body. | Butter, lard, vegetable oil, cheese |
| Vitamins and minerals | Essential for growth and general health. | Fruit and vegetables |
| Fibre | Helps keep the muscles of the intestines exercised, prevents constipation and provides bulk to satisfy appetite. | Vegetables, fruit, cereals and wholemeal foods |

**Monosaccharides** (simple carbohydrates) are known as **single sugars** or **simple sugars**. They are small, sweet to taste and soluble in water. An example is fructose, found in fruit and honey. The liver converts fructose into glucose. Glucose is very important as all the body's cells require it.

**Disaccharides** (simple carbohydrates) are known as **double sugars**. They are small, sweet to taste and soluble in water. They are formed when two monosaccharides join together. Examples of disaccharides include lactose (the sugar found in milk) and sucrose (found in sugar).

Polysaccharides (complex carbohydrates) are made up of many molecules of monosaccharide. Non-starch polysaccharide (NSP) is dietary fibre. There are two kinds of NSP: soluble and insoluble. Good sources of soluble NSP are oats, pulses, and fruit and vegetables. Good sources of insoluble NSP include wholegrain bread, brown rice, and fruit and vegetables.

## Vitamins

Many foods contain vitamins and minerals, which are important to help maintain health. Vitamins fat soluble or water soluble. Fat soluble vitamins are stored in the fat tissue and liver, and include vitamins A, D, E and K. Water soluble vitamins include B vitamins, vitamin C and folic acid. They are not stored in the body and so must be replaced each day. Excess of these vitamins is lost through urination. See Table 10.2 for information regarding important vitamins.

**Table 10.2** Vitamins

| Vitamins | Best sources | Functions | Deficiency signs |
|---|---|---|---|
| Vitamin A Retinol | Fish liver oils, dairy products, liver, eggs, vegetables and fruit | Needed for normal vision, even in dim light. Required for teeth and bone formation. Helps protect against infections. | Night blindness, dry, rough skin and reduced resistance to infection. |
| Vitamin $B_1$ Thiamine | Wholegrain cereals, brown rice, wholemeal bread, nuts, eggs, fish and milk | Helps convert carbohydrate into energy. | Loss of appetite, lack of concentration, muscle weakness and depression. |
| Vitamin $B_2$ Riboflavin | Wheat bran, leafy green vegetables, peas and beans, meat, eggs and milk | Releases energy from carbohydrates, proteins and fats. Maintains healthy skin. | Cracked lips, soreness of mouth and tongue, dermatitis, hair loss, blurred vision and dizziness. |
| Vitamin $B_3$ Niacin | Wholegrain cereals, peas, beans, nuts, meat, eggs and fish | Helps to release energy from fats and glucose. Maintains healthy skin, nervous and digestive systems. | Rare. Loss of appetite, weight loss, nausea, depression. |
| Vitamin $B_5$ Pantothenic acid | Most foods, especially wholegrain cereals, wheatgerm, green vegetables, nuts, eggs and fish | Helps to release energy from fats and carbohydrates. Beneficial for the nervous system. Converts cholesterol into anti-stress hormones. | Exhaustion, abdominal pain, headache, cramps, more prone to infections. |
| Vitamin $B_6$ Pyridoxine | Most foods, wholegrain cereals, wheatgerm, green vegetables, nuts, eggs and fish | Needed for metabolism of carbohydrates, protein and fat, production of antibodies to fight infection, healthy skin | Skin problems, cracked lips, possibly PMS, depression, and kidney stones. |

| Vitamins | Best sources | Functions | Deficiency signs |
|---|---|---|---|
| Vitamin B$_{12}$ Cyanocobalamin | Liver, meat, (pork, beef) fish, animal products | Detoxifies cyanide brought into the body by smoking and food. | Pernicious anaemia, nerve damage so causes tremors, mental deterioration, menstrual disorder, pigmentation of the hands, tiredness. |
| Vitamin C | Citrus fruits, broccoli, peppers, tomatoes | Needed for healthy bones, teeth and gums, resistance against infection and for the body to absorb iron. | Aches, pains, swollen gums, nose bleeds, anaemia, scurvy, haemorrhaging. |
| Vitamin D | Fish, cod liver oil, liver, eggs, dairy products and margarine | Needed for strong bones and teeth, blood clotting, muscle and nerve function. | Rickets in children, osteomalacia in adults, weakened bones, restlessness, poor muscle tone. |
| Vitamin E | Vegetable oils, egg yolks, wheatgerm, nuts, wholegrain cereals, leafy green vegetables | Slows down ageing by protecting cell membranes. Needed for the formation of red blood cells. | Rare. Anaemia and destruction of red blood cells. |

## Fats

There is a lot of hidden fat in the snacks we eat (biscuits, crisps, chocolate). When the body has too much fat, it is stored under the skin as adipose tissue and can be broken down to make energy if required. The body needs some fats to:

✖ protect the organs

✖ transport fat-soluble vitamins

✖ provide insulation and energy.

There are two main types of fat.

✖ **Saturated fat** is found in animal products such as meat, butter and full-fat cheese. These fats are the most

**FAST FACT ❯**

Coconut oil and palm oil, although derived from plants, also contain saturated fats.

damaging to health as saturated fat is converted to cholesterol by the body. This may cause raised levels of bad blood cholesterol, which clog up the arteries and lead to heart disease and strokes.

✖ **Unsaturated fats** are derived from plants. There are two kinds of unsaturated fats: monounsaturated and polyunsaturated. Monounsaturated are the healthier choice as they are said to lower bad blood cholesterol. Olive oil and rapeseed oil are good sources.

## Minerals

The body uses minerals to carry out various functions including building bones, transmitting nerve impulses and producing hormones. See Table 10.3 for more information regarding important minerals.

**Table 10.3** Minerals

| Mineral | Functions | Where it can be found |
| --- | --- | --- |
| Calcium | Needed for teeth and bones; essential for blood clotting and for muscle and nerve function. | Milk and other dairy products, fish and leafy green vegetables |
| Phosphorus | Needed for bones, teeth and nerve and muscle function. | Meat, cereal, dairy products |
| Potassium | Influences nerve function and muscle contraction. | Fruit, vegetables and grains |
| Sodium | Important in fluid balance and the passing of impulses between neurones, also important in muscle contraction. | Many foods, table salt |
| Magnesium | Needed for muscle and nerve function and for bones and teeth. | Nuts, whole grains, leafy green vegetables |
| Iron | Part of haemoglobin, which carries oxygen in red blood cells. | Meat, nuts, egg yolk, dried fruit |
| Iodine | Needed for the production of thyroid hormones. | Seafood, salt, vegetables grown in iodine-rich soils |

# Relationships with other body systems

## Circulatory system

The digestive system changes the food we eat into small, simple molecules that can be absorbed into the bloodstream. They can be used by the body to produce energy or as building materials for repairing itself or growing.

## Endocrine system

The pancreas keeps a check on the amount of glucose in the blood. If the level is too high or too low it produces hormones that stimulate the liver to adjust the balance.

## Lymphatic system

The nutrients are passed into the bloodstream, with the exception of fat. Fat is absorbed directly into lymphatic capillaries, called lacteals, and gives lymph a milky colour. The fat joins the lymphatic system before finally reaching the blood circulation.

## Muscular system

The muscles of the pharynx (throat) push the food down into the oesophagus (foodpipe).

The food is propelled downwards towards the stomach by the process of peristalsis. Peristalsis is a wave of contractions occurring in the muscles of the digestive tract. The walls squeeze and relax to push food along the digestive tract. Sphincter muscles help to control the passage of food.

## Nervous system

Nerve messages are sent from the brain to control the organs of the digestive system.

# Conditions associated with the digestive system

## Anorexia nervosa

This is a condition in which sufferers are obsessed with not eating and have a phobia concerning body fat.

## Appendicitis

Appendicitis is inflammation of the appendix. Too much bacteria in the appendix can cause infection leading to swelling and pain. It can be dangerous if the appendix bursts, so it is removed.

## Bowel cancer

Bowel cancer may occur in the colon or rectum. In the later stages of this disease symptoms include: blood in the faeces, which may be tar-like; a change in bowel habits, such as diarrhoea or constipation, for a period of more than six weeks; there may also be weight loss. Most cases of bowel cancer develop from growths in bowel known as polyps. The exact cause is unclear, but people have a higher chance of getting it if they have a poor diet, do not exercise regularly, are overweight and have close family members with bowel cancer.

## Bulimia nervosa

This involves the sufferer alternately binge eating and vomiting, or purging with laxatives and diuretics.

## Cirrhosis

Cirrhosis is a liver disease caused by cell damage. There is a gradual build-up of scarred tissue that prevents the liver from functioning normally to remove toxins from the blood. It is often caused by a high alcohol intake.

## Coeliac disease

Coeliac (cee-lee-ak) disease is caused by sensitivity to the protein gluten; it often runs in families. Gluten is found in three types of cereal: wheat, barley and rye. It is an ingredient in many foods, including bread. When sufferers eat gluten it results in damage to the lining of the small intestine, which prevents the absorption of nutrients. Severe stress, physical injury, infection, pregnancy or surgery may lead to symptoms developing. Symptoms include diarrhoea, abdominal pain, malnutrition, tiredness, anaemia, mouth ulcers and weight loss.

## Diarrhoea and constipation

✖ **Diarrhoea** is the passing of frequent, loose, watery stools. It results when the contents of the bowel pass through too quickly so there is insufficient time for the water to be absorbed. Diarrhoea can be caused by stress, eating certain foods, food poisoning or drinking too much alcohol. It is the body's way of getting rid of harmful substances in the colon.

✖ If the contents remain too long in the colon, too much water is withdrawn from the faeces resulting in **constipation**. This includes the passing of hard stools, often with difficulty. A common cause of constipation is lack of roughage in the diet.

## Diverticulitis

Diverticulitis is a disorder that affects the lining of the large intestine. There are small pouches, called diverticula, that stick out of the side of weakened areas of the large intestine. The diverticula can become infected and inflamed, causing diverticulitis. The symptoms of diverticulitis include severe abdominal pain and fever. There is a risk of serious complications, including rupturing of the large intestine, which may cause an infection of the lining of the abdomen, which is known as peritonitis. A person with diverticulitis may be treated with antibiotics.

## Gallstones

These are stones made mostly from cholesterol and are found in the gall bladder. A stone may block the flow of bile, causing inflammation. Symptoms include pain in the upper right abdomen, nausea, indigestion and jaundice. It is believed to be caused by an imbalance in the chemical make-up of bile inside the gall bladder, which leads to stone formation.

## Gingivitis (gum disease)

This disease features red and inflamed gums, which may bleed when brushed. It is commonly caused by plaque build-up on the teeth. Good oral hygiene and not smoking can help prevent it occurring.

## Heartburn

This is the result of stomach acid flowing into the oesophagus, causes a burning pain in the foodpipe and chest. It can be caused by overeating, too much alcohol, stress and pregnancy.

## Hernia

When a part of the body, such as an organ, pushes through a weakness in a muscle or surrounding tissue wall, a hernia can result. Muscles are usually strong enough to keep the organs in position, but if they become weak a hernia may occur.

✖ An **abdominal hernia** can occur during exercise, especially lifting a heavy weight, and puts strain on the abdominal wall. The hernia can be seen bulging through the abdominal wall and causes pain.

✖ A **hiatus hernia** results when part of the stomach ends up above the diaphragm; it protrudes through a space usually occupied by the oesophagus.

## Indigestion (dyspepsia)

Indigestion is a pain or discomfort in the upper region of the abdomen and is mostly associated with eating, although it can be caused by an infection or certain medicines. Stomach acid leaks from the stomach and breaks down the protective lining (mucosa) of the digestive tract. This causes irritation and inflammation.

## Irritable bowel syndrome (IBS)

Irritable bowel syndrome (IBS) is a common condition that features bouts of stomach cramps, bloating, diarrhoea, flatulence and constipation. It will often improve after emptying the bowels. Sufferers will often find they have to urgently use a toilet. The exact cause is unknown, but factors including certain types of food, such as spicy foods, alcohol and stress can bring on bouts of IBS. There is no cure, but the condition is not dangerous. The symptoms can often be relieved by changing both diet and lifestyle.

## Jaundice

This is a symptom of various disorders, including hepatitis. It refers to the yellowing of the skin and the whites of the eyes. In bile there is a pigment called **bilirubin**, which gives faeces its brown colouring. If the liver is diseased or the bile ducts are blocked, the bilirubin cannot get out. Therefore, it gradually accumulates in the blood and stains the tissues, giving the skin its yellow colouring.

## Obesity

A person is considered to be obese if their body mass index (BMI) is 30 or over. Obesity is related to diseases such as hypertension, heart disease and diabetes. Experts predict that by 2025 nearly half of men and over a third of women in the UK will be obese.

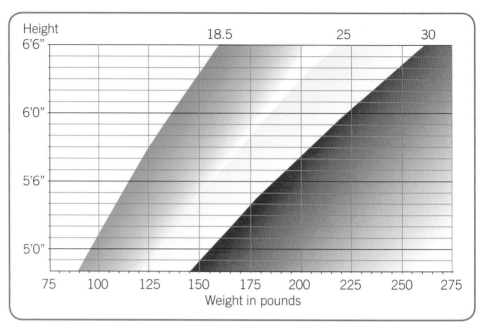

**Figure 10.7** BMI (Body Mass index)

## Reflux oesophagitis

Acid reflux occurs when stomach acid leaks out into the oesophagus, which may cause oesophagitis (inflammation of the oesophagus). Symptoms include heartburn, nausea, discomfort in the chest and upper abdomen.

## Ulcers

### Peptic/duodenal ulcers

A peptic ulcer is an open sore found on the inside lining of the stomach (known as a gastric ulcer), and causes a burning pain in the stomach. Duodenal ulcers are found in the duodenum. Both types of ulcer are referred to as peptic ulcers. These ulcers are commonly caused by a bacterium called *H. pylori*. Painkillers, such as aspirin, may also cause ulcers as they irritate the stomach and small intestine lining.

### Aphthous ulcers

These are mouth ulcers, which are often painful but usually disappear within 14 days. Their cause is unknown.

# What you should know

## Functions of the digestive system

☐ Indigestion, mechanical and chemical breakdown of food, digestion, absorption of nutrients, defecation

## Location, structure and function

☐ Mouth, buccal cavity, lips, teeth, tongue, pharynx, epiglottis, oesophagus, salivary glands, stomach, cardiac sphincter, pyloric sphincter, oblique muscle layer

☐ Small intestine – duodenum, jejunum, ileum, villi

☐ Large intestine – ileo-caecal valve, caecum, ascending colon, transverse colon, descending colon, rectum, anus, anal sphincter

☐ Accessory digestive organs – gastric glands, pancreas, intestinal glands, liver, gall bladder

☐ Process of physical digestion – mastication, peristalsis, churning

☐ Process of chemical digestion – proteases, lipases, amylases

☐ Process of absorption of nutrients – proteins, peptones, polypeptides, amino acids, carbohydrates, monosaccharides, disaccharides, polysaccharides, fats, fatty acids, glycerol

☐ Relationship with other body systems – circulatory, endocrine, lymphatic, muscular, nervous

☐ Growth and repair (see Chapter 1)

## Pathologies

☐ Conditions associated with the digestive system, including their causes, signs and symptoms – heartburn, indigestion, irritable bowel syndrome, constipation, diarrhoea, gallstones, coeliac disease, ulcers, bowel cancer, gingivitis, reflux oesophagitis, obesity

# 11 Urinary system and common pathologies

The urinary system filters the blood and produces urine to ensure that the body gets rid of unwanted substances that could be harmful. It consists of two ① **kidneys**, two ② **ureters**, the ③ **bladder** and the ④ **urethra**.

## ACTIVITY 11.1

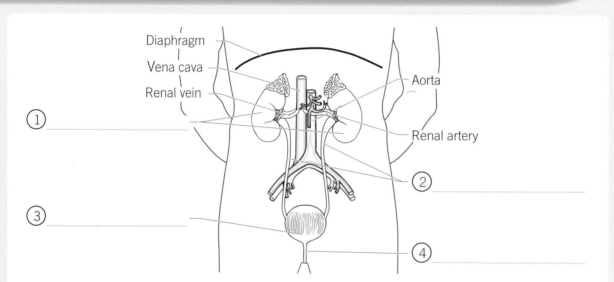

**Figure 11.1** The urinary system

Label the diagram in Figure 11.1, matching the numbers to the numbered terms in the text above. Use this key to colour the diagram.

Brown – kidneys and ureters
Yellow – bladder and urethra

Red – arteries
Blue – veins

# The kidneys

The kidneys are two bean-shaped organs. Each would almost cover the area of a small hand and is about 2 cm thick. They are positioned in the lower back, are mostly protected by the ribs, and are surrounded by a thick layer of fat.

The kidney is surrounded by a tough layer called the **renal capsule** and is divided into the outer **cortex** and the inner **medulla**. The medulla contains about 14 triangular **pyramids**. The tip of each pyramid contains a cup-shaped **calyx** (plural: calyces), which opens into the **renal pelvis**.

The word 'renal' means 'belonging to the kidney'. The renal pelvis is an open space that connects the medulla to the ureter. The **renal artery** and **renal vein** carry blood to and from the kidneys (Figure 11.2).

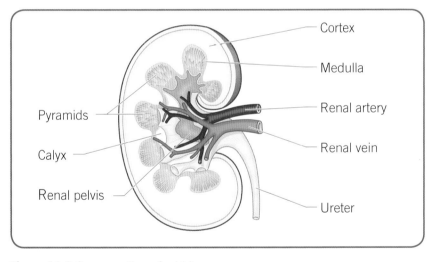

Cortex

Medulla

Renal artery

Renal vein

Pyramids

Calyx

Renal pelvis

Ureter

**Figure 11.2** Cross section of a kidney

## Functions of the kidney

The functions of the kidneys are to:

✖ filter the blood; in other words, to clean it and get rid of any unwanted substances (waste). Many of these substances are toxic and would result in death if they were allowed to accumulate in the body

✖ control the balance of water, salt and potassium levels (electrolytes) in the body. (The balance of electrolytes in the body is important for the normal function of cells and organs)

✖ produce a hormone called erythropoietin, which stimulates the bone marrow to make red blood cells

✖ help control blood pressure by controlling the blood volume in the body and by releasing an enzyme called **renin** into the blood

✖ control blood pH (acid/alkaline level). The normal pH of the blood is around 7.4. All the enzymes in the body can only work if the normal pH is maintained.

## Filtering the blood

A kidney contains about a million filtration units called **nephrons** (nef-rons), in which urine is formed. There are three parts to a nephron:

✖ the ① **proximal coiled tubule**

✖ the ② **loop of Henle**

✖ the ③ **distal coiled tubule**.

Each nephron is joined to a ④ **collecting duct**. The coiled tubules of the nephron lie in the cortex, and the loops of Henle and collecting ducts lie in the medulla. The collecting ducts open into the renal pelvis (Figure 11.3). ⑤ Afferent arterioles are a group of blood vessels that branch from the renal artery and supply the nephrons.

## ACTIVITY 11.2

Label the diagram in Figure 11.3, matching the numbers to the numbered terms in the text on page 272.

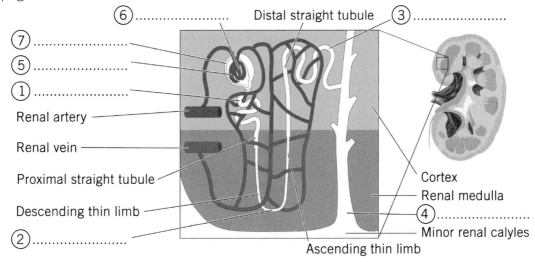

**Figure 11.3** Structure of a nephron

# Processes involved in the formation of urine

There are three important processes involved in the formation of urine: filtration, reabsorption and secretion.

## 1. Filtration

Blood enters the nephron through bundles of capillaries called the ⑥ **glomerulus** (glow-mare-roo-lus) (plural: glomeruli). The glomerulus is surrounded by the ⑦ **Bowman's capsule**. The blood is brought at high pressure to the nephron, so water, amino acids, salt, glucose and waste products, such as urea, are squeezed through the walls of the blood vessels into the Bowman's capsule. The efferent arteriole drains blood away from the glomerulus.

## 2. Reabsorption

The resulting fluid flows along the nephron and substances needed by the body, such as glucose, amino acids, salt and most of the water, are reabsorbed into the bloodstream

### don't forget

Blood cells and proteins are too big to pass through the capillary walls so they remain within the bloodstream.

through nearby capillaries. The remaining water and waste products eventually reach the collecting duct of the nephron and become urine. The urine passes into the pelvis of the kidney. Waves of contraction in the pelvis walls force the urine into the ureter, which then passes it into the bladder.

### 3. Secretion

Substances, such as toxins and excess ions (sodium and potassium), pass from the blood and move into the distal and collecting tubules, where they mix with water and other wastes and become urine.

### Waste products

Unlike iron and certain vitamins, the liver cannot store excess proteins. The liver breaks down these extra proteins, which results in the formation of a waste product called **urea**. Urea is toxic to the body and is passed into the bloodstream to be filtered by the kidneys and excreted in the urine. The kidneys also excrete other waste products called **creatinine** and **uric acid**.

## Control of fluid balance

Two-thirds of the body is made up of water, which is provided by the food and drink we consume. It is excreted from the body through urine, faeces, sweat and the breath. It is important for the body to balance the amount of water coming in with the amount of water leaving it.

The kidneys help to control this balance by removing water from the blood vessels that enter them and producing urine. They do this without affecting the other important substances in the blood.

The kidneys, under the influence of a hormone called antidiuretic hormone (see Chapter 6), control the amount of water excreted from the body. When extra water is needed by the body, for instance on a hot day when a person is active, there is increased sweating, so if little water is drunk, the kidneys return (reabsorb) water into the bloodstream rather than releasing it as urine. This ensures that the balance of water in the body is maintained (see Chapter 6). When there is too much water in the body, the kidneys release it as urine.

## Control of salt levels

Sodium (salt) is taken into the body through food and is absorbed into the bloodstream. If there is too much sodium in the body, such as after eating a salty meal, the kidneys remove the excess from the blood. This restores sodium levels to normal. Eating too much salt tends to raise the blood pressure and results in an increase in urine output. The amount of sodium excreted by the body is controlled by the hormone **aldosterone** from the adrenal gland.

## Control of potassium levels

Potassium is a mineral mostly found inside cells. It has many functions, which include:

✖ maintaining the proper acid/alkaline balance in the body

✖ helping with the passing of nerve impulses

✖ enabling muscle contraction to take place.

The hormone aldosterone also helps to control the levels of potassium in the body.

# The ureters

Urine is formed in the kidneys and consists of 96 per cent water, 2 per cent urea and 2 per cent other substances, including sodium (salt), potassium, ammonia, phosphates, sulphates, chlorides and surplus vitamins. It passes from the kidneys into two tubes called the **ureters**. The ureters are about 30 cm long and join on to the back of the bladder. The colour of the urine is produced by a bile pigment called bilirubin.

## ASK FRAN...

**Q.** Why does drinking alcohol cause more frequent urination?

**A.** When we drink alcohol, it enters the bloodstream and causes the pituitary gland in the brain (see Chapter 6) to block the production of a hormone called antidiuretic hormone (ADH). This hormone causes the body to conserve water by reducing the loss of water in urine. As alcohol interferes with the release of this hormone, it means that the drinker urinates more often.

# The bladder

Urine is stored in a muscular sac called the bladder. When a sufficient amount of urine is collected in the bladder, a message is sent to the brain and the desire to urinate (**micturate**) will be produced. The bladder wall contracts and a sphincter muscle at the base of the bladder relaxes. Fortunately, the release of urine can be controlled voluntarily by another sphincter muscle found at the bottom of the urethra. Small children do not have voluntary control over this particular sphincter muscle, hence the need for nappies.

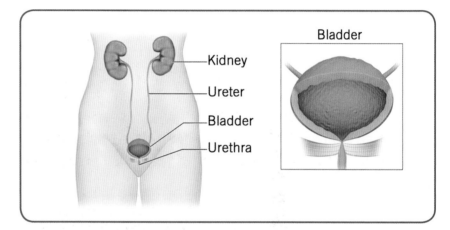

**Figure 11.4** The bladder

# The urethra

The urethra is a narrow tube leading from the bladder to outside the body; it is shorter in females than males. It acts as a passageway for urine and for sperm in males.

## Relationship with other body systems

### Circulatory system
The kidneys filter the blood to clean it and get rid of unwanted substances. They also produce renin, which helps to regulate blood pressure.

### Endocrine system

Antidiuretic hormone is released to help reabsorb water into the circulation. This helps the body to conserve water and reduces the loss of water in urine.

### Skeletal system

The kidneys can produce a hormone that stimulates bone marrow to make red blood cells.

### Integumentary system

Water is lost from the body by sweating through the skin, which may result in decreased output of urine.

# Massage and the urinary system

The kidneys are mostly protected by the ribs and by muscles, and they are deeply embedded in fat. They are delicate organs so care has to be taken when massaging so as not to apply too much pressure.

## Conditions associated with the urinary system

### Bladder stones

Bladder stones are small stones that are produced inside the bladder. These may occur if urine remains in the bladder for a long time. Chemicals contained in the urine will begin to form crystals, which will join and harden to form bladder stones.

They may cause irritation to the wall of the bladder and affect the flow of urine out of the bladder. Symptoms include pain in the lower abdomen and when urinating, more frequent urination and blood in the urine. The sufferer will probably require surgery, which involves using a laser to break up the stones.

### Cystitis

This is an infection of the bladder lining often caused by a bacterial infection. It is more common in women than men because of the shortness of the woman's urethra. It causes an urgent and frequent need to urinate and also pain or stinging when urinating. Mild cystitis can be treated by drinking lots of water and taking painkillers. Severe cystitis may cause abdominal pain or fever, and may require antibiotic treatment.

**Glomerulonephritis (glow-mare-roo-low-nef-rye-tis)**
A bacterial infection may lead to this condition in which the body's antibodies attack the glomeruli. There is inflammation of the walls of the glomeruli, which causes the permeability of these walls to increase. Therefore, blood cells and protein, which usually stay within the capillaries, are able to pass into the urine. Symptoms include swelling of the tissues of the body (oedema), loss of appetite, vomiting and headache. The glomeruli may be permanently damaged, leading to kidney failure.

**Incontinence**
Incontinence involves the loss of bladder control. There is a leakage of urine, which occurs because of problems with the muscles and nerves that help to hold or release urine. More women than men suffer with it and risk factors include childbirth. There are different types of incontinence, but the most common are:

✖ stress incontinence: the pelvic floor muscles are not strong enough to hold the urine, so cause urine to leak in situations such as coughing or laughing

✖ urge incontinence: urine is released as soon as an individual feels the desire to urinate.

Pelvic floor exercises (squeezing the muscles that are used to control the flow of urine) and losing weight can significantly help.

**Kidney cancer**
Kidney cancer mostly affects people between 50 and 80 years old. Symptoms include blood in the urine, pain in the kidney region and a lump in the abdomen. The main risks for kidney cancer include smoking, high blood pressure and obesity.

## Kidney stones

Urine contains many salts and, if little urine is being produced, these salts can crystallise, like salt water left to evaporate. More and more of the salts crystallise and form layers until a stone is made. A small stone can enter the ureter and cause severe pain. It may pass naturally or surgery may be required to remove it.

## Nephritis (Bright's disease)

Nephritis is inflammation of one or both kidneys. Symptoms include decreased urine production, increased blood pressure, swelling of body tissues and fatigue. It may be caused by an infection or conditions such as pneumonia, measles or glandular fever.

## Renal failure

Renal (kidney) failure is the loss of kidney function. **Acute** kidney failure is the rapid loss of kidney function, for example through injury. However, **chronic** kidney failure develops over months and years. The most common causes of chronic renal failure include poorly controlled diabetes and poorly controlled high blood pressure.

## Urethritis

This is inflammation of the urethra and is commonly caused by an infection. Symptoms in men include a burning sensation when urinating, and the tip of the penis may feel sore. Women may experience vaginal discharge and pain in the lower abdomen. The condition is usually treated with antibiotics.

## Urinary tract infections

A urinary tract infection (UTI) affects the urinary tract and causes increased urination, pain and soreness while urinating, and discomfort in the lower abdomen. It is commonly caused by bacteria that have spread from the anus to the urethra, and so results in an infection. Treatment involves a course of antibiotics.

# What you should know

## Functions of the urinary system

- [ ] Distribution of intracellular and extracellular fluid – fluid balance in the body
- [ ] Balance fluid intake with fluid output – fluid balance in the body
- [ ] General electrolyte composition and balance – sodium and potassium
- [ ] Maintain pH values of the body's fluid systems
- [ ] Regulation of blood pressure

## Location, structure and function

- [ ] Kidneys – capsule, cortex, medulla, pyramids, calyces
- [ ] Nephron – afferent and efferent arterioles, glomerulus, Bowman's capsule, glomerulus proximal coiled tubule, loop of Henle, distal coiled tubule, collecting duct

- [ ] Ureters, bladder, urethra, urine production – filtration, reabsorption, active secretion
- [ ] Factors affecting urine production – cold and hot weather, activity and inactivity, stress, water consumption
- [ ] Urine composition – urea, uric acid, ammonia, salts, water
- [ ] Relationship with other body systems – circulatory, endocrine, skeletal, integumentary
- [ ] Growth and repair (see Chapter 1)

## Pathologies

- [ ] Conditions associated with the urinary system, including their causes, signs and symptoms – cystitis, incontinence, renal failure, kidney stones, bladder stones, nephritis, UTI, urethritis.

# Reproductive system and common pathologies 12

The reproductive systems of men and women ensure that new human life can be created. This can only happen when a woman's ovum (egg) is fertilised by a man's sperm.

The female reproductive system consists of a uterus (womb), two Fallopian tubes and two ovaries. In the male, the organs include the testes (which are protected in a sac called the **scrotum**), the **vas deferens** and the penis.

The female reproductive organs are situated within the pelvic cavity – the pelvic bones help to protect them. The pelvic cavity is wider in the female than the male to allow more space for childbirth. The male reproductive organs are found outside the body cavity because the testes need to be kept a couple of degrees cooler than normal body temperature to produce fertile sperm.

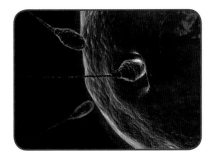

**Figure 12.1** Sperm and egg

# Female reproductive system

When the ovum has been fertilised, a process known as **conception**, it attaches itself to the lining of the uterus. The fertilised ovum is now called a **zygote** and grows to become a baby. The gestation period is around 40 weeks.

The reproductive system contains two (1) **ovaries**, which are about 3 cm long. These glands are found either side of the uterus. Their function is to release the hormones oestrogen and progesterone and to produce (2) **ova** (eggs).

When an ovum (plural: ova) is released it enters the ③ **Fallopian tube**. The Fallopian tubes act as a passageway for sperm to reach the ovum, and it is here that the ovum becomes fertilised.

The ovum enters the ④ **uterus** along the Fallopian tube. The pear-shaped uterus is located in the centre of the pelvic cavity, the bladder being in front and the rectum behind. The uterus connects with the vagina.

The ⑤ **cervix** (neck of the uterus) is a short and narrow passageway found at the bottom end of the uterus. It dilates during childbirth; the amount of dilation can be measured to indicate how soon the baby will be born.

The cervix opens into the ⑥ **vagina**, which serves as a passageway for childbirth and for menstrual flow. Two pairs of skin flaps, called the labia majora and labia minora, surround the vaginal opening. The clitoris is found where the folds of labia join. The external part of the female reproductive organs is called the vulva. The vestibule is the space between the labia minora. The greater vestibule glands are located on each side of the vestibule of the vagina. These glands secrete a small amount of

> **don't forget**
>
> The vulva is the term used to describe the external female genitalia.

## ACTIVITY 12.1

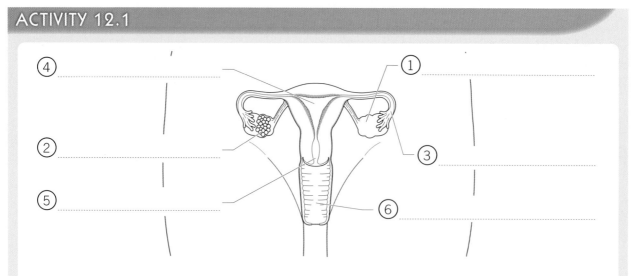

④ ............

② ............

⑤ ............

① ............

③ ............

⑥ ............

**Figure 12.2** The female reproductive organs

Label the diagram in Figure 12.1, matching the numbers to the numbered terms in the text on pages 281–282. Use yellow to colour the ovaries and ova, and brown for the Fallopian tubes, uterus and cervix.

lubricating mucus into the vestibule of the vagina during sexual arousal.

The **perineum** is an area found between the opening of the vagina and the anus; muscles of the pelvic floor are attached to it.

# The menstrual cycle

The pituitary gland, hypothalamus and ovaries play a part in controlling female reproduction. A typical menstrual cycle is about 28 days long and occurs in stages: the follicular phase, ovulation and the luteal phase.

## Follicular phase

This phase begins from the first day of the menstruation until ovulation. **Menstruation** (bleeding) lasts for about five days and is caused by the thickened **endometrium** (lining of the uterus) breaking away. Oestrogen stimulates the growth of the endometrium and of follicles that encase the eggs (when fully grown they are known as **Graafian follicles**). An ovum is produced and matures and the uterus is prepared for pregnancy.

The release of an egg (**ovulation**) typically occurs around 14 days into the cycle. An increase in oestrogen causes a surge in the amount of luteinising hormone (see Chapter 6) from the brain, which stimulates an egg to be released from the ovary. The egg is carried along the Fallopian tube.

## Luteal phase (also known as secretory phase)

After ovulation, the luteal phase occurs, which involves the ruptured follicle (which had released the egg) to produce a structure called the **corpus luteum**. This structure releases progesterone and oestrogen, which encourage continued thickening of the endometrium in preparation for pregnancy. If

**FAST FACT >**

The eggs carry the X chromosome but sperm may carry either an X or Y chromosome. If the sperm is carrying an X chromosome, the baby will be a girl. If it is carrying a Y chromosome, it will be a boy.

**FAST FACT >**

The cervix dilates during childbirth; the amount of dilation can be measured to indicate how soon the baby will be born.

**FAST FACT >**

The proliferative phase is from day six of the menstrual cycle (end of menstruation) to the fourteen day (beginning of ovulation).

pregnancy does not occur, the corpus luteum begins to break down, causing progesterone and oestrogen levels to fall. The egg passes through the uterus and the uterus lining breaks down causing menstruation to begin once again.

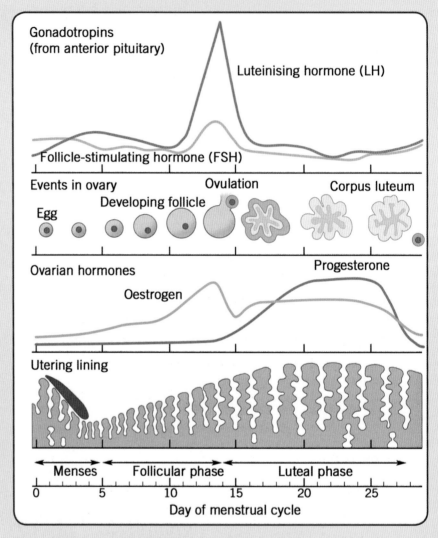

**Figure 12.3** The menstrual cycle

## Stages of pregnancy

### Fertilisation

Fertilisation occurs when a sperm meets and penetrates the egg. This is known as conception. This fertilisation creates a cell called a **zygote**. A thick wall is then made to help prevent another sperm penetrating the egg.

### Post-fertilisation

The zygote divides into further cells and travels to the uterus. The placenta is formed from the outer layer of cells; the inner cells eventually form the foetus. The cells continue to divide and will make the hormone human chorionic gonadotrophin (HCG), which sends a message to the corpus luteum to keep on producing progesterone. (If progesterone production stops, the lining of the uterus breaks down and menstrual bleeding begins.) An **embryo** is formed in the second week after conception.

## Foetal development

At four weeks the body organs are beginning to develop. A neural tube is formed and will become the baby's brain and spinal cord. Defects in this tube are the cause of spina bifida. In early pregnancy women are advised to consume around 400 micrograms (0.4 mg) of folic acid each day, as this vitamin can help to reduce the risk of the baby having a spinal cord problem, such as spina bifida. Women planning a pregnancy are often advised to take a folic acid supplement.

At around eight weeks the baby is about the size of a kidney bean and is continually moving. The arms and legs are formed, and slightly webbed fingers are visible. The face is also beginning to form.

At 12 weeks it is about 8 cm (3 in) long. The foetus is fully formed, including the sexual organs, and it will have also have fingerprints. At 14 weeks the heartbeat is strong and can be picked up by an ultrasound detector.

At 16 weeks it is about 13 cm (5.5 in) long. Its bones are hardening and are changing from cartilage to bone. The heart and blood vessels are formed.

At 20 weeks it is about 27 cm (10.5 inches) long if the legs are stretched out. The baby can suck its thumb, yawn, stretch and make facial expressions. Eyebrows and eyelids are formed. At 22 weeks the baby becomes covered in very fine hair called lanugo, which generally disappears before birth.

*don't forget*

A normal pregnancy lasts for around 40 weeks and is divided into three trimesters.

At 24 weeks the baby becomes plumper and the wrinkled skin becomes smooth.

At 28 weeks the baby is about 40 cm (15 in) long and can open and close its eyes.

Between 32 and 40 weeks the lungs are well-developed and the baby is becoming plumper. Its head is usually downwards and at some point before birth the head moves down into the pelvis, this is called being 'engaged', in preparation for the birth.

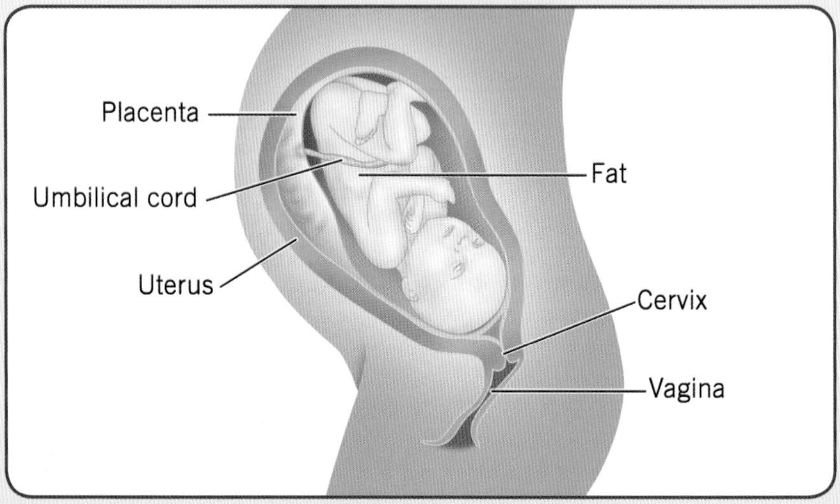

**Figure 12.4** Baby in the uterus

FAST FACT

A pregnancy test measures human chorionic gonadotrophin hormone in the urine or blood.

don't forget

The term menstruation refers to the monthly shedding of the uterus lining. (Menstru means monthly)

Childbirth includes labour and delivery, and is also known as **parturition**.

## Effects of female menopause

The menopause usually affects women between the ages of 45 and 55, and occurs owing to a decrease in oestrogen and progesterone levels (see Chapter 6). Many women experience unpleasant symptoms such as hot flushes, which may be followed by chills. They may suffer with mood changes and depression, insomnia and sleep disturbances, vaginal dryness, and thinning of the hair and skin. Typically, the menstrual flow lightens and decreases until it stops altogether (known as cessation of menses). The reproductive organs will atrophy (waste away) and there may also be bone loss (osteoporosis) (see Chapter 3).

# The breasts

The function of the breasts is to produce milk (**lactation**) after childbirth. They lie over the pectoralis major and serratus anterior muscles and have a vast network of blood and lymphatic vessels. The breasts consist of glandular tissue, fibrous tissue and fatty (adipose) tissue.

## ACTIVITY 12.2

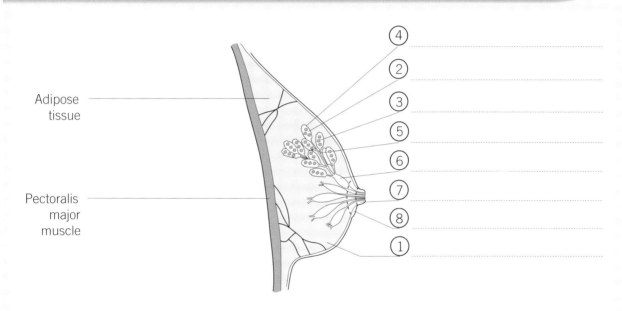

**Figure 12.5** The breast and its structures

Label the diagram in Figure 12.5, matching the numbers to the numbered terms in the following text. Colour the diagram using yellow for the lobes, lobules, alveoli, milk ducts and lactiferous sinuses, and red for the Cooper's ligaments, areola and nipple.

(1) **Cooper's ligaments** are made up of strands of connective tissue and help to support the breasts. The ligaments become slack with age or with prolonged strain, such as long-term jogging, and can become irreversibly stretched, causing the breasts to sag.

A breast consists of about 20 (2) **lobes** and each lobe contains several (3) **lobules**. The lobules contain milk-secreting glands called ④ **alveoli**. The ⑤ **milk ducts** carry the milk from the lobes and expand to form ⑥ **lactiferous sinuses**.

The lactiferous sinuses are found near the ⑦ **nipple** and act as storage for milk. The milk then passes into ducts to be released by the nipple. A pigmented area called the ⑧ **areola** (ah-ree-o-lah) surrounds the nipple and appears rough because of the presence of sebaceous glands, which lubricate the nipple during suckling.

## Blood supply and lymphatic drainage of the breasts

The subclavian and axillary arteries supply blood to the breast. The lymphatic drainage of the breast is extensive and leads mostly into the axillary lymph vessels and nodes under the armpits (Figure 12.6).

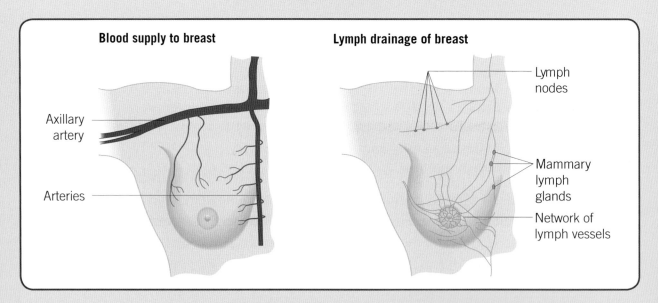

**Blood supply to breast**

Axillary artery

Arteries

**Lymph drainage of breast**

Lymph nodes

Mammary lymph glands

Network of lymph vessels

**Figure 12.6** Blood supply and lymph drainage of the breast

## Puberty

In the female, the breasts are quite flat until puberty. During puberty, breast development is stimulated by the hormones oestrogen and progesterone. **Oestrogen** stimulates the growth of the ducts and **progesterone** stimulates the growth of the alveoli.

These hormones cause additional adipose tissue to be laid down and for the nipple and areola to increase in size.

During menstruation, the hormone **progesterone** causes increased blood flow to the breasts. This results in the retention of fluid in the breasts, causing them to increase in size. This usually happens shortly before a period and can cause discomfort for some women.

## Pregnancy

After the baby is born, the hormone **prolactin** from the anterior pituitary stimulates the breasts to produce milk. The hormone **oxytocin** from the posterior pituitary affects the muscles in the walls of the alveoli, forcing milk to flow from the breasts. Milk is released in response to the suckling of a baby on the mother's nipple. Nerve impulses pass to the hypothalamus in the brain. The hypothalamus signals the anterior pituitary to release prolactin and the posterior pituitary to release oxytocin.

## Menopause

During the menopause, the production of oestrogen decreases; after the menopause oestrogen production stops altogether for most women. The lack of oestrogen causes changes to the body, such as shrinkage of the breasts owing to loss of glandular and adipose tissue. The supporting ligaments lose their strength and so the breasts sag.

# Male reproductive system

The ①**testes** are two oval glands and their functions are to produce sperm and the hormone testosterone. They are held in a pouch of skin called the **scrotum.** Sperm look rather like tadpoles and are produced continually from puberty until about 70 years of age. The ②**penis** contains the ③**urethra**, which acts a passageway for both semen and urine.

Sperm pass along a coiled tube called the **epididymis**, which becomes wider to form the ④**vas deferens**. The vas deferens is about 45 cm long and passes from the testes to the urethra. It acts as a passageway for sperm and has muscular walls to help to move sperm along. The vas deferens passes through a sac-like gland called a **seminal vesicle**, which releases fluid that makes up a substantial amount of semen. The **spermatic cord** supports the testes and contains the vas deferens, nerves and blood vessels.

The ⑤ **prostate gland** is about the size of a chestnut and lies under the bladder and surrounding the beginning of the urethra. It secretes a thin, milky fluid, which is important for the normal functioning of the sperm cell and makes up about 25 per cent of the semen.

> **don't forget**
>
> A <u>gamete</u> is a sperm or ovum.

## ACTIVITY 12.3

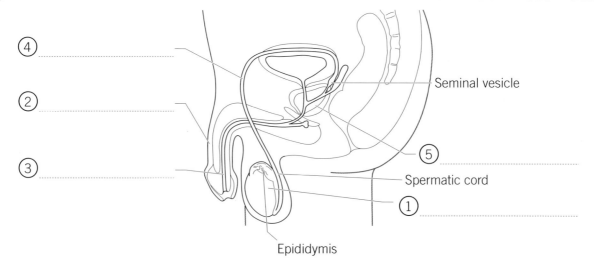

④ .....................

② .....................

③ .....................

Seminal vesicle

⑤ .....................

Spermatic cord

① .....................

Epididymis

**Figure 12.7** The male reproductive organs

Label the diagram in Figure 12.7, matching the numbers to the numbered terms in the text.

Red – testes                      Yellow – urethra and vas deferens
Orange – prostate gland           Pink – penis

## Male reproductive stages

### Puberty

Puberty usually begins between the ages of 10 and 14. The pituitary gland releases hormones that stimulate the testicles to produce testosterone (see Chapter 6). Testosterone causes many physical changes for a male, such as enlargement of the penis and testes, hair growth on the pubic, underarm and facial areas. It is also responsible for the deepening of the voice and muscle development.

### Menopause (andropause)

It is not just women who can experience unpleasant symptoms during the menopause; ageing men can also go through a similar experience known as the andropause (sometimes known as midlife crisis). Men may suffer with fatigue, weakness, depression, loss of sex drive and sexual dysfunction. It is caused by a decrease in the levels of testosterone and occurs gradually over a period of time.

# Conditions associated with the reproductive system

## Amenorrhoea

This is a condition in which menstruation stops, usually owing to a hormonal imbalance. It can be the result of obesity or extreme weight loss, such as someone suffering from anorexia nervosa.

## Breast cyst

This is a fluid-filled sac in the breast and may cause discomfort for some sufferers. It commonly affects women over the age of 35. They are harmless and usually disappear without treatment.

## Cervical cancer

This uncommon type of cancer, which affects the cervix, is mostly caused by the human papillomavirus (HPV). HPV is often transmitted during sex. Symptoms include vaginal bleeding after

**FAST FACT**

A hysterectomy is an operation that involves the removal of a women's uterus.

sex and erratic menstrual bleeding. Depending on the stage of the disease, treatment may involve removal of abnormal cells, surgery, radiotherapy and chemotherapy.

## Dysmenorrhoea

This is the term used to describe painful periods.

## Ectopic pregnancy

An ectopic pregnancy is one that occurs outside the uterus. The commonest place for this to occur is in the Fallopian tube. It is a very dangerous condition and can lead to internal bleeding.

## Fibrodenomas

Fibrodenomas are common painless lumps that are found in the breast. They feel firm, rubbery and marble-shaped, and mostly affect females under 30 years old. Their cause is unknown, and they are harmless.

## Fibroids

These are non-cancerous growths that are found in and around the uterus. Many people will not experience symptoms; however, others may suffer with heavy and painful periods, and abdominal pain. The exact cause is unknown, although oestrogen appears to play a role. Many fibroids will shrink after the menopause.

## Galactorrhea

This disorder involves either one breast or both releasing a milky discharge, and mostly occurs in females. The cause is often too much prolactin production from the pituitary gland, which can be caused by a variety of factors. Medication may be given to help reduce the prolactin in the body or block its effects.

# Infertility

Infertility is when a couple are having a sexual relationship but are unable to conceive naturally. Conditions such as endometriosis and pelvic inflammatory disease (PID) may lead to infertility. Other factors that may cause infertility include a low body weight, being overweight, being malnourished, endocrine disorders, and problems with reproductive system organs.

The uterus lining is known as the endometrium. **Endometriosis** is a condition where parts of this lining begin to grow in areas such as the Fallopian tubes or the ovaries. This can make it difficult for an egg to be released and become implanted into the uterus. It commonly causes heavy periods and pain in the lower abdomen, pelvis or lower back. The exact cause of endometriosis is unknown.

Pelvic inflammatory disease is a bacterial infection, usually sexually transmitted, of the uterus, Fallopian tubes and ovaries. PID can cause harm and scarring to the Fallopian tubes, so the egg is unable to pass through them into the uterus. Both chlamydia and gonorrhea can cause PID.

Male infertility may be caused by endocrine disorders, problems with reproductive system organs, erectile and sexual dysfunction, vasectomy, medication, and low sperm count.

# Mastitis

Mastitis is a condition where breast tissue becomes inflamed and painful, and there may be symptoms such as fever, chills and aches. It commonly occurs in women who are breastfeeding and may be the result of a blocked milk duct or a bacterial infection. However, it can also affect women who are not breastfeeding.

# Menorrhagia

This is the term used to describe abnormally heavy menstrual bleeding.

## Polycystic ovarian syndrome (PCOS)

Ovarian cysts are usually harmless cysts found on the ovaries, but can become large and painful so have to be removed. Larger cysts are often the result of hormonal imbalance and may cause the menstrual cycle to become irregular and periods to be light. In many cases it is caused by high levels of male hormones (androgens) circulating in the body, which can lead to excess hair growth. Other symptoms of PCOS include problems getting pregnant, acne and weight gain. It cannot be cured, but the symptoms can be treated. Many sufferers of PCOS are overweight so are advised to lose weight, and may also be prescribed the combined contraceptive pill.

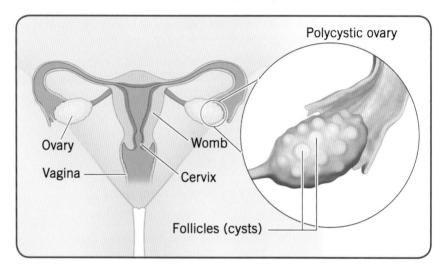

**Figure 12.8** Polycystic ovarian syndrome

## Premenstrual syndrome

Premenstrual syndrome (PMS) usually occurs one week before a period is due. Symptoms include irritability, fatigue, tearfulness and changes of mood. There may also be cramps, backache, bloating, fluid retention, and swollen and tender breasts. Hormonal changes involving oestrogen and progesterone during the menstrual cycle are thought to be the biggest contributing factor to many of the symptoms of PMS. Women affected by PMS may have a deficiency in serotonin (the body's own mood-uplifting chemical) during the premenstrual phase so are often prescribed antidepressants, which stimulate the release of these hormones.

# Prostatitis

This is inflammation of the prostate. It causes symptoms such as pain while urinating and during sex, pain in the pelvic area, increased urination and fever. The cause is mostly unknown, although in some cases it may be caused by a bacterial infection. It is often treated with antibiotics.

# Sexually transmitted infections

These are diseases that are transmitted through sexual acts. Common STDs include chlamydia, gonorrhea and genital warts.

Chlamydia is a bacterial infection and does not generally cause any symptoms. It is easily treated with antibiotics. However, if left untreated the infection can cause infertility and pelvic inflammatory disease.

Gonorrhea is also a bacterial infection and commonly causes an unusual discharge from the vagina or penis and pain when urinating.

Genital warts is a viral infection caused by the human papillomavirus (HPV). The warts appear on, or around, the genital or anal area. They may not cause pain but are unsightly.

# Thrush (vaginal)

Thrush is a common condition and is caused by an excess of yeast (fungus) in the vagina. It may cause itching, irritation and there may also be a creamy white discharge. People who are taking antibiotics, have poor immunity, are diabetic or pregnant are at an increased risk of getting thrush. It is treated with anti-thrush medication.

# What you should know

## Functions of the reproductive system

- ☐ Production of sperm and ova
- ☐ Meiosis (see Chapter 1)
- ☐ Mitosis (see Chapter 1)
- ☐ Cytokinesis (see Chapter 1)

## Location, structure and function

- ☐ The female reproductive tract – ovum, ovary, Fallopian tubes, uterus, cervix, vulva, vagina, labia, clitoris, vestibule and greater vestibular glands, mammary glands
- ☐ Functions of female sex hormones – oestrogen and progesterone (See Chapter 6)
- ☐ Male reproductive tract – testes, scrotum, vas deferens, epididymis, seminal vesicles, prostate, urethra, penis
- ☐ Function of male sex hormones – testosterone (see Chapter 6)
- ☐ Growth and repair – see Chapter 1
- ☐ Define female reproductive stages – puberty, pregnancy, menopause

- ☐ Effects of female puberty
- ☐ Menstrual cycle – menstruation, follicular phase, ovulation, luteal phase
- ☐ Stages of pregnancy – fertilisation, post-fertilisation, cell division, embryo formation, foetal development, parturition, lactation
- ☐ Effects of female menopause – cessation of menses (stopping of periods), mood swings, hot flushes, bone loss, atrophy of reproductive organs
- ☐ Male reproductive stages – puberty, menopause
- ☐ Effects of male menopause – fatigue, weakness, depression and sexual dysfunction

## Pathologies

- ☐ Conditions associated with the reproductive system, including their causes, signs and symptoms – infertility, mastitis, amenorrhoea, dysmenorrhoea, menorrhagia, premenstrual syndrome, sexually transmitted diseases, polycystic ovarian syndrome, endometriosis, pelvic inflammatory disease, galactorrhoea, fibrodenomas, cysts, fibroids, thrush, prostatitis

# Glossary

**Acid mantle**
Sweat and sebum mix together on the skin to produce an acid mantle, which helps to maintain the skin's pH at around 5.5.

**Adenosine triphosphate**
Adenosine triphosphate (ATP) is rich in chemical energy and releases energy when broken down. It is used by the body for metabolic processes such as cell division.

**Adipose tissue**
Tissue that is made up of fat (adipocytes).

**Adrenal glands**
These are found on top of the kidneys and produce corticoids, adrenalin and noradrenalin.

**Adrenalin**
The hormone produced by the adrenal gland that prepares the body for action. It is commonly known as the fight or flight hormone.

**Adrenocorticotrophic hormone**
This hormone controls the activity of the adrenal cortex of the adrenal gland.

**Aldosterone**
The hormone that is released if sodium levels drop in the body; helps to increase sodium levels.

**Allergen**
A substance capable of causing an allergic reaction in the body.

**Alopecia areata**
Patchy baldness.

**Alopecia totalis**
Total loss of hair.

**Amino acids**
The building blocks of protein.

**Anaemia**
This condition can be caused by lack of iron in the diet; symptoms include tiredness, dizziness and shortness of breath.

**Anagen**
The active stage of hair growth.

**Anaphase**
The phase of cell division in which separate sets of chromosomes move to either end of the cell.

**Androgens**
Male hormones, such as testosterone.

**Antibodies**
Antibodies produced by lymphocytes and can destroy harmful matter, such as bacteria.

**Antidiuretic hormone**
This regulates water balance in the body by controlling the amount of water in urine.

**Antigen**
A substance that the body considers to be harmful and which triggers the production of antibodies by the immune system.

**Aorta**
The large artery that carries oxygenated blood from the heart to branch arteries that distribute blood to the body.

**Apocrine gland**
A type of sweat gland found in regions of the body such as under the arms and around the groin.

**Appendicular skeleton**
This is made up of the shoulder girdle, arms and hands, the pelvic bones and the legs and feet.

**Appendix**
The narrow, worm-like tube, closed at one end, that leads off from the large intestine and has no known function.

**Arches**
The bones of the feet fit together to make up arches; these include the medial longitudinal arch, lateral longitudinal arch, and transverse arch.

**Areolar tissue**
Collagen fibres give this tissue strength. It is found throughout the body.

**Arrector pili**
Tiny muscles that raise hair on the skin.

**Arterioles**
Small arteries that carry oxygenated blood.

**Articular cartilage**
This covers the ends of bones. It helps to reduce friction and acts as a shock absorber.

**Atherosclerosis**
A condition involving thickening and narrowing of the artery walls owing to a build-up of fatty substances, such as cholesterol.

**Atony**
Lack of normal muscle tone.

**Atrium**
The upper chamber of the heart, of which there are two.

**Atrophy**
Wasting away.

**Autoimmune disease**
A disease caused by the body attacking its own tissues owing to abnormal functioning of the immune system.

**Axial skeleton**
This is made up of the skull, spine, ribs and sternum.

**Basal metabolic rate (BMR)**
The amount of energy expended by the body, in the form of calories, by a person while at rest.

**Bile**
A substance released by the gall bladder that helps to break down fats.

**Blood vessels**
Tubes that include arteries, arterioles and capillaries; they carry blood throughout the body.

**Blood–brain barrier**
This helps protect the brain from harmful substances.

**Bowman's capsule**
A cup-shaped structure that surrounds the glomerulus in the nephron of the kidney.

**Brachial plexus**
Groups of nerves found at the top of the shoulder.

**Bradycardia**
This refers to a slow resting heart or pulse rate of less than 60 beats per minute.

**Calcitonin**
The hormone that helps to maintain normal calcium levels within the blood.

**Capillaries**
Tiny tubes that carry substances such as blood and lymph.

**Capillary exchange**
The exchange of, for example, oxygen and nutrients through blood capillary walls.

**Carbuncle**
A group of boils.

**Cardiac cycle**
One complete heartbeat that is made up of diastole and systole.

**Cardiac muscle**
Heart muscle.

**Carotid arteries**
Two major arteries on each side of the neck that carry oxygenated blood.

**Cartilage**
Cartilage types include hyaline, elastic and fibrocartilage.

**Cartilaginous joints**
Slightly moveable joints, such as joints between spinal bones.

**Catagen**
The changing stage of hair growth.

**Cell**
A membrane-bound structure that contains organelles. The body is made up of different types of cells, including nerve, fat and muscle cells.

**Cell membrane**
A membrane that surrounds the cell and allows certain substances to pass into and out of it.

**Cell metabolism**
The chemical processes that occur within a living cell, which are necessary for it to live.

**Cellular respiration**
The process by which living cells produce energy. Cells use oxygen and nutrients to produce energy for the cell; carbon dioxide is also produced.

**Centriole**
A barrel-shaped structure found within the cell; it is involved with mitosis (cell division).

**Cerebrospinal fluid**
This protects the brain and spinal cord by acting as a cushion and shock absorber between the brain and the skull bones.

**Cervical plexus**
Groups of nerves found in the neck.

**Cervix**
The neck of the uterus, which dilates during childbirth.

**Cholesterol**
A fatty, waxy substance found in the body; it is needed to produce hormones, bile, vitamin D and cell membranes.

**Chromosomes**
Structures found within a cell that carry genetic material.

**Chyme**
Food that has been turned into liquid form leaves the stomach as chyme.

**Cilia**
Hair-like structures found on specific cells, such as in the respiratory tract; these help to prevent harmful substances from entering the lungs.

**Ciliated cells**
Column-shaped cells containing cilia; these are found in the respiratory tract.

**Cisterna chyli**
The large lymph vessel that leads to the thoracic duct.

**Coccygeal plexus**
Groups of nerves found on the back of the pelvic cavity.

**Collagen**
A substance that is made of protein and gives strength to, for example, the skin.

**Colon**
The large intestine, extending from the caecum to the rectum.

**Columnar cells**
Tall, column-shaped cells that line the digestive tract.

**Conception**
When the egg becomes fertilised by a sperm.

**Cooper's ligaments**
Connective tissue in the breasts that helps to support them.

**Corpus luteum**
A structure that releases oestrogen and progesterone to stimulate thickening of the endometrium in the uterus for possible pregnancy.

**Cortisol**
A hormone produced by the adrenal gland, which is released in response to stressful situations.

**Cuboidal cells**
Cube-shaped cells found in regions such as the kidneys and eyes; these are involved in absorbing and releasing substances.

**Cytoplasm**
Jelly-like substance found inside the cell and containing many organelles.

**Dendrites**
Branches of nerve fibres that extend from the cell body of a neurone.

**Deoxygenated blood**
Blood that contains very little oxygen.

**Dermal papilla**
The structure that surrounds the hair bulb. It contains many blood vessels and provides nutrients for hair growth.

**Dermis**
The layer found beneath the epidermis.

**Desquamation**
The shedding of dead skin cells.

**Diabetes**
A disease caused either by the pancreas producing insufficient amounts of insulin or by the tissues not responding to insulin.

**Diastole**
Relaxation of the heart.

**Diffusion**
The movement of molecules, such as oxygen, from an area of high concentration (where there are lots of them) to an area of lower concentration (where there are fewer).

**Digestion**
A process that occurs in the digestive tract and involves food being broken down into smaller and simpler particles, which can be assimilated by the body.

**Disaccharides**
Double sugars, such as lactose, found in milk and sucrose, found in sugar.

**Dissolution**
The dissolving of substances.

**Eccrine glands**
Glands that are found all over the body and produce sweat on the skin.

**Elastic tissue**
This contains elastic-type fibres to help make the tissue stretchy. It is found in the walls of blood vessels.

**Elastin**
Elastin is made from protein. It gives the skin its elasticity, which helps to keep it flexible.

**Embryo**
An embryo is formed after the second week of pregnancy to around the eighth week of pregnancy. After being an embryo it becomes a foetus.

**Endometrium**
The lining of the uterus.

**Endoplasmic reticulum, rough and smooth**
Rough endoplasmic reticulum makes protein; smooth endoplasmic reticulum makes lipids (fat) within the cell.

**Epidermis**
The top five layers of the skin.

**Epiglottis**
The flap of cartilage found at the back of the throat that prevents food from entering the airways.

**Erythrocytes**
Red blood cells.

**Eustachian tube**
The tube that joins the throat to the middle ear. Bacteria in the throat can travel through the Eustachian tube causing a painful middle-ear infection.

**Expiration**
Breathing out; the movement of air out of the lungs.

**Fallopian tubes**
Two tubes that connect the ovaries to the uterus. They act as a passageway for both eggs and sperm.

**Fascia**
Fibrous tissue that covers the muscle.

**Fibroblasts**
A type of cell that makes collagen.

**Fibrous or immovable joints**
Fixed joints in which no movement is possible, such as the skull bones.

**Fibrous tissue**
Tissue that is made up of collagen fibres to give it strength. It is found in muscles and bones.

**Filtration**
The movement of blood and other substances through a cell membrane owing to pressure from the cardiovascular system. Filtration occurs in the kidneys and involves the blood being filtered.

**Flatulence**
Excessive wind.

**Follicles**
Pits into which hairs sit.

**Follicle-stimulating hormone**
This stimulates the production of eggs and oestrogen in females. In males it stimulates the testes to produce sperm.

**Fracture**
A term that refers to bone breakage.

**Gall bladder**
A pear-shaped structure that is attached to the liver and stores bile.

**Glomerulus**
A bundle of capillaries found inside the nephron in the kidneys.

**Glucagon**
A hormone produced by the pancreas in response to low blood sugar levels. It helps to increase blood sugar levels.

**Goblet cells**
Cells that produce mucus. Mucus helps to trap dust and other unwanted particles, and also aids the passage of food through the digestive tract.

**Golgi body**
This sorts and packages proteins within the cell.

**Gonadotrophic hormones**
These control the ovaries in females and the testes in males.

**Graafian follicles**
Structures that encase eggs in the ovaries.

**Grey matter**
This is made up of numerous nerve cells and blood vessels.

**Growth hormone**
This controls the growth of the skeleton, muscles, connective tissues and organs, such as the kidneys and liver.

**Haemoglobin**
The oxygen-carrying pigment in red blood cells.

**Heart walls**
These consist of three layers: endocardium, the inner layer; myocardium, the middle layer of the heart containing cardiac muscle that contracts to pump the blood; pericardium, the outer layer of the heart.

**Hepatic portal vein**
A large vein that carries blood from the stomach and intestines to the liver.

**Histamine**
This is produced by mast cells in response to an allergic reaction, causing symptoms such as inflammation, itching and sneezing.

**Homeostasis**
The process by which the body maintains a constant internal environment. For example, the regulation of body temperature.

**Hormone replacement therapy**
Treatment that helps restore levels of oestrogen and progesterone in females and so gives relief from menopausal symptoms.

**Hormones**
Chemical messengers that are produced by the endocrine glands and carried in the blood to target cells.

**Hyoid**
Bone found in the neck region.

**Hypertension**
High blood pressure.

**Hypertrophy**
The increase in size of a body part or organ. Activities such as lifting heavy weights can cause hypertrophy of muscles.

**Hypoglycaemia**
Abnormally low levels of sugar in the blood that can lead to sweats, trembles and blurred vision.

**Hypothalamus**
This controls the pituitary gland and autonomic nervous system. It helps control body activities such as body temperature, appetite and sleep patterns.

**Ilium**
The largest of three pelvic bones.

**Ingestion**
To take into the body by mouth, such as food.

**Insertion**
Part of the bone to which muscle is attached that does move.

**Inspiration**
Breathing in; the movement of air into the lungs.

**Insulin**
The hormone produced by the pancreas in response to high blood sugar levels. It helps to bring down the blood sugar levels.

**Interphase**
A phase of cell division in which the cell grows.

**Intervertebral discs**
Pads of white fibrocartilage that are found between the bones of the spine.

**Involuntary muscle**
Also called smooth muscle. It is muscle that is not under the body's conscious control, such as the intestinal muscles.

**Ischium**
The bone that forms the posterior aspect of the pelvis.

**Islets of Langerhans**
Small groups of cells in the pancreas that produce the hormones insulin and glucagon.

**Isotonic**
Activity involving lifting requires isotonic contractions, which involves the muscle shortening as it contracts. For example, an isotonic contraction can be seen when the arm is bent and the biceps contract. Movement of a body part occurs.

**Joint cavity**
The space in between two articulating bones.

**Jugular veins**
Large veins in the neck that carry deoxygenated blood.

**Keratin**
A type of protein found in the skin, hair and nails.

**Keratinised**
The process whereby cells in the skin have become hardened.

**Knots**
Fibrous nodules that may develop in muscles and can be caused by muscle tension, injuries or poor posture.

**Lactase**
The enzyme that breaks down milk sugar (lactose).

**Lactation**
The production of milk in the breasts after childbirth.

**Lacteals**
Lymphatic capillaries that absorb fats in the villi of the small intestine.

**Lactogenic hormone**
Also known as prolactin, it is responsible for stimulating milk production in the breasts after pregnancy.

**Lactose**
The sugar found in milk.

**Leucocytes**
White blood cells.

**Ligaments**
Fibrous bands of tissue that attach bone to bone.

**Limbic system**
Brain structures involved with emotions such as anger, fear, pain and pleasure, and also in the formation of memory.

**Lipase**
The enzyme that breaks down fats into fatty acids and glycerol.

**Liver spots**
Also known as lentigines. They are pigmented areas on the skin associated with exposure to UV light and ageing.

**Lumbar plexuses**
Groups of nerves found between the waist and the hip.

**Luteinising hormone**
This stimulates the release of an egg from the ovary and also the hormone progesterone. In males it stimulates the testes to make testosterone.

**Lymph**
Straw-coloured fluid that travels through lymphatic vessels and nodes.

**Lymph capillaries**
Tubes that carry lymph throughout the body.

**Lymphatic capillaries**
Small tubes that carry lymph throughout the body.

**Lymphatic ducts**
There are two lymphatic ducts, the thoracic duct and right lymphatic duct. They drain lymph into subclavian veins.

**Lymphocytes**
Specialised white blood cells that are produced by the lymphatic system. They recognise harmful substances and destroy them.

**Lysosomes**
These contain enzymes to break down waste material inside the cell. They help to destroy bacteria, worn out parts of cells and other unwanted substances.

**Mastication**
Chewing.

**Medulla oblongata**
Part of the brain stem that controls heart and breathing rates.

**Melanin**
The pigment responsible for the colour of hair and skin.

**Melanocytes**
Cells that produce melanin.

**Melanocyte-stimulating hormone**
This helps to increase skin pigmentation.

**Meninges**
Three layers that surround the brain and spinal cord; pia mater, arachnoid and dura mater.

**Metaphase**
The phase of cell division in which chromosomes line up in the middle of the cell.

**Mid-brain**
Upper-most part of the brain stem, involved with some reflex actions and with the control of eye movements.

**Midline**
The imaginary line that runs through the centre of the body, from the head to the feet.

**Mitochondria**
These provide energy for the cell.

**Mitosis**
Cellular division.

**Monosaccharides**
Single sugars, such as fructose found in fruit.

**Motor nerves**
Nerves that stimulate the sweat glands, arrector pili muscles and sebaceous glands to carry out their activities.

**Muscle fatigue**
This occurs when muscle becomes overworked, perhaps because of vigorous exercise. It is caused by the oxygen and glucose supplies being used up.

**Muscle tone**
Muscle in a state of partial contraction. Exercise improves muscle tone.

**Myelin sheath**
The fatty sheath that covers the axon of a neurone and allows messages to be passed quickly through them.

**Myofibrils**
Long, thin muscle fibres that are found within muscle tissue. Thinner filaments are called actin and the thicker filaments are known as myosin.

**Myositis**
Inflammation of muscle.

**Nephron**
Found in the kidneys, nephrons consist of a proximal coiled tubule, loop of Henle and distal coiled tubule. Urine is formed inside them.

**Nerves**
A bundle of neurones covered by connective tissue.

**Neuroglia**
Spaces between neurones are filled with neuroglia, including astrocytes and oligodendrocytes.

**Neurones**
Nerve cells.

**Non-pathogenic**
Not capable of causing disease.

**Nucleolus**
A small round structure found in the nucleus of the cell. It helps to make ribosomes.

**Nucleus**
The structure that contains DNA and controls the cell's activities.

**Oedema**
Build-up of fluid (mostly water) in the body tissues that results in fluid retention.

**Oesophagus**
Foodpipe.

**Oestrogen**
A hormone released by the ovaries that helps to control menstruation and is responsible for bodily changes girls undergo during puberty.

**Olfaction**
The sense of smell.

**Organ**
Groups of tissues make up an organ, such as the heart or liver.

**Origin**
Part of the bone to which muscle is attached and that does not move.

**Osmosis**
Movement of water from a region of higher concentration to a region of lower concentration through a partially permeable membrane.

**Ossification**
Formation of bone.

**Osteoclasts**
Breaks down areas within bone to form a cavity.

**Osteoporosis**
A condition in which bones become brittle and weak.

**Ovaries**
Found within the female pelvis, one on either side of the uterus. They produce ova (eggs) in the female as well as the hormones oestrogen and progesterone.

**Overactive thyroid**
It is also known as hyperthyroidism caused by an overproduction of thyroxine and leads to symptoms such as fast heartbeat and speeded up metabolism.

**Ovulation**
The monthly release of an egg in females.

**Oxygenated blood**
Blood that is rich in oxygen.

**Oxytocin**
This stimulates the release of breast milk during breastfeeding and is also responsible for contracting the uterus during labour and after birth.

**Pancreas**
Found in the abdomen. It contains islets of Langerhans, which produce hormones that help to maintain sugar levels in the blood.

**Papillary layer**
The upper section of the dermis.

**Papule**
A pimple.

**Parasympathetic nerves**
Nerves that control bodily activities such as digestion and urination. They slow the heart rate and increase gland activity.

**Parathyroid gland**
Found in the throat area and produces the hormone parathormone.

**Parturition**
Childbirth, including labour and delivery.

**Pathogenic**
Capable of causing disease.

**Pepsin**
The enzyme that breaks down protein in the stomach.

**Perineum**
The area of skin between the vaginal opening and anus.

**Periosteum**
Dense fibrous membrane that covers bones and contains blood vessels and nerves. It also acts an attachment for muscles and tendons.

**Peristalsis**
Contraction of the smooth muscles within, for example, the digestive tract to help propel food along it.

**Peyer's patches**
Lymphoid tissue found in the small intestine. These help to destroy harmful substances and prevent infection.

**Phagocytes**
White blood cells that protect the body by ingesting (phagocytosing) bacteria and any other harmful matter.

**Phagocytosis**
Engulfing and ingesting of, for example, bacteria, foreign bodies or cell fragments.

**Pineal gland**
The gland found in the brain that releases a hormone called melatonin.

**Pinocytosis**
The process of fluid intake into a cell.

**Pituitary gland**
Known as the master gland. It contains an anterior and posterior lobe and produces several hormones.

**Pleural cavity**
Fluid-filled space between the pleural membranes that help the membranes slide over each other during breathing, therefore preventing friction occurring.

**Pleural membrane**
This covers each lung and consists of two layers: the visceral and parietal pleura.

**Pons varolii**
Messages pass through the pons varolii from the spinal cord to the brain.

**Pore**
Pit found in the skin.

**Progesterone**
The hormone produced by the ovaries that helps control menstruation and is responsible for the changes girls undergo during puberty.

**Prophase**
The first phase of cell division.

**Prostate gland**
A gland that surrounds the beginning of the urethra. It produces a thin, milky fluid that is important for the normal functioning of the sperm cell and makes up around a quarter of the semen.

**Pubis**
The bone situated on the anterior aspect of the pelvis.

**Pulmonary arteries**
Blood vessels that carry deoxygenated blood from the heart to the lungs.

**Pulmonary veins**
Veins that carry oxygenated blood from the lungs to the heart.

**Pustules**
Pus-filled spots.

**Reflex arc**
A neural pathway that controls a reflex action.

**Reticular layer**
The lower section of the dermis.

**Ribosomes**
Minute, round particles found on rough endoplasmic reticulum that make protein in the cell.

**Sacral plexuses**
Groups of nerves found at the base of the abdomen.

**Sacroiliac joint**
The joint between the sacrum and ilium.

**Salivary amylase**
The enzyme found in the saliva of most people that begins the breakdown of starch.

**Salivary glands**
Found in the mouth and include parotid glands, submandibular glands and sublingual glands.

**Saturated fat**
Fats that are found in animal products such as meat, butter and full-fat cheese.

**Scrotum**
A sac that contains the testes.

**Sebaceous glands**
Glands in the skin that produce sebum.

**Sebum**
An oily substance produced by the sebaceous gland, which helps to moisturise the skin and hair.

**Seminal vesicle**
A sac-like gland that releases fluid, which makes up a substantial amount of semen.

**Sensory nerve endings**
Nerves found in the skin that inform us of sensations such as pain, heat and cold.

**Sepsis**
This condition may occur if the body's immune system overacts to an infection; it can be life threatening.

**Septum (heart)**
The muscular wall that separates the right and left sides of the heart.

**Sinuses**
Air-filled spaces found in the head. Sinusitis may result if the membrane lining the sinuses becomes inflamed.

**Small intestine**
Made up of three parts: duodenum, first part of small intestine; jejunum and the ileum.

**Spasticity**
Abnormal tightness of muscles, which includes muscle contractions and an increase in muscle tone.

**Spongy bone**
Also known as cancellous bone. It is filled with red bone marrow that produces red blood cells in adults.

**Squamous epithelial cells**
Thin cells that allow rapid movement of substances through them, like the movement of oxygen through the air sacs (alveoli) in the lungs.

**Strain (muscle)**
This is caused by muscle tearing, which is commonly a result of overstretching (also known as a 'pulled muscle').

**Stratified epithelium**
A type of tissue that consists of two or more layers, and can be found in the skin.

**Subcutaneous layer**
The fatty layer found underneath the dermis.

**Sympathetic nerves**
Nerves that are responsible for actions in times of stress and are made of a network of nerves (plexuses).

**Synapse**
The tiny gap between two neurones. Chemicals pass messages across it to the next neurone.

**Synovial fluid**
Fluid that lubricates the joint and provides the articular cartilage with nutrients.

**Synovial joints**
Freely moveable joints, such as the shoulder and knee joints.

**System**
A group of organs form a body system, such as the circulatory system.

**Systole**
Contraction of the heart.

**Tachycardia**
A fast resting heart or pulse rate that beats over 100 times per minute.

**Telogen**
The resting stage of hair growth.

**Telophase**
The last phase of cell division in which a cell divides to form two cells.

**Tendons**
These attach bone to muscle, for example the Achilles tendon.

**Testes**
Found in the groin area of the male in a sac called the scrotum. The testes produce testosterone and sperm.

**Testosterone**
The hormone produced by the testes in males, which is responsible for the changes males undergo during puberty. It also helps stimulate sperm production.

**Thoracic plexus**
Groups of nerves found between the upper back and the waist.

**Thrombocytes**
Platelets.

**Thymus**
The gland found behind the sternum; it releases hormones that include thymosin.

**Thyroid gland**
This is found in the throat area and produces the hormone thyroxine.

**Thyroid-stimulating hormone**
This controls the activity of the thyroid gland in the neck.

**Thyroxine**
The hormone produced by the thyroid gland that controls the body's metabolism and also mental development.

**Tissue**
Groups of cells make up body tissue. Types include adipose (fat), nerve and muscle tissue.

**Tonsils**
These are found at the back of the throat (pharynx). They are made up of lymphoid tissue and help to filter bacteria.

**Trypsin**
The enzyme that breaks down protein in the duodenum.

**Underactive thyroid**
Also known as hypothyroidism. It is caused by an underproduction of thyroxine and leads to symptoms such as increased weight and dry hair.

**Universal donor**
People with blood group 0 are known as universal donors because their blood can be given to a patient with either type A, B or AB blood.

**Universal recipient**
People with blood group AB are known as universal recipients because patients with this type can receive blood from all blood groups.

**Unsaturated fat**
Fat derived from plant sources, such as olive oil.

**Urea**
The waste product that is excreted in urine and is a result of the breakdown of protein.

**Ureters**
There are two ureters. These are tubes that join the kidney to the bladder.

**Urethra**
The tube leading from the bladder to outside the body.

**Uterus**
A pear-shaped muscular organ found in the female pelvic cavity. A fertilised egg implants itself into the uterus wall and grows to become a baby.

**Vacuoles**
A structure within the cell that has a membrane and encloses, for example, food, water or air.

**Valves (veins)**
Valves can open and shut to prevent the backflow of blood and so enable it to move in one direction.

**Vas deferens**
A tube that passes from the testes to the urethra. It acts as a passageway for sperm.

**Vena cava**
The inferior vena cava and superior vena cava are veins that carry deoxygenated blood.

**Ventricle**
The lower chamber of the heart, of which there are two.

**Venules**
Small veins that carry deoxygenated blood.

**Vesicles**
Round sacs found inside the cell that transport and store substances.

**Villi**
Millions of tiny structures found inside the small intestine that allow digested food to be absorbed quickly.

**Viruses**
Tiny microorganisms that can cause disease and disorders.

**Voluntary muscles**
Muscles that are under the body's conscious control, such as skeletal muscles.

**White matter**
This is made up of nerve axons that are myelin coated. It carries messages between nerve cells in the brain and the spinal cord.

**Zygote**
When the egg is fertilised by a sperm a zygote is formed.

# Index